Positive Discipline for Single Parents

Revised and Updated 2nd Edition

ALSO IN THE
POSITIVE DISCIPLINE SERIES

Jane Nelsen, Cheryl Erwin, and Carol Delzer

Positive Discipline for Single Parents

REVISED AND UPDATED 2ND EDITION

Nurturing Cooperation,

Respect, and Joy in

Your Single-Parent Family

PRIMA PUBLISHING

Published by Prima Publishing, Roseville, California. Member of the Crown Publishing Group, a division of Random House, Inc.

PRIMA PUBLISHING and colophon are trademarks of Random House, Inc., registered with the United States Patent and Trademark Office.

Illustrations by Paula Gray

All products mentioned in this book are trademarks of their respective companies.

Library of Congress Cataloging-in-Publication Data
Nelsen, Jane.
    Positive discipline for single parents : nurturing cooperation, respect, and joy in your single-parent family / Jane Nelsen, Cheryl Erwin, and Carol Delzer. —Rev. and updated 2nd ed.
        p.   cm.
    Includes index.
    ISBN 0-7615-2011-2
    1. Single parents. 2. Child rearing. 3. Parenting. 4. Discipline of children. I. Erwin, Cheryl. II. Delzer, Carol. III. Title.
HQ759.915.N45   1999
649'.1'0243—dc21   CIP

    03 04 05 06 07 DD 10 9 8 7 6 5
Printed in the United States of America

Second Edition

Visit us online at www.primapublishing.com

To Carol, who convinced me that single parents have special needs; and to Cheryl, who champions the vision that single-parent families are not broken families. Both are shining examples of single parents who are providing nurturing and empowering homes for their children.
—Jane Nelsen

. . .

To my son Philip, who has brought me such joy, and to Tom, whose courage to change made this book possible.
—Cheryl Erwin

. . .

To my daughter Jessica for all her inspiration and to her father for his cooperation in helping me be a single parent.
—Carol Delzer

CONTENTS

INTRODUCTION

Single Parenting: The Journey Begins

IN THE YEARS since this book was first written, some things about single parenting have changed, while many things have not. The statistics have not changed: About half of all marriages still end in divorce, and according to the U.S. Census Bureau, approximately 59 percent of the children in this country will spend some time living in a single-parent home.

Single fathers who have custody of their children are more common now than they used to be, one estimate claiming that the number of single fathers with custody has risen 25 percent from 1996 to 1999. Celebrities such as Jodie Foster and Rosie O'Donnell have drawn attention to the fact that some adults choose to be single parents—and like it that way.

Single parents are more numerous on television. The days when an American vice president felt comfortable publicly expressing outrage over a TV program promoting the idea of a healthy, happy single-parent family (remember *Murphy Brown*?) seem far distant. As with so many aspects of American family life, our perceptions of single parenting are changing, but some fears and other emotions about it are not.

When a group of single parents are asked what it feels like to be a single parent, we expect to be bombarded by emotional reactions. "I feel overwhelmed," says one single mom. "Guilty," says a single dad. And other words come tumbling out: "isolated," "exhausted," "bitter," "scared," "insecure," "vulnerable," "lonely," "depressed," "anxious," "deeply sad."

There are many roads that lead to single parenting. Some parents become single through the death of a spouse. Some never marry at all, either by choice or because of abandonment. Others divorce. Whatever the reason, once you've reached that destination—once you find yourself a single parent—what then?

Being a single parent in this complex world of ours is a tremendous challenge. Single parenting is a kind of "parenting plus": You face all the everyday issues of raising children, plus the problem of doing alone a job that was originally designed for two people.

In addition, many single parents harbor doubts and develop attitudes that hamper their ability to parent (and to live) effectively. Single parents may have become more visible, but they still wonder about their capacity to raise their children successfully. Books such as Judith Wallerstein's *Second Chances: Men, Women, and Children a Decade After Divorce* (Ticknor & Fields, 1989) have led many adults to believe that children suffer inherent damage through having a single parent, and the prospects of happiness and success are automatically dimmed for a child who does not have two parents who live under the same roof.

Being a single parent certainly is not easy. All three of the authors of this book have raised children as single mothers, and we would never underestimate the difficulties—nor the rewards. While many adults begin their single parenting journey by choice, many more do not. The grief and pain that accompany divorce or death make the reality of raising children alone even more daunting. It takes time to heal when you've suffered a loss, and many single parents bear wounds that remain raw. Feelings of grief, hurt, and rejection can be overwhelming at times and can make it difficult to embark with confidence and optimism on the journey of solo parenting.

Parents are usually aware of their own feelings about life in a single-parent family but it sometimes surprises them that their children feel many of the same things. If a parent has died, children have their own grief. If they have known only one parent, they may wonder why the missing parent isn't around. And if they have witnessed their parents' divorce, regardless of the reasons for that divorce, these children must learn to accept their new situation and come to terms with their own anger, guilt, confusion, and sense of abandonment.

Only time can heal the wound left by a spouse's or a parent's death, or by losing a parent or spouse by divorce. However, when divorced parents can work together in a respectful fashion for the good of the child, the trauma associated with the breakup of a marriage can be greatly reduced. Many divorced parents choose to remain actively involved in coparenting their children, which allows those children to have two homes (and two families), each with a parent who loves them. It takes time and a great deal of commitment to rebuild an intimate relationship into a working parenting partnership (we explore in this book ways to accomplish this transformation), but children are able not only to survive but to thrive in a family situation that may not match society's definition of what is "normal."

Single parenting can be an undeniably stressful way of life. Financial worries may seem insurmountable; balancing a job, a home, adequate time with children, and time for oneself is a tricky task. Mention the words *social life* to many single parents and you're likely to get an incredulous snort. "What social life?" they say. "Who has time?"

Is it possible to be both happy and successful as a single parent? Are children harmed by growing up in a single-parent home? Will they have stable relationships themselves when they grow up? Can one parent really provide everything a child needs to grow up healthy and whole? These questions haunt all single parents from time to time.

When single parents gather together, however, and all of the fears and frustrations have been explored, an interesting thing can happen. "Wait a minute," one dad may say. "My home is a lot more peaceful now that we're on our own." Heads may begin to nod, and slowly something wonderful occurs. Though it may take time to realize it sometimes, there are good things about being a single parent.

Regardless of how you became one, you may discover strengths you never realized you possessed. You will certainly encounter opportunities to learn new skills, exercise your creativity, and deepen your faith in yourself and your children. There are other benefits, as well. Many single parents find that they enjoy the lack of conflict in their homes—not having the other parent second-guess their decisions and actions. Single parents are frequently able to be more spontaneous, and find they enjoy their children more.

The movie *Kramer vs. Kramer* is an excellent illustration of how a father was able to develop a close relationship with his son as a result of becoming a single parent. The father would have missed this wonderful opportunity if he had stayed on his hard-driving career track, leaving all the parenting responsibilities to the mother.

Some single parents find their new lifestyle liberating; they like their independence, the new opportunities that arise, and the satisfaction that comes from mastering a challenge alone. And it can be fun to feel open and available!

Children, too, can grow and flourish in a single-parent home. It is tremendously empowering to learn that you can not only survive a trauma but can learn from it—you may even reap benefits. Children being raised by single parents have the opportunity to make a real contribution to their family and to learn a great deal about their own worth and abilities.

If you're reading this book, chances are good that you are (or are about to become) a single parent. It is the goal of this new edition of *Positive Discipline for Single Parents*—and the hope of its authors—that you will discover ways to identify potential problems and develop skills to prevent them. We hope you will discover solutions to the problems that do come your way. While we recognize that not all single parents have experienced a divorce, it is still by far the most common reason for parenting alone. If you have not had to live through a divorce, rejoice—and be patient with us as we share ideas and information with those who have. You will find among these discussions many things that apply to your own situation, as well.

Positive Discipline parenting skills can help you and your children work and live together happily—most of the time, anyway. All of the Positive Discipline parenting tools provided in this book were designed to help parents teach their children important skills for obtaining happiness and success in life, providing a focus that can be very encouraging for single-parent families who might otherwise dwell on grief and failure. We share with you the trials and successes of several single parents, through which we hope you will find encouragement and ideas to make your own journey smoother.

Gardeners tell us that without strong winds blowing against it occasionally, a tree will not develop a strong root system. It is the force of the wind that causes the tree to dig in, to sink its roots deep, to take a firm hold and hang on. The famous cypress trees along the California coast have suffered the lashings of wind and storm, but they are firmly rooted in the rock and they won't let go even in the strongest gale. Their beauty has developed from the winds that shaped them.

Being a single parent may not have been your choice. You may wonder from time to time whether you or your children will survive it. Being a parent at all in this complicated world is often difficult, but being a single parent can be harder still. It is possible, however, to raise responsible, respectful, resourceful children in a single-parent home. If you're open and willing to learn, you may find that life as a single parent holds opportunities you haven't thought of—for you *and* for your children.

Wherever you find yourself at this particular moment, you most likely want what most parents want: a family that works for the benefit of all its members, a life that is rich and fulfilling, and children who are growing into contented, capable adults. No, this isn't always easy; but yes, it *is* possible.

Setting the Stage for Single Parenting

SINGLE PARENTS ARE, above all else, *parents*. They just happen to be parents who are single. Nevertheless, much of what concerns single parents—particularly at the start of their single-parenting—focuses on the "single" part: "Will my children suffer?" "How will I make enough money to survive?" "How can I possibly manage when my children are sick and I need to be with them but I have to be at work?" "How will I deal with the all the emotions I feel—the anger and guilt, the discouragement and depression?" "Will I ever find another relationship? And if I do, how do I squeeze in time for dating and still spend enough with my children?" "How do I deal with the anger and hurt my children display when I want to spend time with other people?" "Will my children be deprived by not having two parents who live together?" "How can I be both mother and father to my kids? I don't have the time or energy to be *one* effective parent, let alone two." "How can I possibly compensate for the hardships my children may experience?"

There is another part to being a single parent, though—perhaps the most important part: the plain old everyday "parent" part. Single parents are just that: parents. They deal with the same mundane but often bewildering issues that all parents deal with: "How do I get my kids to do their chores?" "How can I encourage my teenager to talk to me?" "What do I do about discipline?" "Will my kids believe in themselves?" "Will my children repeat my mistakes?" "How can I enforce the limits I set?" "Is there any way to make my children stop whining?" "What about sibling fighting? Homework? Just getting along?"

Do any of these questions sound familiar? All of these concerns are real, and we will deal with every one of them. Still, single parents *do* find more to worry about than just the everyday issues of parenting. And most harbor at least a few false beliefs and fears about divorce, and about single-parent homes and the children who grow up in them. Some of these ideas have been part of our culture for so long that we rarely stop to question them. But many of these beliefs are untrue and do far more harm than good.

Single Parenting: Myth vs. Reality

LONG AGO—when perhaps the world was a kinder, less difficult place—parents raised children alone only when they had suffered a tragedy (death of a spouse) or somehow violated society's moral codes (conceived a child out of wedlock). Life today is different.

During the past twenty-five years, the number of single-parent homes has doubled; unmarried mothers account for almost 30 percent of all births in the United States, and according to the last census, approximately 16 million children live in single-parent homes.

Some have been through the process more than once, when their parents divorced, remarried, and then divorced again.

Single-parent families may be more common today, but much of what we believe about them dates from an earlier time. These myths sometimes cripple the ability of adults and children to believe in their own potential and a promising future. What are some of these myths our society has cultivated about single parenting?

"My kids are doomed." Many people believe that children who grow up with single parents are far more likely than their peers to struggle in school, get

> During the past twenty-five years, the number of single-parent homes has doubled; unmarried mothers account for almost 30 percent of all births in the United States, and according to the last census, approximately 16 million children live in single-parent homes.

MYTHS ABOUT SINGLE PARENTING

- "My kids are doomed."
- "Children who grow up in single-parent homes will never have healthy relationships themselves."
- "Children of single parents need role models, and the sooner their parent remarries, the better."
- "Children of single parents have lower self-esteem."
- "Single-parent homes are 'broken homes.'"

into trouble with the law, and develop serious social problems. In other words, the children of single parents will become delinquents, dropouts, and drug addicts. Is it true?

Actually, a number of researchers have studied this issue in recent years and have made some interesting—and reassuring—discoveries. Many successful people have been raised by single parents; in fact, researchers have found that good parenting skills can compensate for a great deal of stress and hardship. In other words, in homes where single parents are willing to devote time and energy to parenting their children and building loving relationships with them, children are at no greater disadvantage than are children in traditional nuclear families.

Many of the dire predictions for children of single parents have far more to do with economic hardship than the number of parents a child lives with. Poverty and financial struggles do have a serious impact on single parents and their children: 1994 Census Bureau figures show that the median income for a married couple with children is $47,244, while single mothers (divorced or never

> In other words, in homes where single parents are willing to devote time and energy to parenting their children and building loving relationships with them, children are at no greater disadvantage than are children in traditional nuclear families.

married) average only $14,902. The income of custodial mothers drops an average of 30 percent after divorce, and because the vast majority of custodial single parents are mothers, the results—long hours at low-paying jobs, increased stress, an inability to provide resources and opportunities for children—are serious indeed.

> Single parents have the unique opportunity to teach their children that who they are and what they can accomplish does not depend on what they have.

Although we have no easy solutions to these financial dilemmas, we offer practical approaches for single parents to improve their situation—and their children's prospects for the future. Single parents have the unique opportunity to teach their children that who they are and what they can accomplish does not depend on what they have. The good news is that the children of single parents are *not* "doomed." With hard work, love, and Positive Discipline parenting skills, single parents can raise their children to be capable, contented, successful people.

"Children who grow up in single-parent homes will never have healthy relationships themselves." Not so! In fact, a recent University of Michigan study of more than 6,000 adults found that 43 percent of the adult children of divorced parents were happily married—about the same percentage as those who grew up in two-parent homes! In fact, children of divorced parents seemed to invest more energy in maintaining their relationships, perhaps because their own experience made them less likely to take healthy relationships for granted.

Children learn from their parents, of course. If you become bitter, complain frequently about the opposite sex, and demonstrate through your behavior that relationships aren't worth the trouble or say they "never work out," your children are likely to adopt those attitudes. If, however, you are honest about your own feelings, work to keep an open mind, and model healthy relationship skills yourself, your children can learn that although relationships take commitment and patience, they can add a great deal of joy to life. Finding healing and hope for yourself is the best way to teach your children.

"Children of single parents need role models, and the sooner their parent remarries, the better." Pauline Mays was deeply worried about her son. Justin, eight years old, had never known his father, who had left Pauline before Justin was born. Life seemed to go along well enough for mother and son until Justin joined Cub Scouts. One evening, after Pauline brought Justin home from a Scouts meeting, she noticed that he was unusually quiet.

"You seem a little sad, buddy," she said. "What's going on?"

Justin was silent for a moment, thinking. Then he looked up into his mother's face. "There's a Cub Scout campout this weekend up at the lake. I really want to go, but all the other guys are going with their dads." He hesitated, shooting a worried glance at Pauline. "Mom, you're terrific—but you'd be the only mom there and I'd feel weird. And you don't know how to put up a tent or anything. Clint's dad offered to let me stay in their tent, but that feels weird, too."

Justin sighed. "Mom," he said wistfully, "why did my dad leave?"

Pauline reached out to hug her son, a jumble of emotions and thoughts rushing through her. Should she go on the campout with Justin? Maybe she should ask his uncle or one of the youth leaders at church to go with him. Maybe she ought to start dating again. Her last relationship had ended painfully, but maybe Justin needed a father. She sighed like her son, unsure of what to do and how to help him.

Then Pauline remembered something she had heard at a parenting class for single parents: Instead of feeling sorry for your child when difficult situations come up, get him or her involved in possible solutions. If a solution can't be found, offer support through active listening (we explore this in chapter 2), and then have faith in your child's ability to deal with painful situations without self-pity.

Pauline said to Justin, "Why don't we sit down and brainstorm some ideas that might work for you? I'll start. We could tell all the dads to stay home so mothers get a chance to learn how to pitch tents. Or I could dress up like a dad and see if I could pass."

Justin grinned and said, "I could go by myself and have a tent where all the other kids could come and tell scary stories after their dads are asleep." Pauline said, "You could see if Uncle Joe would like to go, or you could accept Clint's invitation." Justin added, "I could invite Sammy. He doesn't have a dad, either. We could take turns bossing each other around."

By now Pauline and Justin were laughing. Then they took a serious look at their list. Justin said, "Mom, I don't think the other dads will stay home, and you could never pass for a father. If Uncle Joe wants to go, I really would like to invite Sammy, too. If he doesn't, it probably wouldn't be so bad to go with Clint and his dad. After all, like you keep telling me, no one will feel sorry for me unless I feel sorry for myself." Justin leaned over and gave his mom a tight hug. "Thanks, Mom."

Sooner or later, most single parents face moments like this. Children can benefit greatly from the presence of both men and women in their family life—if those men and women are healthy. Children actually suffer far more harm by living with conflict and unhealthy role models than by having one healthy, effective parent. Still, most children occasionally want what they seem to see everywhere around them: a family with both a mom and a dad. So, if a child can't have his birth parents together, should his single parent remarry?

> You may find a loving and respectful partner; however, if you are parenting alone, be assured: You *can* do it!

There are ways single parents can help their boys and girls thrive—things that can be learned about raising sons and daughters (the influence of gender is discussed in chapter 7), but single parents *can* raise their children successfully without a partner. It is wise to build a good support system—to have a circle of friends, relatives, and helpers who can provide what from time to time you may not be able to. You'll discover ways to do this in chapter 6. You may find a loving and respectful partner; however, if you are parenting alone, be assured: You *can* do it!

"Children of single parents have lower self-esteem." Low self-esteem seems widespread in today's world. But the truth is that children of single parents are no more likely to suffer from it than their peers from two-parent homes if these single parents are able to learn and practice the skills and attitudes that empower children and teach them to believe in their own value and potential.

When children believe, "I am capable; I can contribute in meaningful ways; and I have power and influence in my life," they will have self-esteem. Single parents can provide as many opportunities as other parents for children to develop these beliefs. And both two-parent and single-parent families can fail to provide the foundation for self-esteem.

A strong sense of self-esteem is important. It helps children resist negative peer pressure and gives them courage to face challenges and the ability to try new things. This is well worth repeating: Parents—whether single or married—can teach their children life skills, practice the art of encouragement, and give children opportunities to test their wings. In fact, children of single parents have a wonderful chance to learn that they belong, that they can make an important contribution to their family, and that they can face and overcome any challenge.

When children believe: "I am capable; I can contribute in meaningful ways; and I have power and influence in my life," they will have self-esteem.

"Single-parent homes are 'broken homes.'" "Dad," said five-year-old Miriam as she entered the kitchen one evening. "How come everybody else has more people and stuff in their families?"

Mark Singer put aside the vegetables he was chopping and smiled at his daughter. "That's an interesting question," he said. "What do you mean?"

Miriam sat down at the kitchen counter and took a slice of carrot. "Well," she said as she crunched it, "Kitty Parks says I come from a broken home 'cause I only have a dad and my mom lives somewhere else. And everybody else in our neighborhood has a dad and a mom and more kids and stuff. So I wondered why we're different."

Mark scooped Miriam up in his arms and sat down on the couch. "I think we have a pretty terrific family," he said, "but it is a little different. There's you and me and Mugsy, the dog—"

"And Pebbles, the cat," Miriam chimed in, "and my lizard, Rex. Is that really a family?"

"You bet it is," Mark said, gazing into his daughter's eyes. "We have the best family I've ever been in, and no one else has one exactly like it. That makes it special. And you know what? You have another family when you go to see your mom. You have two families!"

Miriam grinned and hugged her dad. "Thanks, Dad," she said. "When's dinner?"

You *Can* Make It Work!

NO HOME—AND NO FAMILY—is broken unless the people in it allow it to be. And even things that have been broken can be fixed. Families come in all sorts of shapes and sizes these days; children are raised by two parents, by single parents, by grandparents, and by gay or lesbian couples. Whatever the shape of your family, learning effective parenting skills, building healthy relationships, and celebrating the ways in which you are special will help everyone in your family do and feel their best.

2

Changing Your Perception of Single Parenting

You MAY HAVE believed that children living with single parents are automatically deprived, but it simply isn't so. As we have said before, many happy, successful people have been raised by single parents—even in orphanages. It is not the circumstances of life but how we perceive those circumstances that has the greatest impact. Each person decides whether challenges will be stumbling blocks or stepping stones to joy and success in life. Understanding this does not eliminate the difficulties and concerns of single parents, but it can offer hope and a basis for dealing with the difficulties in ways that benefit rather than harm children.

Begin by giving up the belief that you have to compensate your child for having only one parent. Don't try to be both mother and father; it's not possible, nor is it wise. One *healthy* parent is enough. Work toward developing a positive attitude about being a single-parent family: "This is how it is, and we're going to benefit from how it is."

Children Follow Your Lead

CHILDREN USUALLY MIMIC the attitudes of their parents, though sometimes they choose the opposite. If you are feeling depressed, deprived, guilty, or tragic, chances are your children will feel the same. If you have a victim's attitude, chances are your children will feel like victims. If you have an optimistic, courageous attitude, your children will most likely be influenced to learn from you. The greatest gift we can give our children is to have a hopeful outlook on life no matter what our circumstances—and all circumstances, no matter how difficult, offer opportunities to learn and grow. Try to focus on how you can make the best of your present opportunities.

Parenting for the Future

THINK FOR JUST a few minutes about the moment you first saw each of your children. Remember the wonder, the awe, the sheer power of those first moments of that precious new life? All too soon you took that baby home and life somehow became an effort to survive each day, deal with each new adjustment and each new phase. The wonder and awe sometimes fade into dim memories, overwhelmed by the sheer amount of work it takes to raise a child.

When will the baby sleep through the night? Stand up? Walk? We spend hours pondering feeding schedules and development charts, and earnestly discussing the varying approaches to toilet training. The weeks and months rush by. Before we know it, our children are toddlers and we must make critical decisions about discipline. Should we spank, and what about time-out? School days arrive, then the teen years. There are so many day-to-day decisions to be made, while often just coping with new behaviors (and misbehaviors) can take all our time and energy. (For more information about parenting young children, see *Positive Discipline: The First Three Years* and *Positive Discipline for Preschoolers* by Jane Nelsen, Cheryl Erwin, and Roslyn Duffy—Prima Publishing, 1998.)

Sooner or later, though, the moment arrives when a proud teenager zooms off in the family car with a group of friends, leaving Mom or Dad to sit in a silent home surrounded by questions. Is she smoking cigarettes? Marijuana? Is he drinking or partying? What about sex? Does she trust me enough

> The greatest gift we can give our children is to have a hopeful outlook on life no matter what our circumstances—and all circumstances, no matter how difficult, offer opportunities to learn and grow.

to tell me what's going on in her life? Does he believe in himself? Can he make good choices about life? Did I do enough? Too much? Was I a good enough parent?

All parents face these moments and these questions. Single parents sometimes worry more than they should; after all, it seems the responsibility rests squarely on only one all-too-fragile set of shoulders. If your children are almost grown when you're reading these words, be assured; it's never too late to make changes—to make things better. And if your children are still young, you have the opportunity to shape the future for all of you—to parent your children in a way that is thoughtful, loving, and focused on the future.

> Perhaps one of the best things you can do right now is to take a moment to ask yourself a very important question: What is it that you really want for your children?

Perhaps one of the best things you can do right now is to take a moment to ask yourself a very important question: What is it that you really want for your children? When they've grown up and set off to lead their adult lives, what qualities do you want them to possess? Is what you're doing now nurturing those qualities in them?

You may want your children to have good judgment, to be responsible, self-reliant, kind, honest, thoughtful, courageous, moral, hard-working, appreciative—each parent's list will be a little different. What matters is that you realize this: What we do today as parents will shape our children's future. If we want our young ones to be responsible, then how we handle the spilled milk, the broken curfew, or the homework left undone must nurture those qualities in them.

These thoughts overwhelm most parents and may make you wonder, "How on earth can I do that? Especially as a single parent?" Just remember that the most important tools are those you already possess: your love for your children, and your wisdom and common sense. Your own life and the decisions you make about it will teach your children a great deal (more, sometimes, than you might like). This book is intended to provide you with additional tools and techniques, and perhaps some new ideas.

If you were to decide to drive across the country from your home to a place you'd never visited before, you would undoubtedly check a map, plan out the best route, and make sure your car was in good running order. Raising children should be an equally careful journey. Spending the time now to set your goals as a parent and to think about the long-range results will save you untold trouble and confusion down the road. As a single parent—with all the distractions and responsibilities that entails—it may be even more important to have a plan and to know what you want the results to be. There will undoubtedly be wrong turns and dead ends along the way, as there are for all parents.

> Just remember that the most important tools are those you already possess: your love for your children, and your wisdom and common sense.

Taking the time to think about what we want our children to learn from life—and from us—is a critical first step on the road to successful single parenting.

Appreciate the Benefits

AMAZING AS IT MAY SEEM, there are benefits to being a single parent. The widely perpetuated myth that parenting is always easier when two people share the job is not necessarily true! It's easy to idealize the advantages of having a partner when you're going it alone, but disharmony often prevails in two-parent households. Mom and Dad almost never agree completely about how to raise their children. As Alfred Adler put it, "Opposites attract, but they usually have difficulty living together." It's amazing how quickly differences that once seemed endearing become faults that are annoying. Couples who have opposing parenting styles usually fail to make this charming discovery until *after* children arrive.

Look around you and see how many couples disagree on the "right" kind of parenting—and how often they do battle over their children. While one believes in strict control, the other believes in leniency. These beliefs become even stronger and more pronounced as each feels the need to compensate for the other's misguided ideas—the strict parent becoming stricter to make up for the "wishy-washy" parent, and the lenient parent becoming even more lenient to make up for the "mean" and "rigid" parent. They argue furiously over who is right when they are both actually being ineffective. In fact, children respond best to something in between called *kindness and firmness with dignity and respect*—something single parents can provide quite effectively.

Strict control is ineffective because it can ultimately produce a dangerous combination of rebellion, resentment, revenge, sneakiness, and low self-esteem. Sometimes overly controlled children become "approval junkies" and spend their lives allowing others to control them, often basing their choices in life on the approval and opinion of others. Permissiveness is equally ineffective because it teaches children to manipulate others into giving them whatever they want without having to put forth any effort on their own. Sometimes children who are raised permissively believe they aren't loved unless someone else is serving them or giving in to them, and may continually test their limits in an effort to feel secure.

Either way, these children are not exploring and developing their own capabilities. They are not learning the skills and beliefs that will help them to solve problems, exercise good judgment, and face the challenges of life with confidence and optimism.

By pointing out the problems of dual parenting we do not mean to imply children will be harmed if they have two parents. Most single parents occasionally long for a helper, while most married parents occasionally disagree with each other. No situation is perfect. Our intent here is to help single parents stop idealizing dual parenting so they will

> In fact, children respond best to something in between called *kindness and firmness with dignity and respect*—something single parents can provide quite effectively.

be more open to other solutions to their problems. Most situations offer both assets and liabilities. You *can* choose to focus on the assets of single parenting.

Assets of Single Parenting

MANY PEOPLE LOOKING back on their failed marriages have said, "I was so devastated by my divorce that I would never have believed I would one day say that it was actually a good thing. I had no idea how much I could grow and learn, and never thought I'd find a relationship that was ten times better than the one I had. When I became stronger and more mature, I was ready for a partner who was stronger and more mature. I thought my divorce was the end of the world, when actually it was the beginning of a much better world."

When we are immature and insecure, we often (unconsciously) look for mates who have characteristics we lack as a way of completing ourselves. We may also have a tendency to choose partners who have the same level of maturity (or immaturity) as we do. But soon after we marry these people, instead of feeling complete we begin a campaign to change our mates—to make them more like us. This does not create a loving, respectful relationship. When we become more mature and secure, however, we want mates who share our interests and lifestyles. When our needs for a shared lifestyle are met, it becomes much easier to create a loving, respectful relationship.

> You can live the rest of your life with anger, resentment, low self-esteem, or whatever debilitating beliefs you allow to run your life, or you can look for the opportunities to learn and grow from whatever circumstances with which you are faced.

Divorce can be extremely painful, especially when it is beyond your control. If you were abandoned, you may be dealing with feelings of rejection, doubts about self-worth, and fear that no one will ever love you again. If you chose to leave your former partner, you may be feeling both guilt and sadness. We strongly suggest that you find a counseling program to help you deal with these issues. You can often find free groups through your church or other community organizations.

Essentially you have two choices: You can live the rest of your life with anger, resentment, low self-esteem, or whatever debilitating beliefs you allow to run your life, or you can look for the opportunities to learn and grow from whatever circumstances with which you are faced. For yourself—and for the sake of your children—we strongly encourage you to use this opportunity to model some of the characteristics you hope your children will develop—courage, tenacity, and confidence in your ability to learn and grow.

Many single parents are fearful of loneliness. They forget that they were often extremely lonely while they were married. Usually so busy dealing with the distractions of a bad relationship, they didn't take the time to focus on their loneliness. But when the distractions are gone, they have a chance to experience the loneliness. Though it may not be a pleasant feeling, you can learn from it. Sit quietly and meditate on whatever is bothering you. Ask your loneliness, "What do you have to teach me?" and you may be surprised at the answers you receive.

Ways of coping with loneliness are explored in chapter 13.

Shared Responsibility and Contribution

Another asset of single parenting is the opportunity it provides the children to feel needed. Single parents have an extra incentive to enlist their children in sharing responsibilities for the family and the household. Children become capable when they are allowed to experience the pride and joy of making a contribution. Participating in shared responsibility—being part of a team—is one way they can gain this experience.

If parents try to do too much for children to make up for the fact that they have only one parent, the children will not have a chance to develop initiative and gain new skills. Strength of character comes from patience, hard work, and delayed gratification. Rather than worrying about deprivation your children may suffer because you are single, concentrate on giving them responsibilities that will nurture a positive outlook and the skills with which to achieve their goals.

> Rather than worrying about deprivation your children may suffer because you are single, concentrate on giving them responsibilities that will nurture a positive outlook and the skills with which to achieve their goals.

Shared Decision Making

A great way to get children involved in sharing responsibility and making a contribution to the family is by inviting them to share in decision making through family meetings. Children feel especially capable when they are genuinely needed and have a sense of belonging and significance. Children are much more likely to be enthusiastic about and motivated to follow decisions they have participated in making. Let your children help you decide on routines for bedtime, morning schedules, chores, homework, planning family-fun events, and anything else needed to help your family run smoothly.

We discuss family meetings in greater detail in chapter 9.

Developing Closeness

LIVING WITH A single parent, children have the opportunity to make meaningful contributions to the family, to feel needed and listened to, and to be taken seriously, all of which develops family closeness. Your circumstances can be seen as an opportunity to build a team relationship with your children. By emphasizing these benefits, we don't mean to imply that problems don't exist. But we do mean to point out that by idealizing other family situations and maintaining a negative attitude about your own simply will not help. Focusing on the benefits is not the same as denying the painful issues and feelings you or your children experience. It can in fact help you and your children work through the negative feelings and difficult issues in beneficial ways, as you will discover in the following chapters.

We can't control everything that happens in our lives, but we can control the way we *deal* with what happens. As a single parent, you have the opportunity to teach your children this valuable principle. If you've been choosing a negative approach to your situation, acknowledge this to your children and ask for their help. It's never too late to start over.

A Few Points to Keep in Mind

PARENTING, ESPECIALLY ON your own, is rarely simple. And no matter how much helpful information you receive, not all things work all of the time for all children—or for all parents! Reading a parenting book can be discouraging, as it might tempt you to think, "I've done it all wrong," and give up before you start—or to think, "This sounds great," and then try to change everything at once. Keeping the following points in mind as you read this book may help you to make the most of what you learn. Also remember that the ideas in this book have been shown to be extremely helpful to many

POINTS TO REMEMBER

- It is always the relationship that matters most.
- Don't try to change everything at once.
- Trust your own wisdom and common sense.

parents—single and married—who have raised or are raising their children using these same Positive Discipline parenting skills.

It is always the relationship that matters most. Tips and techniques for parenting are great and can be very helpful, but what matters more than anything is a relationship between parent and child that is based on unconditional love, respect, and trust. If that relationship is strong—if your children *know* beyond a shadow of a doubt that you love them *no matter what*—you can make a lot of mistakes and still come out okay.

All parenting works best when it is based on a foundation of love. Techniques without love are just techniques. Taking the time to build the proper foundation through talking, laughing, playing, and just being together may be the best investment you make in your children.

Don't try to change everything at once. You may find in this book many ideas you want to try. But changing too much at once—especially in a single-parent family that may have experienced a great deal of change already—may complicate life instead of making it easier.

Pick one or two ideas at a time and try them for a while. See how they feel and how your family reacts before trying anything more. Change that is made gradually and thoughtfully may be more effective than sudden changes that disrupt the family and are then quickly abandoned.

Trust your heart, wisdom, and common sense. No one knows your children better than you do. Your own inner wisdom will tell you when the time is right to make changes in your family. Remember, however, that new skills often feel awkward at first. Learning to trust your own judgment and to follow your heart may take time, and you may have to work at developing the confidence to do it, especially if your faith in yourself has been shaken. As you read and think about what you learn in this book, let your love for your children be your guide. It will help you decide what is needed for your family, when it's right to change, and how to make those changes.

> Remember, however, that new skills often feel awkward at first.

3

Coping with Feelings: Yours and Theirs

ANGRY SHOUTING, irritable nagging, hysterical sobbing, stony silence—the ways in which we choose to express our feelings are often anything but productive. And so many things can cause strong feelings in us: change (such as divorce or death), stress, difficult relationships, sometimes just life itself. What many parents fail to understand is that children have the same emotions they do—and may have even fewer resources for coping with them.

Parents sometimes forget how deeply emotions can influence behavior. And it is often tempting to deal only with behavior and to focus on "fixing" it in the same way you might try to mend a broken doll or find the missing piece to a favorite game. You may find that sometimes you want nothing more than peace, quiet, and an absence of the problems and the feelings they generate.

When children express their feelings, particularly strong feelings, parents sometimes want to take responsibility for those, too, instead of simply trying to understand them. We want to protect our children, so we often find it difficult to share with emotional honesty what we are really feeling. Or we dismiss the messy subject entirely. "Don't use that tone of voice with me, young man!" we say, or "There's nothing to be afraid of." Because of these reactions, children may decide that feelings are dangerous

> What many parents fail to understand is that children have the same emotions they do—and may have even fewer resources for coping with them.

things that shouldn't be discussed. But feelings (both good and bad) will always be part of living, so wouldn't it be better to teach our children (and to learn ourselves) that we don't need to be afraid of our feelings—that we can handle them and even learn from them?

> For all parents—but for single parents in particular—learning to recognize and deal with a child's feelings is a critically important first step in dealing with that child's behavior.

Feelings can be an especially troubling subject for single parents. Depending on your experience, you may be familiar with anxiety, loneliness, guilt, fear, anger, bitterness, confusion, or a host of other feelings. And when you're in the grip of any one of those strong emotions, it can be extremely difficult to deal with the fact that a child's behavior is a sort of code for those same tumultuous feelings. It can be difficult to tell if a child is simply being cantankerous or has actually suffered a loss and is angry and hurt and telling you so in the only way he knows how. For all parents—but for single parents in particular—learning to recognize and deal with a child's feelings is a critically important first step in dealing with that child's behavior.

What Are Feelings?

FEELINGS HAVE A bad reputation, because many people put them in the same category as *emotional displays*. A temper tantrum is an emotional display. Acting depressed is often an emotional display. A feeling, though, is simply a feeling. The truth is: Feelings themselves don't cause problems; it is actions (or a failure to act at all) that can cause problems.

Feelings give us valuable information. In fact, some of them, such as fear, are intended to help keep us safe—to help us sort out foolish actions from wise ones. Other feelings serve as a barometer, a source of information about what is going on in our lives. Both children and adults can be frightened by a new experience or a sudden change; they can be justifiably angry when something alters or threatens their world; and they can be sad, hurt, and depressed. When we are able to tune in to our feelings without judgment or censorship, we can then tune in to our inner wisdom for solutions to the problems that cause these feelings. In fact, there is a great deal of research telling us that *Star Trek's*

Mr. Spock was wrong. Emotions are not just messy annoyances that get in the way of living a rational, logical life; they appear instead to be *critical* to the process of making good decisions and responding to the world around us.

Children learn how to deal with their feelings by watching their parents. And unfortunately, most parents deal with difficult feelings through emotional displays. They either dump their stronger emotions on the people around them or they squelch them entirely. Unexpressed feelings don't go away, however; they simply go underground. When they're finally released, the results may be far more damaging because they have been allowed to fester.

It is important to help children deal with their feelings, such as their disappointments about having only one parent, or their anger and confusion if there has been a divorce. Parents can help children express their feelings in ways that will not hurt themselves or others. Children (and adults) need to know that feelings are different from actions. Feelings are *always* okay—they are never right or wrong. What we *do,* on the other hand, might be appropriate or inappropriate. For example, it is okay to feel angry; it is not okay to use that anger as an excuse to hit someone.

> Feelings are *always* okay—they are never right or wrong. What we *do,* on the other hand, might be appropriate or inappropriate.

Many adults do not acknowledge their feelings, fearing the actions those feelings imply. For example, they may not admit they are unhappy for fear they must consider changes they aren't ready to make. At a subconscious level, they repress their feelings (even though those feelings may leak out in the form of anger or depression). This harmful pattern of denial is passed on to their children.

How many times have you heard this exchange? A child says, "I hate my sister!" An adult admonishes, "No you don't. You know you love your sister."

It would be healthier to say to the child, "I can tell how angry or hurt you feel right now. I can't let you hit your sister, but let's see if we can find a way for you to express your feelings without hurting others."

What About Anger?

One of the trickiest emotions to handle—and the one considered least tolerable by our society—is anger. Anger is often a way in which we attempt to take care of ourselves when we are feeling powerless or hurt; anger usually masks more painful feelings that lie deep within us. Sometimes children display anger because they are frustrated by the demands of their parents or by their own inability to complete a task or satisfy their curiosity. Anger is often a cover-up for other emotions, such as hurt or fear. (It hurts to lose a parent or to feel a lack of unconditional love.) Resisting adults is also one way children (especially teenagers) individu-ate—to find out who they are instead of who their parents want them to be.

Most adults, however, find children's angry behavior difficult to deal with. Children express their angry feelings in all sorts of inappropriate ways—ways that often get them into trouble. Anger properly expressed can be a great way to clear the air and set the stage for a discussion about something troubling. Too often, though, anger rages out of control, closing the door on communication and sometimes even putting those we love at risk.

Dealing with Angry Feelings in Appropriate Ways

Alex was six years old when his father moved out and Diane, Alex's mother, worried about the effect the breakup of the family would have on her son. Alex was a bright, sensitive boy, who was almost always helpful and cheerful. He had never been an aggres-sive child, so Diane was shocked and confused when one night, during a bedtime tickling match, Alex suddenly began punching her in the stomach.

Children express their angry feel-ings in all sorts of inap-propriate ways—ways that often get them into trouble. Anger properly expressed can be a great way to clear the air and set the stage for a discus-sion about something troubling.

Diane and Alex had talked quite openly about his father's decision to divorce Diane, but obviously there were feelings in the little boy's heart that even he had no idea were there. The next day, as she drove her son home from school, Diane asked him how he was feeling about what had happened the night before.

Alex was silent for a moment. "Mom," he fi-nally said, "sometimes I feel so angry about stuff that I just want to punch someone!"

DEALING WITH YOUR CHILD'S EMOTIONS

Dealing with your child's strong emotions can be a great opportunity to get into your child's world and to build closeness, understanding, and trust. Here are a few ideas you might try:

- Ask your child to draw a picture of how the emotion feels. Does it have a color? A sound?

- Ask your child to talk through what he or she is feeling rather than acting it out. Children are often not consciously aware of their feelings (or may not have labels for them), so asking simple questions about them in a calm voice ("Sounds like you may be feeling hurt and want to get even" or "Are you feeling really mad right now?") may help.

- Redirect the behavior in a more appropriate way. Screaming into a pillow, running a race around the backyard, or playing with water or paints or clay may also help vent emotions and restore calm.

- Invite your child to take a cooling-off time-out period before acting on his or her strong feelings.

- Invite your child to notice what is happening in her body when she gets really angry. Because anger is a physical reaction (adrenaline is released, heart rate and respiration increase, blood vessels expand, and so on), most people *feel* anger physically. Both you and your child can learn to recognize your own early warnings (clenched fists or teeth, a pounding heart, or a knotted stomach are common reactions) and provide ways to cool off before anger gets out of control.

Diane was no expert on psychology, but her common sense and love for her son told her that she had to help him work through these overpowering emotions. "Alex," she said, "you know that you can't hit me when you feel this way. We don't treat each other like that. But I understand how you're feeling, and I think we need to find a way for you to be angry without hurting anyone else."

Diane paid a visit to the toy store and came home with an inflatable "bop bag." Then she told Alex that whenever he was feeling angry or hurt, he could punch the bop bag. Diane put the bag in the kitchen so she could talk with Alex while he used it.

Alex and his mother were both surprised at the violence with which he attacked the bag, but with the passage of time, the bop-bag sessions became a source of healing for both of them. Occasionally Diane and Alex would punch the bag back and forth to each other. "Are you angry with Dad, too?" Alex asked one day. "You can pretend this is Dad if you want to." More often than not, the punching sessions ended with laughter and hugs.

Alex punched his way through three bop bags before the fourth one died of a slow leak in the kitchen corner. He learned that although his feelings were sometimes difficult to cope with, they were valid and they were *his*, and they were manageable with a little understanding and help. He also discovered that it was possible to be angry with his dad and still to love him very much. That discovery laid the foundation for strong, healthy relationships between Alex and each of his parents.

Diane did not ignore Alex's feelings, nor did she try to talk him out of them. She did not plummet into depression, despair, or blaming herself. She helped Alex find a way to understand and cope with his feelings in ways in which he did not hurt himself or others. The bop bag helped Alex express his feelings of anger until they were manageable and he could focus on other things.

It is valuable to both you and your children when you learn to explore their feelings by getting into their world and seeing things from their perspective. Children living in single-parent homes may experience a wide spectrum of emotions, particularly if they've had to cope with death, or with the divorce of parents, or simply with being different from their friends. They can feel great anger, guilt, confusion, worry, sadness, and fear.

Acknowledging Children's Feelings

"MY KIDS BEGAN having bad dreams and difficulty sleeping after their father moved out," one mom reported. "I thought they were just being defiant about going to bed, but it turned out that they were afraid of burglars, now that there was no man in the house. I'd never even thought of that."

Many times the everyday tensions and conflicts we experience with our children are a result of what they are feeling. Learning to understand those feelings from a child's perspective—instead of only from our own—can help us solve problems rather than exacerbate them. Sometimes, in fact, understanding and accepting feelings are all that are needed to solve a problem. Children, like adults, need to feel understood and accepted—and careful listening can be a first step to constructive communication.

Heather, six, was planning to go to her father's house for ten days during the Christmas holidays. Although Heather went to her dad's house every other weekend, this visit was different. Her grandmother and her aunt had come in from out of town to spend the Christmas holiday with Heather and her father. It had been planned for months; Heather was very excited about seeing her grandmother again and meeting her aunt for the first time, but she was used to spending her time with Dad alone. She and her father had wonderful weekends together doing many things such as in-line skating, taking walks, and playing games. Heather treasured this special time with her father.

> Many times the everyday tensions and conflicts we experience with our children are a result of what they are feeling. Learning to understand those feelings from a child's perspective—instead of only from our own—can help us solve problems rather than exacerbate them.

On the second day of the holiday visit, Heather called home to her mother, Christie, in tears, because Dad had told her to put on a fancy dress to go see the *Nutcracker Ballet*. "I don't want to wear that dress," Heather had wailed. "I want to wear the sweatshirt you gave me."

Christie was in a hurry when her daughter called. "Wear the dress your dad wants," she told Heather briskly. "Santa probably will be at the ballet, and if you're not being good, he'll know." When Christie hung up the phone, she realized that manipulating Heather with Santa Claus was neither fair nor a solution to the problem. Shame and guilt are not good motivators; they do not empower children to make better choices about their behavior. Christie looked forward to an opportunity to be kinder and more respectful the next time Heather called. Her opportunity came the next day when Heather called again.

"Dad just made me leave the kitchen—he said I was in the way," she sniffed.

Christie tried to get into Heather's world and to understand the feelings behind the child's behavior. "It sounds like you're feeling left out. Is it hard to share your dad with your grandmother and aunt?"

Heather muttered sullenly, "Yeah." She was used to having her dad all to herself, and now he wasn't spending any time with her. "He hasn't played with me at all since I got here, and I'm not having any fun," Heather said sadly.

Christie asked Heather if she had thought about telling her dad what she was feeling.

Heather was silent for a moment. "Maybe I'll do that," she said.

When Christie's phone rang the next day, a much happier child was on the other end. "I told Dad what we were talking about, Mom," she said, "and he agreed to play with me at least once each day. And this morning we went for a walk alone—just the two of us." Heather chattered cheerfully with her mother for a few minutes more, then hung up, leaving Christie smiling.

When Heather felt understood, she was able to approach her problem from a different perspective. Christie avoided the natural impulse to fix things or to assign blame, and by acting as her daughter's coach she helped Heather take responsibility for her own feelings, express them respectfully to her father, and find a solution to her problem.

Active Listening: The Key to Communication

Q. My fourteen-year-old daughter has developed a habit of running into her room, and slamming and locking the door every time she's upset about something. Her dad has never been around and doesn't give us any child support. I do the best I can, but I'm working double shifts and still have trouble keeping up with the bills. My daughter's behavior lately is more than I can handle. I find myself standing outside her door, yelling at her to open it. Last time this happened, I started pounding on the door and rattling the door knob, which only made her scream louder at me. My neighbor told me I should take her door off the hinges so she can't get away from me. What should I do?

A. Your own exhaustion and discouragement are reflected in your question. Raising a child alone with limited means is a demanding task, and sometimes children's behavior makes it even harder. Your daughter is coping with adolescence, which means she is trying to find the balance between establishing independence from you and keeping some sort of connection. Unfortunately, teens sometimes choose arguing as a way of staying connected—and anger does feel like a powerful bond sometimes. After all, there is so much energy between you!

Responding with punishment or attempts to control your daughter (like forcing her to open the door or removing it altogether) may only make matters worse. A good place to begin is by acknowledging the strong feelings both of you are experiencing. Try giving her a while to vent her feelings alone in her room; take several deep, calming breaths yourself.

When both of you are feeling calmer, try standing outside her door and, in a quiet tone of voice (she'll have to be quiet herself to hear you), telling her you can hear how angry, hurt, or afraid she's feeling (your own wisdom will help you know what her feelings are). Tell her that you understand her need for some time alone but that you would like to help. Then tell her she can come and find you if she'd like to talk.

Be patient; children are often slow to trust the changes adults make. But if you are sincere in wanting to listen to her feelings (remember, listening doesn't necessarily mean you agree) and if you can resist the urge to *make* her open her door, eventually she may decide to talk to you face to face instead of yelling through a closed door. Active listening without attempts to control the situation will let your daughter know that what she's feeling is important to you and that you can talk about it together.

Active listening is the art of listening to and reflecting back a child's feelings. It offers the child a chance to feel understood and to gain understanding about—and learn terms for—the often confusing things she feels, and it gives the parent a chance to explore the feelings behind the child's behavior. Active listening does not necessarily mean that the parent is agreeing with the child, but it allows the child to feel understood—something all of us need from time to time—and an opportunity to clarify his own feelings and move on to problem solving.

Ron's ten-year-old son returned home with a sour expression on his face following a visit with his mother. "Hi there, Mitch," Ron called out. "I missed you. When you've had a chance to straighten up your room, we can go have that ball game we talked about."

Mitch, as it so happened, had not had a good weekend. Mom's new boyfriend was visiting—with his two young sons—and Mitch had had to share his room and his possessions with the boys. He was feeling displaced and

angry, and the thought of cleaning his room at Dad's was more than he could bear. "I don't care about playing ball," he told his bewildered father, "and I'm not going to clean my room!" He stomped out into the backyard, leaving Ron to wonder what he should do next.

Ron had several options. He could insist that Mitch clean his room. Or he could ask Mitch angrily, "What's happened now? And don't talk to me that way!" (Doesn't this sound familiar? Parents often tell their children how to behave, instead of just listening and acknowledging the feelings expressed.)

The option Ron chose was to give Mitch a moment to cool off. Then Ron reflected back Mitch's feelings. "Sounds like you're pretty angry," he said gently, when Mark finally came indoors. Mitch grunted noncommittally. "You seem to be feeling hurt, too," his dad continued. "Is there something you'd like to talk about?"

It took a moment, but Mitch began to tell his father about his weekend with Mom and how he'd felt. Once Mitch realized that his dad understood and accepted his feelings, they worked together on finding a solution to the problems, to Mitch's behavior toward his dad, and to the issue of cleaning his room. And later there was still time for the ball game.

Understanding and accepting our feelings and those of our children are the first steps in building relationships of openness and trust; learning to "listen" to nonverbal messages, to express ourselves respectfully and accurately, and to work together to solve problems are the next steps in creating an effective and loving single-parent family.

4

The Fine Art of Communication: Reading the Clues of Energy

COMMUNICATION COMES IN many forms. Adults are comfortable with words; we use lots of them (and then wonder why children tune us out). But much of what we "say" to one another happens without words. The message is contained in our body language and in our energy.

Our emotions create a distinct energy around us. Have you ever entered a room where people have been arguing? There may not be a sound, yet you can feel the static and prickling of anger hanging in the air. We usually communicate more of our message nonverbally (our facial expression, our tone of voice, our posture) than we do with words.

Children are especially sensitive to the non-verbal messages adults send. They can "read" energy long before they learn to read words! When an adult's words and nonverbal messages don't match up, children instinctively trust the nonverbal part. For instance, Katie is telling her mother about the terrific time she had with her dad and his new girlfriend. Katie suddenly interrupts her story about the new doll Dad and Stephanie bought her to ask her mother, "Are you mad?"

"No, Katie, of course not," her mother says (with only a little bit of impatience in her voice). "Why?"

"Well," Katie answers, "you keep doing that sighing thing and your eyebrows are all scrunched up."

Katie's mom now has an opportunity to let her daughter know that sometimes she feels hurt or lonely—but that she isn't angry with Katie and she's happy Katie can enjoy being with her father.

Parents must learn to be alert to their children's nonverbal clues, too. A normally cheerful child who comes home from school and goes silently to his room may be giving you clues that he needs to talk. A slammed door, a quivering chin, or an inability to sleep at night may be evidence that your child needs to sort through some feelings with you.

When you can learn to reflect back and empathize with the statements—both verbal and nonverbal—made by your children, it allows them to think about what has happened—a moment to probe for the true feeling. When you contest what they have said (or lecture, or offer solutions before they are ready), you are only challenging them to argue their position or to refuse to talk at all. And you may miss important opportunities for healing, showing love, and building trust.

How to Listen Actively

A CHILD MAY SAY, "No one wants to play with me." An ineffective response from a parent would be, "Oh, come on now, you have lots of friends." Although the parent's statement may be true, it doesn't acknowledge the child's feeling at that moment—and it effectively closes off any real communication about what's going on.

An active response would be, "You seem to think you don't have any friends. I can see that makes you sad." When the child has had a chance to respond, a parent might follow up with, "Is there more?" This question often brings out deeper, buried feelings. And it is important to ask with genuine interest and curiosity, rather than judgment. (After all, no one enjoys being interrogated!) Sometimes all children *really* need is for someone to listen and understand. Thoughtful, active listening encourages empathy in both adult and child, and gives parents the chance to understand so that they can then deal with what's really important.

EXAMPLES OF ACTIVE LISTENING

Imagine that these statements are made by a child. How would you respond?

- No one ever invites me to parties.
- It hurts when I go to the dentist.
- I don't like my teacher at school.
- You're not fair!

Active listening might lead you to offer responses like these:

- Sounds like you're feeling disappointed and left out. Do you want to talk about it?
- It can hurt sometimes when you go to the dentist—sometimes I don't like going either!
- You seem frustrated with your teacher. Is there more you can tell me?
- Sounds like you think I made a mistake. Can you tell me why you feel that way?

These statements invite children to feel heard and to know that it is okay to feel what they feel. Validating a child's feelings through love and understanding is a wonderful way to open the door to real communication, and to build a relationship of trust.

Dealing with Loss:
The Miracle of Time and Patience

ONE OF THE hardest things for parents to accept is that we can neither change our children's feelings nor protect them from unpleasant ones. Children feel grief and loss just as acutely as adults do. It is tempting to try to reason our children out of their pain, not because we don't understand but because we don't want them to suffer. Most of the time, however, the most helpful thing a loving parent can do is simply to listen, to accept, and to be patient with the process.

Jackie had always been careful to plan with her children for emergencies. They knew their phone numbers, who to call, and what to do if Mom was late picking them up from school. So when a long meeting and several red lights made Jackie about ten minutes late one afternoon, she wasn't overly concerned. Seven-year-old Charles knew that he could talk to the school secretary if he was worried, and that he should wait in front of the school for his mom to arrive.

Jackie was both surprised and alarmed when she pulled up at the school to find the principal sitting on a low wall next to a hysterical little boy.

"What's wrong?" she called out, almost tripping in her rush to get out of the car. She knelt down next to Charles, looking anxiously into his tearstained face. "What happened, Bud?"

The principal gave her a gentle, sympathetic smile. "Your little boy was afraid you weren't coming," she said. "He panicked a little."

Charles's sobs subsided into occasional sniffles as they drove home. "Charles," his mom began, "I can see you're really upset, but I don't understand why. You didn't used to be so clingy. We've talked about what you could do if I was late. Why didn't you just wait for me to come?"

There was a long pause; Charles's answer was almost a whisper. "I thought something might have happened to you, Mom," he said. "I thought you weren't coming."

"But honey," Jackie began, "you *know* I would never leave . . ." And then in a sudden flash of insight, Jackie understood what Charles was feeling. His dad had died unexpectedly only a few months before, and now Jackie realized just how fragile life must seem to her small son. What would happen to him if Mom were gone, too?

Jackie pulled the car over at the first safe place and scooped Charles into her arms. "I miss your dad, too, and sometimes I'm just as scared as you are. I guess I can't always control what happens, but I would never *choose* to leave you, Charles. You and your sister are the most important people in my life and I'll always do my best to be there for you."

The pain and fear her son felt almost broke Jackie's heart. Even harder was the realization that she couldn't make those feelings all better the way she'd cured his "owies" when he was tiny. Children do grieve, whether for a parent, for a lost pet, or for a shattered dream. The hope that all parents have, for themselves and for their children, is that time is indeed a healer.

It is normal for children who have suffered the loss of one parent, for whatever reason, to cling to the parent who remains, to cry when that parent leaves, and to worry when they're even a little late returning. Though such dependency can be frustrating, the simple rhythm and routine of normal life can be soothing. It helps, too, to talk about your schedule with your children, to make contingency plans with them, and to reassure them that you will do your best to be there when you're expected (and that you'll call if your plans change). Active listening can also let them know that you understand their feelings and help you find ways to get through the healing process together.

> Children do grieve, whether for a parent, for a lost pet, or for a shattered dream. The hope that all parents have, for themselves and for their children, is that time is indeed a healer.

Experts tell us that it can take two or three years to heal from the loss of a loved one. Whatever the reason for the loss of a parent about whom your children are grieving, you can't rescue them from the pain. Only time and understanding will ease it. You *can* listen, understand, and when appropriate, share your own feelings. Be patient; it may not seem possible, but it will get better.

What About My Own Feelings?

FEELINGS—SAD ONES AND GLAD ONES—are a part of the human condition. They aren't likely to go away any time soon. Parents are often struggling with their own topsy-turvy emotions: rejection, worry, stress. And as with our children, feelings can influence how we behave. Parents don't do their best work when they're tired, hurting, or overwhelmed; and sometimes our children bear the brunt of our feelings—without understanding why.

"But I'm furious at my ex-wife," you may think. Or, "I'm feeling so panicky and afraid that I can't function." "Sometimes," you may say, "those kids make me so angry I can't help myself."

How much of their own feelings should parents show? Is it wise to let children see when we're angry or sad or afraid?

Covering up or denying our feelings rarely works. Those who know us well generally sense them. In fact, children possess incredibly sensitive antennae when it comes to detecting moods and emotion. Lacking a better explanation, children may assume that *they* are the cause of whatever their parents are feeling. Even worse is first denying our feelings then taking them out on our children—yelling and screaming about a messy kitchen instead of saying, "I'm feeling scared and overwhelmed right now. I need some time to myself until I can feel better."

As tricky as it can be sometimes, it's best to talk honestly about what you are feeling, especially when the family is going through times of change or stress. Not only does a parent's emotional honesty help children understand what's really happening, it encourages them to express their own feelings honestly as well. You can share what you're feeling simply ("I'm really angry at your dad right now") *without including details or accusations that children don't need to know.*

Parents can even express their feelings of displeasure with their children's behavior in a nonjudgmental way. All too often our "constructive criticisms" of our children are accompanied by a great deal of finger-pointing and unpleasant tones of voice.

One helpful way to express your feelings is by using "I statements." An "I statement" helps us know what (and what not) to say—especially when we may be too upset to stay calm. For instance, it is possible to say calmly, "If you don't come home when you've promised to, I feel scared and upset because I love you and I worry that something has happened to you. I'd appreciate it if you would phone me when you're going to be late."

Or, "I'm feeling really frustrated because the washing machine isn't working and we all need clean clothes. I'd appreciate it if you could help me by getting ready for bed now." Children are far more likely to understand the true situation—and parents are far less likely to lose control—when feelings can be expressed honestly but with respect.

Laura, a single mother, had just arrived home after a long day at work. She was late getting dinner together, and she was exhausted; in addition, she had an early meeting scheduled the next morning and still needed time to herself to prepare for it. She longed for peace and quiet—and her two daughters were arguing about who would get to use the bathroom first. As the argument gathered steam, they clamored for Laura to decide who was right.

Laura felt her own tension level begin to rise. Finally, she could take no more and she began to yell, too, lecturing the girls about getting along. When she paused for breath, she realized that what was happening was more her problem than the children's: She was too tired to respond rationally to their arguing.

Laura drew a deep breath and faced her daughters. She said quietly, "Girls, I am too tired tonight to have the patience for your arguing." She explained that she had had a long day, would have another tomorrow, and needed to take care of herself. She asked the girls if tonight they would please work their problem out between themselves and then put themselves to bed. Laura said goodnight, gave them each a hug and kiss, and went off to her room.

Because Laura rarely needed to ask for this kind of time alone and had shared her feelings with sincerity instead of lecturing and blaming, her daughters were able to allow her the time alone—and to work out on their own their dispute over the bathroom.

Parents often overreact in frustration or disappointment, or insist on an irrational form of discipline when they are low or tired. What they really need to do is take care of themselves by letting their children know what they are feeling, helping them to understand what is going on, and teaching them to be supportive. Children should *never* be asked to bear burdens too heavy for them or to take the place of a missing adult. Still, simple explanations of how you're feeling can make all the difference between causing anger and guilt, and creating a loving and cooperative atmosphere.

Going Too Far: What if I Lose Control?

LEARNING TO DEAL with our emotions honestly and constructively can do more than keep our homes peaceful—it can prevent injury to those we love. No parent intends to hurt a child, but stress, frustration, and anger can lead us to behave in ways we regret later.

Picking up his sons, Billy and Eric, at the day-care center was the high point in Joe's day. Joe, a single dad, worked hard and was often tired, but he loved to scoop the boys up for a hug, inspect their art work, and talk about how their day had gone. When they arrived home, Joe would prepare dinner and unwind a bit—with a few drinks. And the more Joe "unwound," the more annoyed he became with Billy's and Eric's behavior.

One evening after dinner, Joe slumped in his chair watching his sons as they tried to help clear the table. There were bills to be paid—too many bills—and the car wasn't running properly. Joe had had an argument with the boys' mother about visitation, and his anger led him to unwind a bit more than usual. Just as Joe finished his third drink, Billy dropped a casserole dish—and Joe exploded. He dragged the crying child into the boys' room, where he lectured him about his clumsiness. *I need some fresh air,* he thought. He locked the door to Billy's room, told Eric to watch TV, and headed out to the neighborhood bar.

Several hours later, the police stopped Joe and cited him for driving under the influence of alcohol. When it was discovered that the boys were left at home alone, child neglect was added to the charge. With intervention of the legal system, Joe was able to get weekly counseling to deal with his drinking. He also attended a parenting class to learn some new skills.

Despite his unquestionable love for his sons, Joe had gone too far. And so do many parents, who resort to physical punishment, or emotional and verbal abuse. How does a stressed-out parent, particularly a single parent who may be raising children alone under difficult circumstances, stay in control?

It helps to have a support network of friends (see chapter 6) who can offer a listening ear. And it is vital to learn to recognize in yourself certain danger signals. A tense jaw, clenched fists, pounding heart, or rising voice may tell you it's time to be careful. Drugs and alcohol are never solutions to problems.

Do We Control Our Feelings?
Or Do They Control Us?

IT IS TEMPTING to let our emotions control us or to use them as excuses for our less brilliant parenting decisions. When we become aware of our true feelings, and listen to, accept, and learn from them, we are able to act thoughtfully and make the best choices in even the most difficult situations.

Andrea had been out of town for the weekend at a workshop, and she was looking forward to picking up her eight-year-old daughter, Amy, at Amy's father's house. Amy usually missed her mother when they were separated, and Andrea hummed cheerfully to herself as she drove, looking forward to a big hug. After she picked Amy up, Andrea took her out for pizza. When they got home, they unpacked and took a walk, talking about what each had done while they were apart. Then they curled up to read together before Amy went to bed.

Andrea was sitting at the kitchen table sorting through the weekend mail when she saw her daughter walking hesitantly down the hall toward her. "What's up, honey?" she asked. "Can't you sleep?"

"I'm going to call my dad," Amy responded.

Andrea waited quietly while Amy talked to her dad, trying not to glance impatiently at the clock. It was a short conversation; Andrea could tell that John, her ex-husband, was busy with something. Amy slowly hung up the phone, and when she turned to face her mother, there were tears trickling down her cheeks.

Andrea reached out for her daughter. "You look awfully sad, pumpkin," she said. "Do you want to tell me what's wrong?"

Amy hesitated, and Andrea could see that she was reluctant to speak. Finally, out it came. "I can't sleep because I miss my dad, Mom. We had *such* a good time this weekend, and I just want to be with him right now."

Andrea was stung. It had been more than three years since she and John had divorced, and the adjustment had been terribly difficult. But Andrea had been determined to do what was best for her daughter, even helping her maintain her relationship with her father when Amy was feeling hurt and disillusioned. It had been a painful process, but in recent months the emotional trauma and upheaval had subsided. Andrea had begun to feel secure and optimistic about both her own life and her daughter's. John was going to remarry soon, and Amy was thrilled with all of the wedding plans. Andrea had managed to cope with that; but now she saw Amy was obviously still caught in the middle.

"Well, what do you want to do, Amy? What would make you feel better?" Andrea asked.

Amy's answer was immediate. "I want to go back to my dad's house. I want to sleep there and then he can take me to school in the morning."

Andrea's face must have mirrored her hurt. "But honey, I just got home," she said. "Don't you want to be with me?" She watched her daughter struggle, realizing that Amy was caught between her own wishes and the desire to avoid hurting her mother. Pleasing her mother won.

"Oh, never mind, Mom," Amy suddenly said. "I'll be okay. I'll just go back to bed." She turned toward her room, but not before her mother saw Amy's trembling chin.

Andrea took a deep breath. "Amy," she said, "I'm not sure what your dad will say, but we can call him and ask if he's willing to come and pick you up. Is that what you really want?"

"Oh, yes!" Amy replied, and ran for the phone. This time the conversation was longer and when Amy hung up she was smiling. "He's going to come right away, Mom," she said, and ran off to pack some clothes for the morning.

When John arrived, he had a sympathetic smile for Andrea. "Are you sure you're okay with this?" he asked. "I don't want to interfere with your time with Amy."

"Well," Andrea replied as Amy came down the hall, "it's what she seems to need right now. Yeah, it hurts a little, but I'll be okay."

Andrea managed a smile and a hug for her daughter and then closed the door behind her. "Oh well," she told herself as she walked back to the kitchen table, "it doesn't really matter. I'm really glad she's able to tell me what she needs. . . ." Andrea's thoughts trailed off and suddenly she was crying.

It hurts, she thought, sitting down in a heap on the couch as the reality of how she felt hit her. *How can it still hurt so much?*

Amy called the next morning before school. "I'm really sorry, Mom," she said softly. "I guess sometimes I want both you *and* Dad, and I don't know what to do."

Andrea was able to respond with a smile in her voice. "Amy, it took courage to tell me the truth about how you felt. I'm glad you did." They chatted for a few minutes before Amy, reassured, went off to school.

"I still feel so insecure and afraid sometimes," Andrea told her best friend later that day. "I guess I still think I'm going to lose her somehow. I don't really like sharing her, even with her own father. I think I did the right thing, but

Amy's wanting to leave me really hurt. I've had a knot in my chest ever since last night."

Her friend smiled sympathetically. "You did what you thought was best for Amy. And Amy learned she can trust you with her feelings, and that she can love and enjoy both of her parents. Have faith, Andrea—in your daughter and in your relationship with her. You'll both be just fine."

It may not always be necessary (or wise) to go along with what your children want. You could be encouraging your children to be manipulative when you jump in and try to fix every emotional upset. But in this case, Andrea trusted her instinct that Amy was struggling with an emotional conflict involving a genuine need to work things out in her own way. Even though it hurt, Andrea was willing to listen and accept her daughter's feelings, trusting that this would eventually lead to a greater degree of closeness between them. If Amy repeats this sort of behavior, Andrea may need to give more thought to her response so that Amy learns both to trust her mother with her feelings, and that emotions, no matter how genuine, aren't an excuse for manipulation.

> Choosing what is best for our children can be difficult, even painful. It is nevertheless possible to act in spite of the painful feelings rather than allowing yourself to be controlled by them.

It is tempting to believe that doing the "right" thing will always feel good, but as Andrea learned, choosing what is best for our children can be difficult, even painful. It is nevertheless possible to act in spite of the painful feelings rather than allowing yourself to be controlled by them.

When Amy came home the next afternoon she gave her mother an extra-big hug before she went out to play. Later that evening Andrea talked to Amy and explained a little about how she had felt. Both mother and daughter learned that it was okay to be honest with each other and that difficult situations, handled without anger or accusation, can be opportunities to build trust and closeness.

Feelings Are Just Feelings

REMEMBER, EVEN THE most difficult feelings are still just feelings, and it is how we deal with them that can be either constructive or destructive. When anger and stress become overwhelming, both children and adults can learn to take a time-out—not as a punishing confinement but as a way to cool off and feel better so that a situation can be dealt with calmly. And we can find alternate ways of expressing frustration; yelling into a pillow rather than at a person, for example, can work wonders.

> When anger and stress become overwhelming, both children and adults can learn to take a time-out—not as a punishing confinement but as a way to cool off and feel better so that a situation can be dealt with calmly.

Children and adults alike can learn to count to ten, to take deep breaths, and to discuss problems calmly. One dad reported that when anger threatened to take over, he took out the garbage and dumped it forcefully and noisily in the can. By the time he returned to the house, he was in control and ready to find constructive solutions to the problems at hand.

Changing the way we handle our stronger emotions takes time and energy, and we won't always be successful. But teaching our children—and ourselves—to deal positively with feelings not only allows us to be truthful, it saves all that energy we would otherwise spend suppressing or dumping our emotions to be put to far better uses. Taking the time to practice active listening, to understand our children's feelings, and to help our children understand ours are wonderful and highly practical ways to build relationships of trust and closeness, which will carry us through years of growing, changing, and coping with difficult times.

5

Balancing, Juggling, and Other Single-Parenting Skills

I T HAD BEEN a frustrating day at work, and Lynne felt tired and cranky as she flopped down on the couch to figure out what she could accomplish before the end of the day.

A pile of bills waited on the desk, the carpet was speckled with pebbles from the shoes of three children who had obviously had a fine time in the school sandbox, and the kitchen floor was spattered with sticky spots where some Kool-Aid had missed its target. Come to think of it, Lynne mused, the bathrooms probably needed cleaning, too. And the car needed an oil change.

Lynne's mind began to whirl. It was almost time for dinner. Was there anything in the refrigerator? She gazed wearily out into the yard, but that only reminded her that the lawn needed watering, fertilizing, mowing, and edging. And at that moment, Lynne's children plopped down by her side with a stack of books. "Can you read to us, Mom?" they asked.

It was a moment of revelation. The sea of emotions calmed, the dust settled, the mist cleared, and

> It doesn't matter whether you are divorced or widowed, male or female, custodial or noncustodial; being a single parent can be one of life's trickiest balancing acts.

the sunlight revealed the handwriting on the wall. "Welcome," it said, "to the land of single parenting. Watch your step."

It doesn't matter whether you are divorced or widowed, male or female, custodial or noncustodial; being a single parent can be one of life's trickiest balancing acts. There is too much to be done, and, all too often, too little time in which to do it.

How does a single parent balance all of the demands on his or her time, raise children effectively, and still find time to learn, to grow, and to enjoy life?

In a "traditional" home, a couple may share the tasks of running a household and caring for children. In a single-parent home, there are those same tasks but only one pair of adult hands to do the work—and the prospect can seem overwhelming.

Single parents often report that it's the little things that send them over the edge. There is no one to watch the kids for a minute while you take a quick shower or run to the store; no one else to catch the mutilated but still living mouse the cat has brought in; no one to help mend a torn garment, explain why the car won't start, do the laundry, mow the lawn, or shovel the snow.

Worst of all, there is no one else to talk to at the end of the day when the children are asleep, no one to share concerns and small triumphs with. The traditional partner in raising children, the other parent, may

be completely out of the picture or completely unsympathetic. Single parents frequently complain of feeling isolated, and no wonder! There is never enough time to get everything done. The result is often a stew of frustration, guilt, worry, and exhaustion—not exactly an atmosphere that encourages the kind of relationship we want to have with our children.

How, then, do you cope? When the grieving is done, the adjusting has been accomplished, and life settles into a semblance of normalcy—however stressful—what then? How does a single parent balance all of the demands on his or her time, raise children effectively, and still find time to learn, to grow, and to enjoy life? Is it even possible?

We will show you that it *is* possible—but it requires thoughtful planning, patience, and some old-fashioned hard work.

Sorting Priorities: What's Most Important, Anyway?

SINGLE-PARENT FAMILIES can function just as effectively and efficiently as the two-parent variety (and have just as much fun), nurturing and encouraging children who grow up to be capable, healthy adults. It is essential, however, to know just how and when to spend your all-too-limited time and energy.

Time, as they say, is money. Yet we frequently budget our dollars carefully while we spend our time without thought or plan, wondering at the end of a frantic day why we got so little accomplished. Carefully sorting out priorities may be one of the most effective things any parent—but especially a single parent—can do.

There are some things in life we can't avoid—work or school, for instance—but we demonstrate which things are important in our lives by the amount of discretionary time we spend on them. Some of those choices can be difficult: Should you concentrate on work and career, or make time with children a priority? Should you hop on the career fast track, hoping for advancement and the benefits it might bring to your family? Or do you spend less time at work, settling for fewer financial rewards but being more involved in your children's daily lives? What are the long-range results of each decision, for you and for your children?

> Carefully sorting out priorities may be one of the most effective things any parent—but especially a single parent—can do.

Answers to such fundamental questions will differ for each parent and will require a great deal of thought. However, deciding where the time goes day by day can be a bit easier to manage.

Try the following experiment: Make a list of what you value most in life, then prioritize this list. Your children will probably be at the top. Next, keep track for a week or so of exactly how much time you actually spend on each activity in your life. The results are often surprising. When you discover just how you're spending your time now, it is fairly simple to look at the time available each week and decide what is *really* most important.

Ideally, how we spend our time reflects what we value most—and what we believe is most important for creating home and family. Many parents are surprised to learn that they spend most of their time on activities low on their priority list (such as watching television), and devote too little time and energy to the people or things at the top. It may be helpful to budget time during each week for family activities. (If you don't plan them, sometimes they don't happen at all.) Looking at the way you approach unavoidable chores can be helpful: A little advance planning may make one weekly trip to the grocery store possible, for example, instead of daily ones.

There are any number of creative ways to adjust priorities and responsibilities so that they fit better into a limited amount of time. Here are just a few suggestions for streamlining and simplifying your life:

Eliminate unrealistic expectations. Your mother may have kept her floors spotless, ironed her pillowcases, and placed elegantly prepared meals on the dining-room table each evening precisely at 6:30, but that doesn't mean you have to—or even should. Look at what is possible and keep your expectations of yourself realistic.

Make a list of all your "shoulds" and "oughts." Spend some time thinking about—and paying attention to your feelings about—the items on this list.

> Ideally, how we spend our time reflects what we value most—and what we believe is most important for creating home and family.

How much time are you spending on things you believe you "should" do—because you've "always done it that way" or because at some point in your life you were told you "had to"—that are not truly adding to the quality of your life? It will take time and some experimentation, but learn to be content with what you want to do, what you believe is truly worthwhile, and what you actually can do effectively.

Try making lists. Prioritize on paper each day's tasks and do the most important ones first. Not only will lists help you get things done, crossing items off can be one of the most satisfying parts of your day! Try to do small tasks

SIMPLIFYING LIFE AS A SINGLE PARENT

- Eliminate unrealistic expectations.
- Try making lists.
- Organize meal preparation.
- Share housecleaning duties.
- Take time to teach.
- Make time for fun.

(such as paying a bill or sewing on a loose button) as they come up, rather than piling them up for later.

Organize meal preparation. Getting dinner on the table after a day of work can be a single parent's recurring nightmare. Try preparing dishes (when you have time) that will provide several meals, such as casseroles or a roast turkey. Keep your cupboard stocked with items that will help you turn leftovers into tempting dishes. Invest in one of the many cookbooks designed to help you prepare nourishing meals in a short time. Or prepare double portions on weekends and put what's left in the freezer for a busy day. Get older children involved in planning and preparing meals—it can be a great learning experience for all of you.

One mother made a list of ten meals her children liked. They were simple things, such as tacos, spaghetti, tuna-noodle casserole, meat loaf, soup and toasted cheese sandwiches, hamburgers, and lasagna. She then made an index card for each item, with the recipe on one side (along with side dishes, such as salads and vegetables) and the shopping ingredients on the other. During their weekly family meeting, the kids and Mom would take turns drawing five of the cards out of a hat. They would list the meals on a calendar. Each child was responsible for checking the pantry to see what ingredients might still be on hand for the meals they had picked, and they would make a list of the things that were needed to go on the weekly shopping list. (The younger kids got an older child or Mom to write up their list.)

Once a week they would all go shopping together. Each child helped find the ingredients for the meals they had chosen (and which they would help cook). This mother explained, "Our plan eliminated so much hassle. It was much more stressful to wonder what to cook than to do the cooking. What used to be a chore is now a fun family activity."

Share housecleaning duties. This is one part of family life that seems to get out of hand for many single parents. Cleaning can be more fun when everyone in the family works together. It's surprising how much can be done when everyone pitches in for ten minutes a day or two hours once a week. Try doing a little bit every day, rather than a lot all at once. Provide each member of the family with baskets for laundry—even young children can learn to put white clothes in one basket and dark clothes in another. Tackle cleaning one room each day. Agree on some family rules about picking up toys and clothes, and follow through on agreements (more about that later).

Given the choice between an evening cuddle with a child who needs to talk and scouring the bathroom, it may be wise to choose the cuddle.

Again, life will be more enjoyable if children are involved in the process. During a family meeting, let children help you make a list of what needs to be done. Then create fun ways for kids to choose chores to do. One way is to put each chore on a card and let the kids pick several cards out of a hat. Another way is to create a wheel chart (maybe one for each room) with pictures of what needs to be done on the outside of the wheel and a spinner attached in the middle. Then the kids can spin to see which chore or chores they will tackle during cleaning time.

Take time to teach. Though it may not seem so at the time, teaching children how to help out with domestic duties can save you time later on—as well as giving your children the basic skills they will need to be self-reliant and successful. Work alongside them, showing them how a job can best be done; next, supervise in a friendly way as they do it alone. Before long, they'll be able to do the work to your satisfaction without your involvement. Just be careful not to set your standards too high! (We'll explore teaching, encouragement, and self-esteem in greater depth in chapters 8 and 13.)

Make time for fun. Housework and chores seem a lot easier to bear when a good time is waiting at the end. You may choose to have the entire family do housework and yard work on Saturday morning, saving the rest of the day for an activity you have planned together. Be sure to leave time in your week for togetherness and fun: These times will make you feel like a family. It is important to put plans for fun on your calendar; otherwise they may become only good intentions.

Some other things may need to be moved far down the list of priorities. Given the choice between an evening cuddle with a child who needs to talk and scouring the bathroom, it may be wise to choose the cuddle. The house may not be as spotless as you'd like, but housework will wait; moments missed with children may never come again.

Keeping Things in Perspective

MAINTAINING OUR PERSPECTIVE on what is most important can take some of the frustration out of balancing priorities. Lisa is a single mother whose three-year-old daughter, Abby, always seemed to come home from preschool dirty—so dirty that the task of cleaning her up and doing the laundry each night had become a constant source of irritation to Lisa.

"It's more than I can handle," Lisa complained to a group of single parents. "This afternoon when I picked Abby up, she was soaking wet from playing in a stopped-up water fountain, and she was muddy, too." Lisa heaved a sigh. "My days are hectic enough without this. I'm angry at Abby, and I'm angry at the preschool."

The group understood what Lisa was saying: Staying abreast of a busy life can leave single parents without the energy to handle unexpected mishaps with grace and patience. But they suggested to Lisa that active three-year-olds are bound to get dirty. The group encouraged Lisa to do something about her suspicion that the preschool might be lax in their organization and supervision of the children. A father who had experienced a similar situation suggested that visiting the preschool and observing for a while might help Lisa decide what, if anything, could be done to change the situation. Spending the time to observe might seem time-consuming now, he told her, but it would eventually save the time

> It is easier to maintain a balanced outlook when you have interests in life besides your children. Regardless of how busy you may be, one of your priorities should be you.

Lisa was now spending worrying and fretting about her dirty daughter, and it might put her mind at rest about the quality of care Abby was receiving. Realizing that other parents faced similar problems, and thinking through some solutions helped Lisa regain her perspective.

And What About You?

IT IS EASIER TO maintain a balanced outlook when you have interests in life besides your children. Regardless of how busy you may be, one of your priorities should be you. It won't just happen; you have to make time to nurture yourself. You cannot answer every demand made on you, no matter how hard you try, and you'll have nothing to give if you allow yourself to become exhausted. Recognize your limitations. Say no to new demands on your time when you must.

You and everyone around you will benefit if you take time to do something you enjoy, whatever it might be, on a regular basis. Read a book, take a hot bath, listen to music, tinker with machinery, spend time with friends. (Yes, your children can survive without you once in a while.) You can model self-esteem for your children by being good to yourself. Your children will learn that taking care of oneself is important and they will learn to respect others' needs. And you will find yourself a healthier, calmer parent—and a happier human being. (We spend more time on nurturing yourself in chapter 13.)

What About Leaving My Children?

FOR MANY SINGLE PARENTS, leaving their children, whether it's to go to work or to have some time to themselves, is a real problem. We yearn to get away; but once we're gone, we worry ourselves silly. Quality child care is expensive and can be difficult to find. You may be lucky enough to have a trustworthy teenager nearby, or you may be able to share child care with neighbors or form a baby-sitting co-op. There is one option that, however tempting it may seem to harried single parents, must be considered very carefully before you try it: leaving children home alone.

Unfortunately, not all children are as resourceful as the young hero of the *Home Alone* movies. Leaving children home alone may be convenient for parents—and sometimes it may seem to be the only option available—but it can be an invitation to disaster for children. Is it ever okay to leave children on their own? If so, when?

Judging when a child can handle staying alone depends on many things, and age isn't always the best clue. Never leave a preschooler or toddler alone, and it may be wise to check with your local social services agency to see whether your area has specific laws about how young is "too young." Otherwise, before leaving her on her own, consider carefully your child's maturity, confidence, and ability to exercise good judgment. If you have *any* doubts, don't leave—and never leave for longer than an hour or so. Even if you believe that your child is mature enough to understand the situation and the rules involved in keeping herself safe, be sure you structure the situation carefully.

Be sure your *child* feels comfortable with being alone. Branches scratching the window or a cat yowling outside can be terrifying to a child alone in an empty house. Of course, the situation can become a lot more volatile when more than one child is involved. Unless you've got a teen or a responsible preteen to rely on, never leave children in charge of their younger siblings. The responsibility is just too great and too many things can go wrong.

> Leaving children home alone may be convenient for parents—and sometimes it may seem to be the only option available—but it can be an invitation to disaster for children.

If you are confident that your child can handle being alone for a short time, there are some steps you should take to make the situation as safe as possible:

Talk with your child about what might happen while you're gone. Leave a key for doors that may be bolted. Outline a way out of the house in case of fire or emergency. Write down emergency numbers and be sure your child understands how and when to use them. The number of a friend or neighbor who is home may be helpful as well.

Discuss with your child what to do if someone comes to the door or calls for a parent who isn't home. You may want to make some rules about who

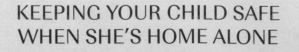

KEEPING YOUR CHILD SAFE WHEN SHE'S HOME ALONE

- Talk with your child about what might happen while you're gone.
- Discuss with your child what to do if someone comes to the door or calls for a parent who isn't home.
- Set guidelines for activities that are allowed.
- Be *sure* your child understands.

may or may not be in the house while you're away, and brainstorm possible responses to phone calls. (One twelve-year-old girl tells callers that her mother is in the bathroom and takes a message.) A recent Oprah Winfrey show illustrated how easy it was for strangers to get into a house when children were alone. A well-dressed stranger would ask to use the phone because his car had broken down, and the kids would let him in. Later, parents said they had told their children never to let strangers in the house. This show illustrated that children may not have the wisdom or ego strength to "do what they know they should do," and it is not wise for parents to expect them to.

Set guidelines for activities that are allowed. For instance, watching television and playing video games are fine, but cooking or experimenting with the chemistry set may not be appropriate without adult supervision. You also may want to agree on whether or not outdoor play is acceptable.

Be *sure* your child understands. Never simply ask a child if he understands the rules—he'll almost always tell you he does. Write down the rules you've agreed upon, post them where they can easily be seen, and have your child repeat them to you to check his understanding. If he isn't comfortable with the rules you have agreed on, don't leave!

Single parents frantically juggling too many responsibilities may be tempted to leave children alone "just for a little while." And if the child is responsible and mature, it may be just fine to do so. But before you close the door behind you, think for a moment about all that can happen while you're away. Our children are precious and irreplaceable, and our convenience is never worth putting them at risk.

Balancing Work and Family

Q. I am a single mom with three young children. I'm lucky; their dad helps with child support and does spend time with them. Still, the support isn't enough for all of us to live on, and I have to work. I hear so much on the radio and television about how good parents stay at home with their children. I don't have a choice about working, but I worry all the time that I'm hurting my children by not being with them more. Is it okay for parents to work? Will my children be hurt by being in child care?

A. Experts have been debating this issue for years and will probably continue to do so. We believe that neither staying home with children nor putting children in child care *guarantees* healthy children; that task requires thoughtfulness, energy, and good parenting and communication skills. Regardless of your situation—whether you must work or choose to stay at home—your attitude is an important element in your child's health. If you believe that you are doing your best and you have confidence in your choices, your children can do well. If you feel insecure and guilty about your choices, your children will sense your attitudes and mirror them in their behavior. All that single parents—or any parents—can do is make the best decisions they can, learn the skills they need, and accept that they will make mistakes. As we illustrate many times throughout this book, mistakes are wonderful opportunities to learn. Positive Discipline parenting skills, encouragement and active listening, and confidence in your choices will help your children (and you) do just fine.

For the vast majority of single parents, working is simply not an option; it is a necessity. Yet balancing the demands of the workplace with parenting can be a difficult task. Many single parents find that their jobs keep them from attending school conferences and music programs, soccer games, or other activities, and that the choice between working and staying home with a sick child is agonizing. Some employers offer on-site child care, flexible hours, and family leave; others do not. Single parents frequently find they do not feel satisfied with their work life or their family life: There just isn't enough time (or enough energy) to do both as well as they would like.

Unfortunately, there is no simple solution to the dilemma of balancing life as a single parent with the need to earn a living; each adult—and each family—is different. Nevertheless, here are a few ideas you can consider to help ease the burden:

Be sure of what you "need." Determining your priorities may help you decide how much effort to put into work and career. And, as we will learn in chapter 6, managing money wisely will help relieve the financial strain that drives so many single parents to work long hours or double shifts. Take time to weigh the benefits of your job (salary, insurance, and so on) with what it costs you in time away from your children. You may decide that a less demanding job actually provides a better life for your family.

Investigate community resources. There are many single-parent families out there these days, and more and more communities are realizing that single parents need occasional support. Many hospitals and family clinics now offer "sick-child" care. These facilities provide for sick children to be cared for by health professionals, allowing parents to go to work without undue

> Single parents frequently find they do not feel satisfied with their work life or their family life: There just isn't enough time (or enough energy) to do both as well as they would like.

BALANCING WORK AND FAMILY

- Be sure of what you "need."
- Investigate community resources.
- Explore your options.
- Synchronize your schedule with other family members.
- Stay in touch.
- Do the best you can—then relax.

worry. Fees will vary, but you may decide that the peace of mind is worth the cost.

Explore your options. Some single parents discover that running their own business allows them more flexibility to be with their children, such as in-home child care or other services that allow them to work at home. Although it is not possible (or preferable) for every parent, developing your own business may help you to be more available to your children and provide for them at the same time.

Synchronize your schedule with other family members. Children love to have their parents attend their important events—and full-time employment usually means that attending all of those events simply isn't possible. Rather than expecting yourself to make it to every athletic event and dance recital (and blaming yourself when you fail) invite other members of your family and network of friends to share these special times.

If your child's other parent is available and involved, be sure he or she knows what is going on. You can both attend (and sit apart if it isn't feasible to sit together), or you can arrange a schedule so that at least one of you is present for your child's special times. Friends and members of your extended family may also enjoy sharing this responsibility with you—and you are likely to feel less guilt and regret about working when you know your child is supported by a circle of caring people.

Stay in touch. Single parents often find themselves running frantically from work to the soccer field to child care to meetings to school and back again. We are not the only ones these days who are busy; our children have a whirl of activities and obligations, so do what you can to ensure that your children are able to find you when they need you— and that you can find them. Cellular phones and pagers can help single parents and children stay in touch, particularly as children grow older and more independent. Be sure you agree on schedules, transportation, and other plans; most families find it useful to have a large calendar posted, with all activities and drop-off and pick-up times listed. Let your children know when to expect you; do your best to be consistent and reliable.

> Take time to weigh the benefits of your job (salary, insurance, and so on) with what it costs you in time away from your children.

Be sure that your workplace allows your children to contact you when necessary. Children can be taught when it is—and is not—okay to call you at work. One single dad installed a private telephone line in his office (at his own expense) so that his children could call him whenever they felt the need.

Ask coworkers and office personnel to be sure that you receive messages from your children as soon as possible.

Do the best you can—then relax. Worry, blame, and guilt do no one any good. When you know you have made the best choices possible and are doing your best to provide for your children, relax—and focus your energy on helping everyone in your family adjust to what must be done. Routines, consistency, encouragement, and good communication skills will help you build a close relationship with your children, even if you must work more than you might like. Your children will not only survive, they will benefit from the opportunity to learn cooperation and other life skills, and to make a real contribution to you and to their family.

> When you know you have made the best choices possible and are doing your best to provide for your children, relax—and focus your energy on helping everyone in your family adjust to what must be done.

Choosing Quality Child Care

JUST AS WORKING is a fact of life for most single parents, child care is a fact of life for their children. Most of the research that has been done on how child care affects children is reassuring: Children do very well in a *quality* child care setting. Many studies have found that "family factors" (parenting skills and parental responsiveness) appear to be more powerful predictors of how children do than child care—assuming, that is, that you find good quality care for your children.

When finding child care for your child, don't be in a rush; there are a number of factors to consider. Ask friends and professionals for recommendations. If you choose to use a nanny or sitter, interview carefully, check references, and allow time for the caregiver and child to become comfortable with each other. If you choose to use a child care center, visit several and take notes on what you see. Are the children busy and happy? Do they move around the center confidently? Is the building clean? Do the caregivers appear frazzled or angry? Are

SELECTING CHILD CARE

Identify quality child care using the following criteria, which you may want to write down to take with you:

1. The center or home has:

   Current licenses displayed

   Low rate of staff turnover

   Local, state, and/or national accreditation

   Loving, child-centered environment

2. The staff is:

   Well trained in child development and care

   Working as a team

   Staying up-to-date through training programs

   Adequately paid (which reduces turnover and dissatisfaction)

3. Discipline is:

   Positive rather than punitive

   Kind and firm at the same time

   Designed to help children learn important life skills

4. Consistency shows:

   In the curriculum and daily activities

   In the way problems are handled

   In day-to-day center management

5. Safety is demonstrated by the:

   Physical setting

   Program health policies

   Preparedness and training for emergencies

For more detailed information on child care, see *Positive Discipline for Preschoolers*, Nelsen, Erwin, and Duffy (Prima Publishing, 1998).

the children encouraged to learn, be active, and explore—or to sit quietly and "be good"?

Choosing good child care can be confusing, but succeeding will give you a great deal of peace of mind when you must be away from your children. A list of important qualities you will want to investigate in choosing care for your child is provided here. If you have questions, *ask*. You are entitled to the information you need to feel comfortable. If a center is reluctant to answer questions or allow you to observe them in action, it's probably wise to look elsewhere.

Selecting child care may be one of the most important decisions you make as a single parent. Yes, quality child care can be expensive, but your child's well-being and your own peace of mind are worth the cost. Some communities have grant money available to provide subsidized child care for working parents; a call to your local family resource organization may provide you with both referrals and financial aid.

Keeping the Balance

YOUR PRIORITIES, the demands on your time, and life itself will change periodically, and you may find that what works one month may need adjustment the next. But investing some time and thought into sorting out all the things you must do will pay off in reduced stress and frustration, healthier children, and a more peaceful home.

6

Conquering the High Wire: Skills for Creating Balance

THERE COMES A time in the life of most single parents when it all just seems to be too much to cope with. You may find yourself dreaming about Tahiti or Alaska or some nameless deserted place where you can be at peace and "they" (whoever "they" are) can't find you. Single parents may be more susceptible than most to becoming overwhelmed and burned out. They can feel alone and overburdened, without help or resources—all alone up there on the tightrope with no safety net.

But there *should* be a net. One of the most important tasks for a single parent is to build this net, by developing a support system that will provide resources to rely on when the anxieties and pressures in your life threaten to engulf you. Learning to deal with all the demands on your time isn't easy—but it's critical to your effectiveness and peace of mind as a single parent.

Coping with Financial Pressures

AMONG THE MOST overwhelming aspects of single parenthood, especially in the first months, are the insecurity and anxiety that come from financial stress. As we have already learned, research shows that the greatest risk factor for single parents and their children is lack of money.

Each single parent has his or her own litany of woe: "I don't earn enough." "I don't have any skills, except waiting tables." "My ex-spouse doesn't pay child support; how will I ever make it?" "My family lets me live with them, but they don't have much money and my children and I are a real drain on them financially and emotionally—to say nothing of the arguments we get into about how to discipline the children." "Can I go back to school? Get a better job?" "How on *earth* will I ever pay for college?"

One of the most important tasks for a single parent is to build a net, by developing a support system that will provide resources to rely on when the anxieties and pressures in your life threaten to engulf you.

Sometimes it seems unavoidable to give in to panic about money. But panic and fear often short-circuit constructive approaches to problem solving. If financial worries are overwhelming, start solving them by taking small steps that you can handle. And pay attention to your attitudes and perceptions about your situation; changing an attitude is usually the first step in changing a life.

Don't be ashamed to ask for help if you need it. Seek assistance from community services or welfare agencies if you have to, and then make a plan to learn a skill and support yourself as soon as you can. Many churches and social agencies have food and clothing closets that can provide you with a boost over the difficult places. Subsidized housing may be available in your community. If

MANAGING FINANCIAL STRESS

- Find other single parents in the same boat.
- Consider starting a child-care co-op.
- Beware of self-pity and anger.
- Be open to new experiences and perceptions.
- Become a learner.
- Learn to manage your money.

your pride gets in your way, simply promise yourself that one day you will be in a position to help someone else.

Find other single parents in the same boat. Consider sharing housing and child care responsibilities with another single parent. Use family meetings (see chapter 9), at which all the parents and children get together to create routines, solve any problems that have arisen, and prevent further problems by developing solutions before they are needed.

Consider starting a child-care co-op. If you don't have extended family or a spouse who shares time with your children, start a children's play-group swap. Find two to four other single parents who are willing to swap kids for one weekend day. If there are four parents, each one takes all the

> If financial worries are overwhelming, start solving them by taking small steps that you can handle.

kids for one weekend day a month. That leaves three free weekend days for each parent. The play groups can be well organized and include art activities, games, stories, and simple cooking experiences. Even if only two parents are swapping, they each have two free weekend days, and two weekend days during which they can enjoy their children more because of thoughtful planning.

Beware of self-pity and anger. Bitterness can keep you stuck in negative thinking and can make it difficult to take positive steps. It may take time, but work on giving up your "victim mentality" and anger. Focus your energy on finding solutions, take time to nurture yourself, and remember that your attitude really does make all the difference.

Be open to new experiences and perceptions. You may want to visit the library to check out motivational books or tapes or inspirational stories of others' successes under similar circumstances. Be open to new ideas and to learning from someone else's experiences.

Become a learner. If you don't have an education, get one. Start by taking one class a semester at a local university, community college, or technical school. Scholarships and grants are often available to help with tuition, and local organizations, such as Rotary and Kiwanis, may offer scholarships. It took one of the authors eleven years (while raising five children) to obtain a bachelor of arts degree; she started because someone advised her to take one class at a time. Improving your education not only will ease your financial burden, it will set examples of courage and determination for your children, and will increase your own self-esteem.

Marcia's children were six and nine years old when she decided to take the plunge and return to school for a graduate degree. It seemed like a good idea, but she couldn't help wondering how it would affect her relationship with her children—and her own stress level. She introduced the idea to her sons, Kevin and Bradley, at a family meeting.

> Focus your energy on finding solutions, take time to nurture yourself, and remember that your attitude really does make all the difference.

"Guys, I have something I want you to think about," Marcia said after she and the boys had shared compliments, appreciations, and a funny story or two. "I'm thinking about going back to school part-time at the university so I can get a master's degree. I think it would help me get a better job so we could move to a nicer neighborhood—but it will mean being gone more often and studying when I'm at home. I'm really going to need your help."

The boys were silent, digesting this new plan. Bradley was the first to speak. "Will we have to stay at day care longer? I don't want to do that."

"You may have to, Brad," Marcia said. "I'll tell you what. Let's brainstorm all our questions and ideas about my plan. Then we can look for solutions."

Together Marcia and her sons explored what it would mean for Mom to go back to school. Kevin and Bradley voiced their concerns about day care, spending more time at Dad's house, and possibly not having enough time to spend with Mom. They worried about her safety and her ability to do everything she would need to. The family brainstormed solutions to a few of the potential problems; others they left for another time. But at the end of the family meeting, all three had agreed that it would be a good idea—and that they would work together to make it happen.

"Hey, Mom," Kevin said as Marcia got up to make popcorn. "Can you get football tickets if you're a student?" When Marcia smiled and said that it might be a possibility, both boys whooped with glee.

Returning to school is a big obligation, but many adults find that it is well worth the effort—one reason so many schools have reported huge increases in the number of "older" students. Invite your children to become part of the effort; create a family vision of the benefits you will experience. And remember: It does take courage, but sometimes you just have to make the leap and build your wings on the way down!

Learn to manage your money. We live in an age of affluence and materialism. Some financial problems have less to do with being a single parent than they do with attitudes and poor budgeting skills. It is true that you may have to go without a fancy wardrobe and car, nice furniture, and eating out, at least for a while. However, many successful people can tell you stories of strict budgeting and "going without" during their early days.

> When you adopt a positive attitude about budgeting and the long-range benefits of delayed gratification, you teach your children many skills that will serve them far better than materialism.

Too many single parents think their children will be deprived if they have to do without luxuries, and it can be tempting to try to give children material things to make up for their not having a two-parent family. Take a moment to think about the message this attitude may give children about the importance of *things*. When you adopt a positive attitude about budgeting and the long-range benefits of delayed gratification, you teach your children many skills that will serve them far better than materialism. Though it may not seem so at the moment, your children can learn far more from "going without" than from living in affluence.

Another Opportunity to Respectfully Involve Your Children

ALTHOUGH CHILDREN MAY be spoiled by too much affluence and may develop unhealthy attitudes if you use material possessions to make up for losses, involving them in the realities of budgeting can teach them important values and life skills.

Teach your children about budgeting by involving them in the process. During a family meeting, discuss how much money is available for the week.

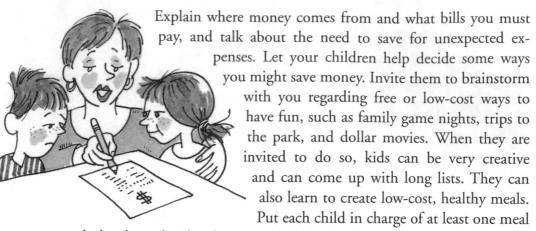

Explain where money comes from and what bills you must pay, and talk about the need to save for unexpected expenses. Let your children help decide some ways you might save money. Invite them to brainstorm with you regarding free or low-cost ways to have fun, such as family game nights, trips to the park, and dollar movies. When they are invited to do so, kids can be very creative and can come up with long lists. They can also learn to create low-cost, healthy meals. Put each child in charge of at least one meal a week; let them decide what to cook, help do the shopping, and then cook (or help cook) the meal.

Expectations vs. Reality: Learning to Thrive in the Real World

IT ALL SOUNDS EASY; however, life in the real world is often anything but. Jenny was a single mom who worked as a paralegal assistant. Jenny had two children, aged eight and eleven; their father had not given her any child support in more than six months, and the small salary she received each week did not cover her bills. Feeling overwhelmed and afraid had become a way of life.

Jenny had gone to the district attorney about collecting her child support payments, but there were no guarantees for collection. Not knowing where else to turn, she let her boss know that she was very disappointed that she was not making enough money to pay her bills. She threatened to look for another job. Her boss knew Jenny was receiving a fair salary for her skill level and was neither able nor willing to pay her more. The more Jenny complained, the more her boss began to think about looking for a new paralegal.

Jenny's becoming overwhelmed and her ineffective way of expressing herself almost cost her her job. Being unemployed would certainly have been more stressful than having a job that didn't quite pay the bills.

What were the options for Jenny? She could have looked for a higher-paying job; however, it was doubtful that her skills were good enough to merit a better salary. Or she could have taken a closer look at her situation to see if budgeting would help. As it happened, Jenny was spending a large portion of her income on clothes and a new car. She was an excellent example of someone caught in the trap of materialism. Jenny's expectations and her reality were far apart.

Financial worries often come from the belief (or the reality) that we do not have enough of what we need. This in turn creates a feeling of deprivation. Changing a feeling can be a difficult task, but *recognizing* an attitude is the first step to *changing* it. Feelings of scarcity often lead to self-pity and blaming, which usually hamper productivity.

Jenny was feeling deprived and afraid, and it was hindering her productivity at work and her ability to see solutions to her financial problems. Once she recognized her feelings, she was ready for the next step. Jenny began by making a budget. She wrote down all her necessities: food, shelter, basic clothing, child care, and transportation. Then she looked at her necessity budget and decided where it could be cut. She decided to find a housemate to help pay the rent. She and the kids started planning meals together and decided they would eat out only twice a month instead of twice a week. Jenny had purchased an "ego" car that was expensive to maintain. She sold that car and bought a used car—one that had a reputation for low maintenance.

Jenny also made a vow that she would not use her charge cards anymore. She made a plan to pay them off and to buy things only if she had the cash to pay for them—and only after necessities were purchased. An important part of Jenny's new direction was to focus on improving her skills as a paralegal. She started taking one class each semester at a community college. She wanted to make sure that when her boss was ready to pay more, she would deserve a raise.

> Most communities offer counselors, low-cost legal clinics, and financial advisors who can help you find your way through the maze of legal and financial issues.

Statistics tell us that the vast majority of custodial single parents are women, and that lack of money and financial management skills are important reasons so many single-parent families struggle. If you are in debt or are not managing the money you do have effectively, consider looking for help. Most communities offer trained credit counselors who can help you make a budget, consolidate debt, and plan for improving your financial health.

IDEAS TO CONSIDER: CREATING SECURITY FOR YOURSELF AND YOUR FAMILY

- Learn to budget wisely.
- Use credit cards with care.
- Make a will.
- Explore investments, retirement, and financial planning with a reliable, certified advisor.
- See a credit counselor if you need help.

There are a number of other issues single parents should take time to consider but often do not. Among them are making a will, providing for children's college expenses, obtaining adequate insurance coverage, investing wisely, and planning for retirement. If these ideas make your head spin, take one issue at a time and ask for help when you need it. Most communities offer counselors, low-cost legal clinics, and financial advisors who can help you find your way through the maze of legal and financial issues.

Your Attitude Is the Key

HAVE YOU EVER noticed those rare people who seem to have very little, yet who live their lives with joy and gratitude? Then there are others who always want more, no matter how much they have. Happiness truly is based more on attitude than on circumstances. Develop an attitude of gratitude for what you have. Take time at family meetings, or as a mealtime ritual, to invite each member of your family to share at least one thing he or she is grateful for. (There is *always* something!) Not only will you be happier, you will have the kind of positive energy that will help you create abundance in your life—and in the lives of those around you.

It's difficult to view hard times as opportunities and problems as challenges to be conquered, but remember that your children will be quick to follow your lead. If your attitude is one of deprivation and "Oh, poor me," your children will be likely to adopt this perspective. However, if you work at keeping a positive attitude and remaining open to learning beneficial skills, your children are likely to catch your spirit.

> Develop an attitude of gratitude for what you have.

Of course, your attitude will be tested. Your children (and you) will be bombarded by television commercials and other advertising designed to brainwash you into materialism. Your children will be faced with the name-brand mentality of their peers. You may want to discuss with them the wisdom of thinking for themselves rather than accepting the values of others.

Learning to budget wisely and to handle the demands of a job will help bring one of the biggest pressures of single parenthood under control. But what about the parenting itself? Can we do an adequate job in one area of our lives without neglecting another?

Learning to Lean: Building a Support Network

BEING A SINGLE PARENT can often seem like being the Lone Ranger, only without Tonto and Silver. There is so much to be done and so little help—or so it seems.

Carla, a talented professional woman with a growing career, had been a single mom for most of her six-year-old daughter's life. Ashley was a wonderful child—bright, friendly, and busy—but sometimes she could be *such* a handful. So, when Carla walked into her friend Alice's kitchen one afternoon, the tears seemed to come out of nowhere.

"I love my daughter more than anyone in the world," Carla explained after she'd calmed down a bit, "but I hate parenting sometimes. It feels like a trap. I just don't know how to be a good parent and still have a life of my own."

"You sound pretty overwhelmed," Alice said gently. "What's going on?"

Carla sighed. "I feel like I don't have time for myself or for the things I need to do. I'm always having to pick Ashley up from school or take her somewhere. Getting child care is such a hassle, and then I worry that no one else will take care of my daughter the way I do or that I should be spending more time with her. And the more frustrated I feel, the more controlling and impatient I get with Ashley. I feel like crawling into a closet—in fact, I guess that's what I do. I'm ashamed to talk about the way I feel. I want to be such a good parent—and so often I'm not."

Alice smiled at her friend. "You know," she said, "I bet you're not the only one who feels this way. I heard about a parenting class for single parents—maybe it's worth checking out."

Carla was skeptical, but she figured that anything was worth a try. And so one evening she found herself sitting in a room full of other single parents, who were saying many of the things she herself had said and thought and felt. *I'm not alone— and I'm not a horrible parent,* she realized. *Maybe there are ways to work through everything I'm feeling.*

Because it takes two to create a child, it seems to follow that parenting was designed to be a partnership. Sometimes when that partnership is no longer available, single parents feel they must be both mother and father to their children. So, in addition to the stresses of running a home, providing a living, and taking care of children, harried single parents find themselves trying to fill a double role: playing baseball and Barbies, soccer and video games, cooking, sewing, coaching, helping with carpentry projects, being a pal and a parent and a teacher. If you can do all of those things without breaking a sweat, congratulations. But is it really necessary?

There are times when two heads are better than one, when you need a safety net to fall back on. And there are ways to go about building a support system for yourself.

Businessmen have long known the value of networking. Doctors frequently recommend a second opinion. And single parents have a special need for a network—people who can offer advice, help, skills, another perspective. It is a wonderful thing when you realize you don't have to know everything—you only need to know who to ask. But how do you find out who to ask? How does a single parent go about building a support network? Here are some suggestions:

Check your community for parenting classes. They are not only wonderful places to learn new skills but they are also places to meet other parents, some of whom may be in similar situations and who may have already discovered solutions to your problems. Parenting classes also allow you to realize that you're not alone—and sometimes that can make all the difference.

Ask for help when you need it. Our culture has traditionally valued the "rugged individual" who has the ability to succeed on his or her own. But rugged individualism is not only overrated for single parents, it may be downright dangerous. Keep your eyes and ears open and don't be afraid to ask for assistance. A neighbor may be glad to help out with batting practice; someone at church may be thrilled to teach your child to knit or sew. A coworker with children of the same ages as yours may be able to help with parenting ideas, child care, or transportation. And friends may have expertise in areas you don't: home repair, gardening, sports. Ask and see what happens.

Keep relationships with extended family strong. Even if you're no longer related by marriage, grandparents, aunts, uncles, and other family members can remain a wonderful source of advice and nurturing. Children, too, benefit from healthy relationships with other family members; these often provide a sense of stability and heritage in times of transition, and children usually

LEARNING TO LEAN: BUILDING A SUPPORT NETWORK

- Check your community for parenting classes.
- Ask for help when you need it.
- Keep relationships with extended family strong.
- Make time for friendship.
- Look for organizations or other support groups.
- Don't write off the other parent.

appreciate knowing that they still belong to their extended family. When it isn't possible to maintain existing family relationships, create a new "extended family" with friends and support groups.

Make time for friendship. Friends are not only wonderful listeners, they can be sources of wisdom as well as great problem-solvers. Don't be afraid to talk with people who care about what you're experiencing and feeling.

Look for organizations or other support groups. Check in your local area for single-parent organizations, such as Parents Without Partners. If there aren't any, consider starting one yourself. It only takes one other single parent who is willing, and you may find your group growing by leaps and bounds as other single parents realize its value and the opportunities it creates. Your local family service agency may be able to give you referrals.

The world of computers has also opened exciting new opportunities for single parents. It is now possible to learn parenting skills, share experiences, and simply "chat" with other single parents over the Internet. Web sites exist for single mothers, single fathers, custodial parents, noncustodial parents, parents who are single by choice—the list is almost endless and no child care is required! You can search for your particular single-parenting topic of interest through any of the major search engines; Yahoo, Excite, and 800go.com are all good places to begin. Major providers such as America Online also provide parenting and family-oriented sites. As always when "surfing" the Internet, use caution (for both yourself and your children). Still, you may find a new world of information and support right at your own keyboard.

Don't write off the other parent. An important part of dealing with the overwhelming pressures of being a single parent may be allowing your child's other parent, if he or she is available, to play his or her part in your child's life. Although that may be an emotionally difficult thing to do (see chapters 15 and 16), it may be the best thing for your child in the long run—and it may take some of the burden off of you. Even if your child's parent isn't in the picture, it is enough if you are simply yourself: one parent, doing the best job you can.

> It is enough if you are simply yourself: one parent, doing the best job you can.

Your relationship with your child's other parent can be complicated and emotional—but sometimes that parent will see an aspect of a situation that you've missed, or may know a more effective way of dealing with a problem than the ones you've tried.

Learning to listen (and learning that you may not be right all of the time) is occasionally humbling—but it's liberating too.

"Mom," seven-year-old Cody yelled as he burst through the door after a weekend with his dad. "Come out here—I've got a surprise for you!"

As she followed her excited son into the garage, Janet wondered what could have happened. She was flabbergasted when Cody climbed on his bicycle, wobbled just a little, and rode proudly off down the street, flashing her a grin you could read by on a dark night.

The bicycle had become a difficult topic for Janet and Cody. Everyone in the neighborhood had been riding for months, but Cody couldn't seem to learn. Janet had tried everything she could think of to help, but a few bad falls had shaken Cody's confidence; each time he realized he was on his own, the teetering began. Nothing worked—not practice sessions, not running alongside him, not encouragement, not ignoring the whole thing. The bicycle had become larger than life.

> Learning to listen (and learning that you may not be right all of the time) is occasionally humbling—but it's liberating too.

Now, after a weekend with his dad, Cody was cruising proudly around the neighborhood. And as Janet watched him, she began to wonder what had made the difference.

It turned out that Dad had bought him a bike to keep at Dad's house, and the miracle had occurred when they went to try it out. "What did Dad do that I didn't?" Janet asked her son. Cody thought for a moment or two. "Well," he said, "he didn't tell me when he let go of me. And he taught me how to crash."

Janet was floored. She never would have thought of those things, but they had made all the difference in the world. Cody had possessed all along the skills he needed to ride a bike; what he'd lacked was confidence. Learning that he could survive his crashes had given him the courage to try again. Janet felt an odd mixture of joy for her son and disappointment that she hadn't been the one to help him; but as she watched him circling with his friends, she decided to be grateful that Cody's dad had done what she could not.

Janet and Cody both learned a valuable lesson—learning to crash successfully is a pretty important part of life itself. Being a single parent can be frightening. We feel responsible for our children, for their well-being, for their happiness. We feel we should always know what to do—and so often, we simply don't. One of the most important assets we can acquire is the courage to risk "crashing," to learn we can fail or lose our dreams and still survive. Sometimes we are even stronger for the experience.

Perfection Isn't Required

IT HELPS TO KNOW that our inadequacies and failures as parents need not be permanent. Parents can't be perfect, no matter how hard they try; but children don't need perfect parents. They only need parents who love and accept them, who are willing to learn and to do the best they can.

Being a single parent *can* be overwhelming. It can also be an exciting opportunity to build special relationships with your children. Budgeting our time and money and learning to find help when we need it will make single parenting less overwhelming and more joyous with each passing day.

7

Life with a Single Mom or Dad: Your Relationship with Your Child

MATTHEW IS NINE years old. "I love my mom and she works really hard," he says, "but one thing I hate is that since my dad moved out, I'm the only guy. My mom and my sisters sort of stick together, and I don't think they understand that sometimes I just feel different than they do. Plus they never want to do the things I want to, like play baseball or street hockey. I really miss having Dad around."

"My mom won't talk about my dad," thirteen-year-old Shannon says. "He left when I was a baby. My grandma says my dad used drugs and I don't need to know about him. But it's really hard. My friends mostly have their dads, even if they don't live together, and I don't even know mine. My mom is pretty cool and I like living with her. But I wonder where my dad is; I wonder if he ever thinks about me."

"I miss my mom so much sometimes that I can't even do my schoolwork," says seven-year-old James. "She died two years ago, and what makes me really sad is that it's getting hard to remember what she looked like. Dad has a new girlfriend and she's really nice—but she's not my mom. Dad tells me that Mom is in heaven but I feel sorta mad at God for taking her away from me, and when I see other kids with their moms I feel mad at them, too. I'm mad or sad almost all of the time. I don't tell Dad, though. I don't want to hurt his feelings."

Ten-year-old Daniel has a different story. "I'm glad my mom and dad got divorced," he says firmly. "They were both upset all the time. Mom cried a lot. My brother and I stayed in our rooms most of the time and we never went anywhere all together. Now that they're divorced, things are better. We get to spend time with both of them, and because no one's upset we can do more fun stuff. I know some kids are sad when their parents get a divorce, but for me, it's better this way."

Carina is sixteen. "All I know is that my mom and dad fight all the time. They fought when they were together and they fight now that they're divorced. They yell on the phone and they yell at my school, and Mom had to get a restraining order to keep Dad from coming to our house. Whenever I'm with either one of them, all I get to do is baby-sit my little brothers. There's never enough money for me to do stuff with my friends: Mom says it's because Dad won't pay child support, and Dad says it's because Mom took him for everything he owned. Sometimes I hate both of them. I'm never getting married!"

Getting into Your Child's World

ALL SINGLE PARENTS wonder from time to time how their choices affect their children. As do their parents, children will have all sorts of feelings about their situation—and those feelings will shape a great deal of their behavior, as well as their relationship with you. But because they are young and they often feel powerless to change their situation, and because they usually feel strong loyalties and protective instincts toward their parents, children may not share their world openly with you. And no two children will react to life in a single-parent home in precisely the same way.

For most of the first decade of their lives, children are egocentric; that is, they see themselves as the center of their own world and may believe that most of what happens around them is somehow related to them. A child may wonder if a parent isn't around because the child was bad or unlovable; he may believe that his parents' divorce was somehow his fault. Many adults spend hours explaining reasons and placing blame, but a child is usually most concerned about what will happen to her. There is one thing about which all children agree: They don't want to find themselves in the middle of a war between angry adults!

Coping with Chaos

Q. My son's dad moved out of our house about six months ago. Jeremy is five. He seemed okay at the beginning but lately he seems very defiant toward me. His dad says he is cheerful and loving at his house, but Jeremy screams at me or comes into the room and kicks me without warning. Five minutes later he'll be hugging me and telling me he loves me. I've tried ignoring his behavior or putting him in time out and I threatened to make him sit alone in the garage if he couldn't be nice, but I know that doesn't help. I just feel so confused and scared. What should I do?

A. There are many reasons why a five-year-old might behave differently with you than he does with his dad.

> There is one thing about which all children agree: They don't want to find themselves in the middle of a war between angry adults!

Children often vent difficult feelings on the parent with whom they feel "safest," which may explain why Jeremy doesn't behave this way with his father (the parent who "left"). In some way, your son senses that you will not abandon him, no matter how unlovable his behavior. Do your best to be both loving and consistent in setting boundaries. And be patient; the greatest healer of all is the passage of time.

It may help you deal with these difficult moments if you remember to be kind and firm at the same time. You can use active listening to validate Jeremy's feelings (and help him understand his own overwhelming emotions) and be firm about not allowing hurtful or disrespectful behavior. Punitive time outs and other punishments won't help. In fact, they are likely to escalate your son's behavior with you.

Although it can be difficult to remember when emotional energy is running high, you should try not to take your child's behavior personally.

Children sometimes blame themselves for their situation; sometimes they blame parents. Remember that this blaming is usually about a child's anger and fear; listening without judgment, offering support, and working toward trust will help you through the difficult moments.

The Importance of Belonging

MOST ADULTS BELIEVE that the most important ingredient for raising a healthy child is love. Although we certainly won't argue with the miracles love can produce in a family, we do question what some people call love. Some parents pamper their children in the name of love. Others push, protect, or punish in the name of love. We need to ask, "What makes a child feel loved?"

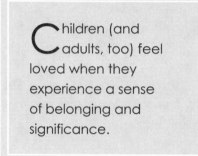

Children (and adults, too) feel loved when they experience a sense of belonging and significance.

Those who study human beings and their relationships have found that children (and adults, too) feel loved when they experience a sense of belonging and significance.

We all need to believe that we fit in, that we have a special place in the world, and that we can make a contribution to those around us. We need to feel that we have worth and value simply for being who we are. When we are not able to feel a sense of belonging (and we all have our moments), we may try to create that feeling for ourselves in other ways, often with mistaken or self-defeating behavior.

We'll take a closer look at the mistaken goals of misbehavior (and how to deal with them) later on, but it is essential to realize that belonging begins in the family. Being part of a single-parent family may, for a multitude of reasons, challenge a child's sense of belonging and her ability to form a close, trusting relationship with her parent.

Take a moment and, as best you can, stand in your child's shoes. Look at the world through her eyes. What changes has she experienced? What losses has she suffered? Does she see herself as being the same as those around her, or different? Does she feel loved? Wanted? Special? And regardless of how you became a single parent, how has your situation affected your child's ability to feel that she belongs and has a special place in the world?

We can create belonging for our children in dozens of ways. We can spend time with them, listen to them, and invite their ideas and help. Helping others and making a contribution are two of the best ways to feel significant. Parents can learn to value children's unique gifts and qualities, to accept them as they are instead of as we wish they could be. We can provide opportunities for them to develop life skills so they will feel confident and capable— other key ingredients to a sense of belonging.

> Remembering the importance of belonging will help you see past your children's behavior and into their hearts.

We can make an effort to get into their world and understand how their sense of belonging may have been damaged or dented by the choices (no matter how necessary or justifiable) of their parents. We can find ways to stay connected in a world that seems to do its best to push us apart. Remembering the importance of belonging will help you see past your children's behavior and into their hearts.

Building Trust

CHILDREN ARE HIGHLY SENSITIVE to the differences they perceive between their families and those of their peers. And being different in this world of ours can be a painful thing. As we have learned, children will feel grief, anger, loss, and fear as keenly as will their parents. As difficult as it is for loving parents to accept, no amount of wisdom, good parenting skills, and caring will remove all the pain from hurtful experiences. However, we can use these experiences to build a strong sense of belonging and significance by helping children learn that they can handle life's challenges. Good communication skills help immensely, but it almost always takes time and patience for single parents and their children to become comfortable with life as it is—and to see opportunities where they once saw only problems.

How can parents build a relationship of closeness and trust with their children? Regardless of the reasons you are a single parent, these suggestions will help.

Listen, listen, listen. One father told the leader of his single-parenting class that the most important skill he had learned was active listening because it allowed his children to share their real feelings. "I don't always like what I hear," he said with a rueful grin, "but I understand what's going on for them much better now. They feel safe telling me how they feel and what they think; and even when it makes me uncomfortable, I usually have a much better idea of what to do than I used to. They trust me more now and we can solve problems together."

As difficult as it is for loving parents to accept, no amount of wisdom, good parenting skills, and caring will remove all the pain from hurtful experiences.

It is impossible to overemphasize the importance of listening to your children. When you can get into their world, you'll be far better able to use your wisdom and love for them to help you make decisions and deal with their behavior.

Be "askable." Children certainly do not need to know all the grisly details of your private life. But when adults put sensitive subjects off-limits because of their own discomfort, children may decide that parents are too hard to talk to and may form their own mistaken beliefs about what has happened—and why.

Carl believed he was protecting his four-year-old daughter Myra by not telling her about her mother. Trish, his girlfriend, hadn't wanted her baby daughter and had left town soon after Myra's birth. Becoming the single father of an infant had been a tough adjustment for Carl but he'd managed, and now Myra was the delight of his life. He hadn't heard a word from Trish and he

BUILDING A RELATIONSHIP OF TRUST AND CLOSENESS WITH YOUR CHILDREN

- Listen, listen, listen.
- Be "askable."
- Check out your child's feeling—don't assume.
- Spend special time,
- Practice mutual respect.

allowed himself to believe that she would never return. When Myra eventually asked about her missing mother, Carl hesitated in confusion, then told Myra that her mommy had been sick in her head and had to go away. After that conversation, whenever Myra asked questions Carl changed the subject.

Myra stopped asking about her mother, but her behavior began to change. She had frequent nightmares and refused to sleep without her old "blankie." She avoided the other children at her preschool and sat alone during lunch and snack time. Myra's teacher decided to spend some time with the solitary child, and approached Carl one evening when he arrived to pick up his daughter.

"Is Myra ill?" the teacher asked Carl.

"Not that I know of," a perplexed Carl replied. "Why?"

"Well, she's been keeping to herself lately, and she's always been such a friendly little person that we were concerned. When I asked her why she didn't play with the other children anymore, she told me she was sick in her head and shouldn't be around anyone."

Carl sighed. He knew that the time had come to set things straight. He spoke to a counselor; then, one evening when the dishes had been done and Myra was cozy in her pajamas, he held her on his lap and began to tell her, in simple words, about her mother.

It was a long talk. Once Myra realized she could ask her dad questions, she had lots of them. Carl told Myra that her mother was a sweet lady but she just wasn't ready to take care of a little baby. He showed her a picture of her mom and told her how much he loved being her daddy. Most important, he told Myra that he had been afraid to tell her the truth and that he had made a mistake; Myra's mom wasn't sick and neither was she. No, he didn't know if her mother would ever come back, but perhaps one day they could see about finding out where she was. And no, Carl would never choose to leave Myra.

"You're the most important person in my life, angel," he said, and felt a lump forming in his throat. "From now on, ask me anything you need to know. I may not have all the answers and I'll make mistakes sometimes, but I'll do my best."

Myra kept the picture of her mother and, for a while, asked endless questions about her. Carl occasionally felt frustrated and discouraged, but he did his best to listen to Myra's thoughts and feelings, and to give her calm, honest answers. It took time, but life eventually returned to a comfortable routine—and Carl realized that he felt closer to his daughter than ever.

It can be difficult to decide just how much children need to know about your history—and theirs. Still, practicing emotional honesty and being approachable will go a long way in helping you build trust with your children. If you're not sure what—or how much—to say, consider asking a counselor who specializes in working with children. Building a relationship of trust and closeness now can save you untold trouble as your children grow and mature.

> Still, practicing emotional honesty and being approachable will go a long way in helping you build trust with your children.

Check out your child's feelings—don't assume. It's easy to believe the cliché that children are resilient and can handle anything; after all, it often seems that way. Still, it can be a mistake to assume that your children are fine just because they don't complain or misbehave. Some children work very hard to please and protect their parents while their own needs and fears go unspoken.

Parents are sometimes afraid to ask their children how they're doing. But if you ask with genuine curiosity and interest (rather than as an accusation or complaint), children may respond with honesty and confidence and allow you farther in to their own special world. Children often respond to questions with "I don't know"—and there are at least three reasons why. One is to avoid what they perceive as an "inquisition" or an invasion of their privacy. Another reason is that they don't believe you really want to know what they think but are looking for a specific response. A third reason is that they really don't know—at least not on a conscious level. They may need your help to acknowledge and verbalize their feelings, and in doing so will feel validated.

One way of initiating a conversation with your child is to use "what" and "how" questions, or to begin with "I notice that. . . ." For example, a mom may say to her son (with a smile and a warm tone of voice), "I notice that you've been kind of quiet today, honey. What's going on with you?" Or a dad may ask, "What things do you think I could do to help you feel better?"

If your child really doesn't understand her own feelings, try active listening and make guesses that she can correct or affirm. "You seem to be scared," or sad, angry, or happy—whatever your intuition tells you. If you are truly curious, your child will usually let you know when you are on or off target. You can then invite her to "Tell me more." Showing genuine interest often is an invitation to children to open up and let adults get closer.

Spend special time. As we've already learned, if we don't schedule time for family activities—even those as simple as talking and just being together—sometimes they don't happen at all. Yes, it takes time; but setting aside even ten minutes a day to spend one-on-one with each child in your life can make a huge difference in the quality of your relationship. You can go for a walk or read a book together; you can make cookies or wash the dishes. You can make special time together a part of your bedtime routine, inviting your child to share with you her happiest moment of the day (and her saddest) and then sharing yours with her.

One single mom and her son decided that they would go out to dinner together every Thursday night. They took turns choosing an inexpensive place to eat, with the understanding that neither would argue with the other's choice. Aaron always chose pizza; his mom stretched Aaron's horizons by choosing Chinese, or Mexican, or Italian. Both found that dinners out—just the two of them—gave them uninterrupted time to talk, to learn about each other, and to just be together. However you arrange it, regular special time can be a wonderful step to a closer relationship with your children.

Practice mutual respect. Mutual respect may be the single most important ingredient in a healthy relationship, but all too often we're better at demanding respect than offering it—especially with children. Children do not have equal rights with adults, nor should they; but they do have equal worth as human beings and they deserve to be treated with dignity.

Take time at a family meeting to invite your children to explain what respect means to them. Brainstorm ways that you can show respect for yourselves and for each other. For instance, respect can take practical shape in the way we speak to one another, treat others' property, and enter one another's

> Children do not have equal rights with adults, nor should they; but they do have equal worth as human beings and they deserve to be treated with dignity.

space. Offering your children kind, firm discipline and respect is a potent way to build a relationship of trust.

The Problem of Enmeshment

LOVE, TRUST, AND CLOSENESS are important elements in making a single-parent family work, but sometimes the members of a single-parent family can get a little too close.

Nancy, a single mom, had been alone for almost three years, and Stephanie, her five-year-old daughter, was the center of her life. In fact, since Stephanie's father moved out, Nancy had never spent a night away from her daughter. Because Nancy was disabled and didn't work outside the home, her days with Stephanie had been a succession of picnics, trips to the park, tea parties, and other shared activities.

However, change was looming on the horizon. Stephanie was ready to begin kindergarten, and her mother found the thought of entire days without her daughter unbearable. In addition, Nancy realized that Stephanie would begin to make new friends and develop new interests, and Nancy began to be afraid that somehow she wouldn't be as important in her daughter's life.

Perhaps, she thought to herself, *I can school Stephanie at home.* The more she thought about it, the more she liked the idea of keeping Stephanie with her and shielding her from the difficulties and influences of the outside world.

Nancy was wise enough, though, to realize that she needed some help in making such a big decision. There was free counseling available through her church, and though it was hard to leave Stephanie with a sitter even for an hour or two, Nancy made an appointment to discuss her situation with a counselor.

It wasn't difficult for the counselor to grasp Nancy's dilemma. Single parents often focus a huge amount of their time and energy on their children. They may be struggling with the transition from being part of a couple to being single. They may be feeling lonely and afraid. They may be worried about—and trying to compensate for—the effects on their children of growing up in a single-parent family. And because they love their children, they sometimes become over-involved in their lives, blurring the healthy parent-child boundaries and becoming enmeshed.

When this happens it's difficult for a single parent to let children grow up and develop relationships outside the family—or for the parent to develop a life of his or her own. Children may eventually feel trapped or overwhelmed, and when they try to break free, the parent feels hurt and betrayed.

Nancy's counselor understood the deep love and bond between mother and daughter. But she suggested to Nancy that letting go of Stephanie a little at a time was a healthy and loving thing to do. Stephanie needed to have friends her own age; she needed to learn how to get along in the world and to have all the experiences and adventures that school would bring. Nancy could share in all of that without restricting it.

Just as important, the counselor added, Nancy needed to begin a new life of her own. Joining a single parents' group would be a beginning; taking a class or going out for dinner or a movie with a friend would be a good step as well.

Nancy knew in her heart that the counselor had given her wise advice. She knew she and Stephanie would be healthier if they learned to spend some time away from each other. What surprised Nancy was how hard it was for Stephanie to make the break. The first time Nancy hired a baby-sitter so she could go to a movie with her friend, Stephanie cried and clung to her mother as she tried to leave. Nancy was tempted to give in and stay home, but instead she peeled Stephanie off of her body, said, "Honey, I'll be home in three hours," and left.

> A parent's job is to raise a capable, successful adult—and that means allowing a child to try her wings, explore beyond the nest, and, eventually, fly away.

Nancy did not have a good time with her friend and didn't remember one scene from the movie. But when she got home, Stephanie was happily playing a game with the baby-sitter.

"She quit crying as soon as you drove away," the sitter reported, "and we've had a great evening." Nancy quickly realized that the next time she went out it would be easier—for both her and her daughter.

It took a while for Nancy to face her fears of losing Stephanie, and for Stephanie to face her fears of losing her mother. Each had to develop the courage to let the other have some independence. Gradually, though, Nancy discovered that both she and Stephanie were happier as they developed new friendships and interests, and they enjoyed even more the time that they spent together.

A parent's job is to raise a capable, successful adult—and that means allowing a child to try her wings, explore beyond the nest, and, eventually, fly away. The comfort parents have is that our bond with our children can be both flexible and strong: flexible enough to allow them room to stretch, and strong enough to keep their hearts close for a lifetime.

The Issue of Gender

Q. I'm worried about the things my ex-wife tells our son about men. I understand that she's angry with me; I did choose to leave her for someone else. But she's constantly telling our son Jack, who is eight, that men are jerks (and worse) and that he'd better be careful or he'll grow up just like me. How can my son have any self-esteem if he believes men are bad?

A. Anger and hurt sometimes lead parents to say and do things they shouldn't. But you are correct: Your son will be happier and healthier if you and your ex-wife can keep from attacking each other, particularly about gender. Believing that one's own sex is "bad" may complicate development of a healthy sense of self-esteem. It is possible to use emotional honesty to express feelings in simple, unaccusatory ways. Perhaps seeing a therapist or mediator (or giving your ex-wife a copy of this book) will help her learn more effective ways of expressing her feelings without confusing your son.

> Boys and girls (and moms and dads) express and cope with emotions in different ways and our culture sends messages to our sons and daughters that often are unhealthy and damaging.

In recent years, researchers and writers have devoted a great deal of energy to the subject of gender, studying whether girls and boys with single parents do better with their moms or dads—or either, or both. Will children do better with same-sex parents? Can opposite-sex parents raise healthy children and understand what they're going through? Do children need role models of both genders to be healthy?

Research findings on the issue of gender are mixed, but we can be fairly certain of a few things. Respected authorities such as William Pollack, Ph.D.,

(*Real Boys: Rescuing Our Sons from the Myths of Boyhood*, Random House, 1998) and Mary Pipher, Ph.D., (*Reviving Ophelia: Saving the Selves of Adolescent Girls*, Ballantine, 1994) believe that boys and girls (and moms and dads) express and cope with emotions in different ways and our culture sends messages to our sons and daughters that often are unhealthy and damaging.

Girls may be particularly susceptible to the messages of a materialistic culture, especially as they approach adolescence. They learn from advertising, the media, and their peers that it is best to be sexy, thin, sophisticated, and grown-up. Close attachment to parents is not cool. Girls may be more comfortable expressing emotion than boys, but they frequently do so in angry, defiant ways, yelling in a parent's face.

> In fact, fathers who feel unable to connect emotionally with their children sometimes substitute money and entertainment, the well-known "Disneyland Dad" syndrome.

Boys may learn that being male means appearing strong and macho at all times. It's acceptable to be happy and it's acceptable to be angry (after all, anger is a "strong" emotion), but feelings such as fear, worry, or loneliness may indicate weakness. Studies have shown that boys often repress such feelings, putting on, in William Pollack's words, a "mask" and withdrawing into isolation and depression.

It isn't only "little" boys who suffer, either. Fifty percent of divorced fathers see their children only once a year; 30 percent never or rarely do. Many fathers report feeling unable to communicate with their children comfortably about difficult subjects. This "emotional disconnect" may lead to the cessation of visitation and support; fathers who feel unable to connect emotionally with their children may substitute money and entertainment, the well-known "Disneyland Dad" syndrome.

Mothers struggle, too. Society praises fathers for remaining involved with their children, but mothers must be careful to keep their involvement at just the right level; too much is considered smothering, while not enough makes her distant or cold. In fact, loving one's mother is associated with negative qualities such as passivity and dependency, while leaving mother is seen as an act of independence and strength. Our culture may actually encourage both boys and girls to reject their mothers as part of growing up.

In truth, healthy relationships are interdependent, neither enmeshed and stifling nor detached and cold. Each person needs space to be an individual and to explore separate interests while still having the warmth and closeness of love and trust to rely on. And both boys and girls can benefit greatly from healthy relationships with both men and women. Is one healthy parent enough? Yes. Will children benefit from healthy ties to both sexes? Again, yes.

Mothers and fathers can use Positive Discipline parenting skills to get into their children's worlds, to build confidence, self-reliance, closeness, and trust. Both men and women need to learn how their own sons and daughters express emotion; both need to be very careful of the messages they send about the opposite sex. Both need to practice respect, active listening, and good communication skills.

HOW TEACHERS CAN HELP: GENDER AND SINGLE-PARENT FAMILIES

You might want to share the following suggestions with your child's teacher:

- Be sensitive to art and holiday projects that may relate to only one parent (Mother's Day, Father's Day, Christmas, and so on). Allow children some flexibility, inviting them to make a project for both parents, if they choose.

- Be aware of your own attitudes toward boys and girls, and toward children living with single parents. Some studies have shown that teachers call on boys more often and allow them to talk longer than girls, and expect more misbehavior from children of single parents. Students will "catch" your attitudes regarding their fellow students and regarding themselves.

- Don't take outbursts or occasional misbehavior personally.

- Make an effort to learn what a child's living arrangements are; provide two invitations to music programs and plays, if appropriate.

Fathers and mothers can be aware of the messages our culture sends to our children and can learn to discuss these openly. And both can pay attention to what happens at school, where their older children adopt so many beliefs about their own sex—and the opposite one. Teachers, who sometimes spend more hours with our children than we do, can help children deal with both family and gender issues.

> Mothers and fathers can use Positive Discipline parenting skills to get into their children's worlds, to build confidence, self-reliance, closeness, and trust.

Danger or Opportunity?

THERE MAY BE nothing more important in life than the relationship we build with our children. It will shape their lives and ours and determine the nature of life in our homes and families. Take time to consider thoughtfully what you want your children to learn about trust, belonging, men, women, love, and life itself. Every moment we spend with our children is an important moment.

8

Single-Parent Families Aren't "Broken": Practicing Cooperation and Encouragement

THERE'S NO DOUBT single parenthood can be challenging for everyone concerned, and that we and our children may arrive at being a single-parent family laden with heavy emotional baggage. But as we're learning, life for single parents and their children holds some wonderful possibilities as well.

"Wait a moment," you may be saying. "When are we going to get to the 'discipline' part of this book? When will I learn how to deal with my child's behavior?" As we will discover, the best sort of discipline is *prevention,* creating a relationship with children that encourages cooperation, good judgment, and trust. When your relationship is strong and healthy, misbehavior simply doesn't happen as often. (Notice that we say "as often." Neither we nor our children will ever be perfect!)

> The best sort of discipline is *prevention,* creating a relationship with children that encourages cooperation, good judgment, and trust.

There are many ways single parents can practice positive discipline, preventing problems before they occur. One important way is to know your child and to understand his temperament, personality, and special qualities. (For more information on these important subjects, see *Positive Discipline: The First Three Years* and *Positive Discipline for Preschoolers, Revised 2nd Edition,* both by Nelsen, Erwin, and Duffy—Prima Publishing, 1998.) Other tools for preventing misbehavior are teaching, encouragement, and family meetings.

Drawing Children into the Circle

IF WHAT HUMAN BEINGS really need is to belong and to feel significant, worthwhile, and needed, then a single-parent family can provide tremendous opportunities for young people to fulfill those needs. Single parents rarely have to manufacture things for their children to do; they can say with absolute honesty, "It really makes my life easier when you help me and I really appreciate you. Thanks!" And that can make a child feel truly important.

It may be tempting occasionally to make children too important, to cast them in the role of the missing spouse. A son becomes the new "man of the family"; a daughter becomes Mom's best friend and confidante or "Dad's little homemaker." It's natural for a single parent to want someone to lean on, someone to share the responsibilities of keeping this new sort of family together.

Frazzled parents may believe it is easier simply to do things *for* children than to find ways to work *with* children.

But children are still children and the weight of being the "little man" or the "little woman" can be far too heavy for young shoulders.

Occasionally parents go to the opposite extreme, taking all of the responsibility for chores, schoolwork, and decisions. Their children, they may believe, have suffered enough by losing the active involvement of one parent in their home and shouldn't be expected to work or be responsible. Frazzled parents may believe it is easier simply to do things *for* children than to find ways to work *with* children.

Neither overfunctioning nor underfunctioning works well in the long run for adults or children. As we've mentioned, overly responsible children can become their parent's caretakers, bearing unnecessary stress and emotional burdens, while children who aren't involved in family work at all may begin to simply slide through life, expecting others always to make decisions for them—and to clean up after them. In either case, what children are thinking, feeling, and deciding about themselves and others may not help them become capable, happy adults. Parents *can* give children experiences that encourage perceptions of confidence, capability, and the desire to contribute.

The Value of Cooperation

ONE EFFECTIVE APPROACH is to acknowledge that life in a single-parent family is a cooperative effort. "We are a team," a parent might say to his children, "and this family needs each one of us to work well." Children want to make a contribution (even when they aren't aware of it, and seem to resist it); a parent needs to know that her children are learning to live successful, happy lives. Family life is a circle, and when each person in it is carrying just the right amount of weight it rolls along smoothly.

Family Work: Opportunity or Oppression?

FAMILY WORK—those tasks that need to be done to keep a home running smoothly and peacefully—can be either an accepted part of life in a family or an endless hassle. It's probably best not to define these tasks as "chores," things you do because you have to, things you'll get nagged or penalized for not doing. Family work means cooperation, making a contribution that helps the entire family.

Believe it or not, most children react with enthusiasm when they are given opportunities to be valued contributors to their family. Young children in particular learn by imitating adults and usually want to do whatever you are doing, whether it's vacuuming the carpet, changing the oil in the car, or mashing potatoes. (How many times has your little one exclaimed, "Me do it, Mommy!"?) Nevertheless, children's "helpful" efforts sometimes create more work for parents (after all, they rarely do things exactly the way we do), and we may tell them to "go play" so we can get our work done. But allowing them to participate (and teaching them the skills they need to do so) is an effective way of encouraging cooperation. Being part of the family team, especially when it's approached with love, humor, and respect, can be a wonderfully empowering and encouraging experience for parent and child alike.

> Being part of the family team, especially when it's approached with love, humor, and respect, can be a wonderfully empowering and encouraging experience for parent and child alike.

Every member of a family, from youngest to oldest, can do something worthwhile. A three-year-old can put napkins at each place at the table; older children can clear away and wash dishes, take out trash, or water plants; teens can help out in a variety of ways. Too often, though, what parents notice (and nag about) is what *didn't* get done. Or they set their standards and expectations too high and provide little or no on-the-job training. Or parents fail to get their children involved in the process of helping to decide what needs to be done and creating plans for doing it. Family work then becomes a discouraging experience for young people—and getting them to participate turns into a major hassle. When parents take the time not only to notice what *did* get done but to teach, encourage, appreciate, and give positive feedback, the entire process can actually become an enjoyable part of family life. (For more on inviting your children's cooperation with family work, see *Chores Without Wars,* Lynn Lott and Riki Intner—Prima Publishing, 1998)

What if Children Won't Cooperate?

Q. My oldest son is fifteen years old, and no matter what I do, I can't get him to help me around the house. I have to nag and lecture him, and even then he does only the bare minimum. Usually I give up and do everything myself, and then yell at him for not helping. I hate hearing myself scream. I've tried taking away his privileges when he doesn't do his work, and last weekend I told him he had to cancel dinner with his dad because he hadn't helped me, but that didn't feel right. What should I do?

A. It may help to remember that children do what works—and your son's behavior is working very well. He has learned that if he resists long enough, you will give in and do the work for him. Changing this pattern will require patience and some thought.

Begin with small steps and encouragement. What is he doing right, at home and at school? Be sure he hears about those things as well as the things he doesn't do to your satisfaction. Have a family meeting and ask him which jobs he would be most willing to do; be sure to set a time for the job to be done. If it feels reasonable, respectful, and related, you can ask that his work be done before he goes out. (It isn't helpful to take away time with his father; chances are good that he only resents you more for interfering with a relationship that is important to him—and which is separate from his chores and relationships at your home.) Be sure that if you decide to impose a consequence, he knows what it is in advance and you can follow through kindly and firmly. Avoid yelling; don't do the work for him. When he sees that you mean what you say, his behavior will change.

It is important to know that nothing will work all the time and forever. Normal children will not cooperate all the time no matter what you do because of their individuation process. For a child to *individuate* means to discover who they are separate from their parents. How can children discover who they are separate from their parents unless they test their own power? Parents will save themselves a great deal of stress if they understand that this process is normal (and create kind, firm limits and routines) instead of getting upset about it.

Another reason children may not cooperate is simply because they *are* children and have other priorities. Household work is not high on their priority list—in fact it is usually not on their list at all. This does not mean they should not have to do anything that is not on their priority list. It does mean, again, that parents will save themselves a lot of frustration and anger when they accept this and then find ways to get children to cooperate and do the things they need to do. The methods we suggest usually have to be repeated many times. Parents usually nag and lecture over and over. Positive Discipline methods are much more effective and pleasant, but they still require repetition.

Emily looked forward to her weekly dinner out with her two best friends, single parents like herself, but tonight she plopped into her seat with a heavy sigh. "Sorry I'm late," she said, "but I was cleaning the kitchen—again. I swear, I can't get Joanna to do anything! Have you all ordered yet?"

"No, we just got here ourselves," Martha said. "What's going on with Joanna? You do seem to be having a tough time with her. How old is she now?"

"She's eleven." As the three women read the menu and placed their orders, Emily continued with her story. "Actually, Joanna is a great kid," she said. "She gets good grades and is so sweet and loving. She just hates to work around the house. I ask her to clean up the kitchen after school, but when I come home everything is stacked in the sink and the counter is covered with crumbs. I hear myself nagging and lecturing—I hate that, because I sound like my mom—but I don't know what else to do."

> Parents usually nag and lecture over and over. Positive Discipline methods are much more effective and pleasant, but they still require repetition.

"You know," Karen said with a smile, "I went through that with Corey. I nagged and nagged, but things were never done the way I wanted. One day I asked him what he thought cleaning the house meant, and he looked at me and said, 'I don't know.' And I realized he really didn't. I'd just assumed he knew what I wanted him to do—and he got discouraged because it was never right. I wonder if Joanna has the same problem?"

Emily was thoughtful. "You know, I never even thought of that. I guess I need to sit down and talk with her."

A much more relaxed Emily arrived for dinner the next week. "You look a lot happier," Martha teased. "You must have a clean kitchen."

Emily laughed. "I do—I cleaned it myself. When I talked to Joanna, it turned out that she thought stacking the dishes was enough—after all, it looked neater to her. But when I stopped nagging and criticizing and just listened, it turned out that she hated doing the kitchen. I told her that I really did need her help. I asked if there was something she'd rather do, and she told me she wouldn't mind doing the laundry. So I took the time to show her how. Now I clean the kitchen and she does the laundry, and we're both much happier!"

Adults often assume that children will somehow magically understand what we need them to do—and just how to do it. But that assumption usually leads to discouragement on both sides: Adults feel discouraged because children won't help and children feel discouraged because they can't do things right. And discouragement frequently leads to misunderstanding—and misbehavior.

Take Time to Teach

ONE MEANING OF the Latin word from which *discipline* is derived is "to teach." Did you know that teaching—communicating to those around us what needs to be done and what is involved in doing it—is one of the most effective forms of discipline? Note that teaching is not the same as lecturing or criticizing. Teaching is a truly encouraging and loving act, and it provides young people with the skills they need to develop a healthy sense of self-esteem.

Chances are that Emily and Joanna could have avoided arguments about the kitchen if Emily had recognized and shown appreciation for the efforts (no matter how small) that Joanna made, and had shared with her the basic skills required to do an effective job. Teaching children does require that we invest time and effort up-front, but the rewards are well worth the energy it takes.

Separating the Child from His Behavior

WE'VE ALL HEARD the term *self-esteem*; we all know that it is important for children to have a healthy sense of it. But exactly how does that happen? Is it harder for children of single parents to believe in their own worth and significance?

Absolutely not! Teaching your child life skills and allowing him to experience the satisfaction of accepting a challenge and succeeding will go a long way toward developing self-esteem (we call these "competency experiences").

HOW TO TEACH A CHILD

1. Let her watch you. Invite your child to observe as you prepare dinner, mow the lawn, or make a bed. Explain in simple terms what you are doing and why.

2. You do it with her help. The next time you perform the task, encourage your child to help you. Explain what you are doing; be sure to let her know that you appreciate her help.

3. She does it with your help. Now it's time for your child to try the task herself—with lots of support and encouragement from you.

4. You watch her. By now your child should feel confident enough to tackle the job on her own. Remember to keep your standards realistic (expecting perfection can discourage both of you) and offer appreciation. Making "helping out" a pleasant adventure will take much of the hassle out of doing chores as the years go by.

Have you ever noticed that healthy self-esteem is not constant? It seems to come and go. Sometimes children may feel really good about themselves, and then something happens and they feel terrible about themselves. When children have had many competency experiences and have learned that they are able to solve life's problems, the periods of low self-esteem will not last as long.

Learning to notice and acknowledge what's *right* with our children is also very important. Much of a child's perception of herself is created by the feedback she receives from her parent and other adults in her life. Parents sometimes equate children with their behavior. In other words, a misbehaving or discouraged child is a "bad" child, while

> Teaching your child life skills and allowing him to experience the satisfaction of accepting a challenge and succeeding will go a long way toward developing self-esteem.

one who behaves well (or pleases adults successfully) is "good." Self-esteem allows a child to learn from mistakes instead of believing that she is worthwhile and belongs only when she is perfect, and parents can help by learning to separate children from their behavior.

Children are never "bad." They do, however, misbehave occasionally and sometimes frustrate, irritate, and provoke the adults around them. Wise parents learn to give children the message that while who we *are* is okay, some of what we *do* is not.

Encouraging Uniqueness

HELPING CHILDREN DEVELOP their full potential is a top priority for all caring parents, and one that can be all too easily neglected when the hassles of daily life intrude. Have you ever stood outside the door of a young child and listened?

"Pretend your guy is riding up on his horse," one child will say. "Yeah, and then pretend that my guy is in the castle," another chimes in. "And then there's an earthquake!" another shouts, and the room echoes with the sounds of falling Legos and laughter.

> Imagination and creativity are wonderful gifts. Creative children see many possibilities and are able to believe in themselves and in their ability to tackle and solve a problem.

Imagination and creativity are wonderful gifts. Creative children see many possibilities and are able to believe in themselves and in their ability to tackle and solve a problem. Experts also tell us, however, that creative, thoughtful children are the ones who ask those steady streams of irritating questions. They love to invent new rules for games and new ways of doing things—often to the annoyance of their harassed parents.

Unfortunately, it is often the most creative children who are labeled "troublemakers," because they ask too many questions and because they seem to find it impossible to be still and do what everyone else is doing. Perhaps every child has the potential to be creative—but because creative, energetic children can complicate life for busy teachers and parents, they are often taught early to squelch their enthusiasm and to conform with the crowd. We may never know what talents and ideas have been lost in exactly this way.

Life as a busy single parent may leave little time for special and out of the ordinary things. It is difficult enough to listen to everything your children say and to deal with the endless crises of daily life. Encouraging specialness takes time and energy that you may not feel you have.

Creative children are not always those who play the violin at three or the piano at five, or who read or paint or study ancient history at an early age. What about the child whose gifts are less obvious? What about the child who simply has a knack for solving a problem? Or who has a vivid imagination and a talent for storytelling? Or a deep and genuine love for ideas?

We need to learn both to recognize and to encourage the uniqueness of our children. It helps to turn off the television and read or talk about what our children find interesting. Be patient with their questions, their different approaches. Let them try new things occasionally or experiment with a new idea. Ask yourself whether they're challenging the status quo just to be contrary or because they really do have a better idea.

Above all, let them know you love and value them for exactly who they are, differences and special qualities included. The pressure to go along with the majority is overwhelming enough as it is. Though it takes patience and perseverance, teaching our children to value their own uniqueness strengthens their self-esteem and may be just the thing that sets them on the road to a creative and productive life.

The Magic of Encouragement

THE WORD *encouragement* means "to gladden the heart." Encouragement does not mean we tell children that everything they do is okay. But many well-meaning parents withhold acceptance and the sense of belonging from children until they become "good" or succeed at a task. Remember, children and adults alike do better when they feel better, when they know that they belong and have worth. Encouragement does not mean accepting inappropriate behavior; it does mean noticing effort, acknowledging improvement, and offering appreciation and gratitude.

Children also feel encouraged when they know that mistakes are wonderful opportunities to learn instead of evidence that there is something wrong with them. It is very encouraging to help children learn from inappropriate behavior by helping them explore what happened, what caused it to happen, how they feel about it, what they learned from it, and what they can do in the future to solve the problem. In this way we can help them learn to become "good-finders."

Becoming Good-Finders

People who succeed in life and relationships tend to be good-finders. That is, they are able to notice the good in other people and in situations, and they are quick to point those things out to others. There may be nothing else so important in creating a family atmosphere of optimism and confidence. Unfortunately, most of us are far more apt to notice negatives than positives. How do we become good-finders? And how do we share that marvelous gift with our children?

Look for positives. Denise was just hanging up the phone when her boss poked his head in the door. "When you have a minute, Denise," he said, "I'd like to see you in my office."

Denise's stomach curled into a tight little knot. What had she done wrong? Had she forgotten something? Made a mistake? As she walked into her boss's office she expected the worst.

Ken, Denise's boss, waved his hand at an empty chair. "Sit down, Denise—and don't look so worried!" He grinned. "Actually, I've been meaning to talk to you for some time. I've been noticing what a terrific job you do. I know you've been under a lot of pressure at home, yet your attitude here has been wonderful. Our clients love you, the quality of your work is great, and your sense of humor keeps us all going sometimes. I just wanted you to know how much we appreciate everything you do."

Denise realized that her jaw had dropped, and Ken laughed. "We supervisors don't do this sort of thing often enough, do we?" he asked. "Did you think I was going to fire you or something?" When Denise smiled ruefully, Ken continued, "I guess I don't blame you. Somehow it's harder to find time to say good things than it is to criticize. Anyway, keep up the great work."

> Encouragement does not mean accepting inappropriate behavior; it does mean noticing effort, acknowledging improvement, and offering appreciation and gratitude.

BECOMING GOOD-FINDERS

- Look for positives.
- Offer compliments and appreciation.
- Build on strengths.
- Teach that mistakes are wonderful opportunities to learn.

When Denise opened her own front door that evening and looked around, she had a flash of inspiration. Some chores hadn't been done, she could see, but the kids were playing quietly together and it was obvious they had all done their homework—the books and papers were neatly stacked for her to check.

"Hey, guys," she called out to her children. Three faces turned toward her with apprehensive looks, and she realized they probably felt much as she had when Ken had spoken to her. She smiled as warmly as she could.

"I just wanted you to know how much I enjoy coming home. You look so cozy there together and I can see you've done your homework. You know, I really appreciate it when you do what I ask without my nagging. What do you say we rent a movie and make some popcorn tonight?"

Later, as Denise prepared dinner, she noticed her oldest son quietly doing the job he'd neglected to do earlier. And there was an unmistakable warmth in the atmosphere that night. She smiled to herself. A little encouragement, she'd learned, made everyone feel good and worked much better than lectures.

Take a moment right now and make a list: What things do you love about each of your children? What qualities, quirks, and special gifts make you smile? When you have a good list (and if you've struggled with your children, it may take a while to make one), put it somewhere where you will see it often. Then, at least once each day, tell each child something you appreciate about him or her. You needn't gush; in fact, children can spot insincerity a mile away, so say only what you truly believe. But there is always something good in each person and each situation; learning to find it and share it can give you and those around you courage and hope.

Ask your children what they like about their family (and you, and each other); encourage them to share these observations. Becoming a good-finder takes some practice (after all, we're usually so much more comfortable with complaining than complimenting) and it does not mean you should ignore misbehavior. It will, however, set the stage for the Positive Discipline parenting skills that both manage behavior and build relationships.

Offer compliments and appreciation. Many parents learned somewhere along the way that "pride goeth before a fall." So sometimes we fear that complimenting our children will make them boastful or arrogant. But think for a moment: Don't all of us love to have our efforts and abilities acknowledged?

Family meetings are the perfect place to share the good that you and your children discover about each other. As we'll see, beginning each meeting with spoken appreciation for each person's contributions and achievements can create a sense of belonging for everyone. Compliments fit well in the daily flow of life, too. Smile, say "thank you," and offer hugs daily!

Build on strengths and manage weaknesses. The book *Soar with Your Strengths* by Donald O. Clifton and Paula Nelson (Dell Publishing, 1992) begins with a delightful parable about a duck, an eagle, an owl, a squirrel, and a rabbit who attend a school with a curriculum that includes running, swimming, jumping, and flying. Of course, each of the animals has strength in one area but cannot succeed in others. It is sobering to consider the discouragement and punishment these animals encounter when parents and teachers insist that they do well in every area in order to graduate. A major idea in the book is that excellence can be achieved only by focusing on strengths and managing weaknesses, not through the elimination of weakness.

> There is always something good in each person and each situation; learning to find it and share it can give you and those around you courage and hope.

Parents often take from children those areas in which they excel, such as sports and the arts, when they do not earn A's in school. How much more encouraging would it be to help children learn to get by in difficult classes and encourage them to spend time on the activities and abilities that make them soar?

Help children discover their strengths; we don't all know them instinctively. Read to them; encourage curiosity and a spirit of discovery. Yes, extracurricular activities take time and energy that single parents may believe is in short supply, but how many children have been encouraged and supported by the acceptance they found doing something at which they excelled? Remember, children need to belong. If we cannot help them discover positive ways to belong, they will discover negative ways.

Teach that mistakes are wonderful opportunities to learn. It takes courage to accept that each of us is imperfect and will inevitably make mistakes—and still get up each morning determined to be the best parent and person we can. Our children, too, will struggle with their inevitable missteps and mistakes. But mistakes aren't fatal disasters or unforgivable sins; they are simply mistakes.

When you or a child you love has made a mistake, you have the opportunity to teach valuable lessons and to grow even closer. When the mistake is yours, acknowledge it and ask for forgiveness. Then you can model the importance of doing whatever is necessary to make amends. When your child makes mistakes, one way she can learn from them is through "what" and "how" questions that help her explore the consequences of her actions. Some possible questions are, "What are your thoughts on what happened?" "What did you learn from this experience?" "How could you use what you learned in the future?" "What ideas do you have to make amends or to solve the problem?"

"What" and "how" questions are effective only when done after your child has had time to calm down, and when she senses that you are truly curious about her perceptions. Sometimes a friendly discussion is all that is needed to resolve a problem.

9

Family Meetings: Making Your Family a Team

IT'S EASY TO view children as weighty responsibilities or as lesser beings who get in the way of what we need to accomplish. Actually, children are remarkable resources. They are—or can be, when given the chance—creative, energetic, and ingenious. How can single parents go about tapping into that energy and creativity? And how can we make life in our family a well-balanced circle, embracing everyone and rolling along smoothly?

The Family Meeting

ONE IMPORTANT WAY to create a spirit of family teamwork and cooperation is the family meeting. It doesn't matter whether your family consists of one parent and one child or one parent and several children, you are a family, and family meetings will strengthen your family team.

Family meetings may be a new idea to you. You may wonder what the benefits are and how to go about holding them. And you may wonder how you'll manage one more thing to do. There are many excuses for not having family meetings: "With all I have to juggle, how can I find time?" "There are only two of us and we solve problems while driving in the car." "My kids are so good we don't need meetings." All of these excuses ignore the long-range benefits you can reap from family meetings.

When parents truly understand the many benefits of family meetings, they realize they can't afford not to find the time—which becomes a valuable investment because of the prevention of problems and the cooperation gleaned from this valuable process.

How Do You "Do" Family Meetings?

JUST AS FAMILIES come in different shapes, sizes, and personalities, family meetings will differ in their priorities and their details. There are a few important points to keep in mind, though.

Family meetings should be a priority. Most families find that setting aside a certain time each week works best. This may be an evening when no one has activities to dash off to, or after a meal when everyone is present. Try not to make other plans for that time, and don't allow yourself to be interrupted by the phone or other distractions. Let your children know that you consider this time with them a very important part of your week.

Begin each meeting with compliments and appreciations. Look for—and comment on—the positive things each member of your family has done, and teach your children to do the same. This can be awkward, especially for siblings who are more accustomed to put-downs, arguments, and hassles. However, with time, they will learn the skills of giving compliments and will catch the spirit. The feelings of worth and significance that result will be worth the effort, and your entire meeting will be off to an encouraging start.

A tradition of family meetings can become the foundation for special times together and cherished memories for the future.

Keep an "agenda board" in a handy place. (Refrigerators seem to be a perennial favorite.) Encourage members of the family to write down during the week ideas and problems for consideration at the next family meeting—and then be sure to discuss each item. You will find that you can often resist the temptation to nag when you can instead write your own concerns on the agenda. Sometimes, too, having a place to vent their frustration is all children really need, and by the time the meeting rolls around the problem will have been solved—or forgotten. At other times, the family will need to brainstorm for ideas to solve the problems.

LONG-RANGE BENEFITS OF FAMILY MEETINGS

Regular family meetings accomplish many positive goals:

- Setting aside time to gather as a family demonstrates a commitment to the family. So often we keep appointments with coworkers, friends, even strangers, but not with our children.

- Family meetings are an opportunity to teach important life skills, to create mutual respect through brainstorming, to do joint problem solving, and to make time for conversation, understanding, and staying in tune with one another.

- Family meetings allow children to learn that their thoughts, feelings, and ideas are listened to and taken seriously (while parents gain ideas and insights they didn't have before). What could be bet-ter for building healthy self-esteem, confidence, and feelings of capability?

- In our busy, stressful lives, time for relaxed meals together and long conversations afterward may be difficult to find. A tradition of family meetings can become the foundation for special times together and cherished memories for the future.

Brainstorm to solve problems and plan activities. It is important to invite the opinions of each member of the family. During brainstorming, *all* ideas, no matter how unworkable they may appear at first, should be accepted respectfully. All it takes is one "Well, *that's* a stupid idea!" to sour a child on family meetings for good. Once everyone has had a chance to brainstorm ideas, you can proceed with figuring out which ideas will work and why, and everyone can agree on the best plan. In this way, brainstorming becomes a learning experience and an opportunity to teach your children valuable problem-solving skills.

Decisions should be made by consensus rather than by a majority vote. Voting only builds resentment in those who "lost." If your family can't agree on something, put it off until the next meeting. Everyone will have cooled off and may have had time to come up with new ideas.

Have a chairperson and a secretary to record decisions, and rotate these positions. Children love to be in charge and can do a good job once they understand the procedure. This also demonstrates that the parent is willing to listen and to consider the thoughts and abilities of each child.

End on a positive note. Conclude each family meeting with plans for a family activity in the coming week, or with a game or favorite dessert.

But Does It Really Work?

IT WAS A BUSY MORNING—as usual—at the Taylor home. Marlene was preparing for her day at work, and trying to see that her three daughters had some breakfast before they left for school. She was sipping coffee when a loud wail echoed down the hall.

Mandy, her fourteen-year-old, stormed out of her room with a crumpled blouse in one hand. "Mo-om!" she howled. "I wanted to wear my favorite blouse to school today, but Kim wore it and got it all dirty—and she didn't even ask me first."

Kim, thirteen, was not far behind. "Well, Mandy took my best jeans," she sulked. "And Caitlin keeps taking my hair stuff."

"Do not!" came eight-year-old Caitlin's voice from the bathroom.

Marlene closed her eyes for a moment and took a deep breath. "Sounds to me like you're all feeling frustrated with the borrowing that's going on," she said. "Have you written it down on the agenda for our next family meeting?"

The girls looked at each other and shook their heads. Marlene sighed, then smiled. "Well, why don't you write it down?" she said. "Our next meeting is Thursday night and we can work on the problem then. Now it's time for school—you'd better finish getting dressed."

Thursday evening rolled around and Marlene gathered her daughters around the cleared kitchen table. "Kim," she said, "it's your turn to be chairperson. And Mandy, you're secretary."

"Okay," Kim began. "I want Mandy to quit taking my stuff."

"Whoa," her mom said. "How do we begin our family meetings?"

There was a stubborn silence. The girls were still angry and found appreciating one another a tricky task. Finally Kim said, only a little sullenly, "I appreciate that Mandy helped me with my math homework the other night." That broke the ice. Other compliments and a funny story followed, and before too long the family was ready to begin problem solving.

Kim took charge. "The agenda says we need to talk about borrowing each other's things. Does anyone have any ideas?"

It didn't take long to brainstorm quite a list. The girls decided that Mandy and Kim, who shared a bedroom, should have separate drawers and racks for their things. The owner's name could be written on each item's label with a laundry pen. Each girl agreed to ask her sisters *before* she borrowed something, and to make sure it was returned clean, pressed, and ready to wear.

The girls agreed that baskets on the bathroom counter would help them keep their hair supplies separate. And Mandy and Kim, who were almost the same size and were most likely to borrow each other's clothing, agreed that taking something without permission or returning it dirty (or not at all) would give the other sister the right to borrow and wear the article of her choice for a day—and to return it without laundering it.

Marlene looked at the list of solutions Mandy had written down. "Are you all willing to try this for a week?" she asked. The girls nodded their heads. "We can check at our next meeting to see how it's going, but if you're happy with this, it's fine with me. Now, what shall we do this weekend?"

"Go shopping for more clothes!" exclaimed Caitlin, and they all laughed together.

Before family meetings, Marlene had lectured to the girls about asking before they "borrowed" things. The lectures never produced results. However, when the girls chose the same plan, they were willing to do what "they" decided.

Family meetings aren't the solution to every problem. But they do provide a time and a place for family members to listen to one another's thoughts, ideas,

grievances, and accomplishments, and to learn to work together to find mutually acceptable ways out of the dilemmas and controversies of everyday life.

Meetings Can Include Everyone

REMEMBER, TOO, that your "family" can include just about anyone. And
family meetings often work best when they include all of the people who are
directly involved in a situation, such as baby-sitters, close friends, or even
teachers.

For example, Phyllis was a single mother with one six-year-old son,
Matthew. Matthew was a bright child—a little too bright for his own good.
He was creative and verbal, and usually had no trouble getting around people.
Phyllis had recently started a new business and found herself needing to work
long hours, but she worried about child care for her son. The solution presented itself in the form of an older woman who was willing to live in. Phyllis
drove off to work whistling the first morning the sitter moved in—and arrived
home late that night to find disaster awaiting her.

Matthew, it turned out, had used all of his intelligence to manipulate his
new sitter, knowing Mom wasn't around to enforce the rules. He was still up
when Phyllis came home, although it was a school night. He had been out
playing in the neighborhood until 7:30 that evening and had thrown a
tantrum when the sitter managed to make him come inside then—even
though he knew Mom expected him in at 5:00. Phyllis scolded and punished
but the situation was hopeless. After a week of power struggles with Matthew,
the sitter gave up in despair and Phyllis shortened her hours and went back to
the hassle of trying to make arrangements with neighborhood sitters.

A few months later, as Phyllis found her business thriving and demanding
more of her time, she decided to try a live-in sitter again. But this time Phyllis
planned to include the sitter in family meetings. The sitter, Aggie, was in-
trigued with the idea. They involved Matthew in looking at all of the possible
problems and making all of the rules—and they found that Matthew enjoyed
putting his creativity to constructive use. Because Matthew was involved in
creating the rules, he was more inclined to obey them.

Life ran much more smoothly, although it was far from perfect; still, when
there was a problem, Phyllis, Aggie, or Matthew would put it on the agenda

and they would work on solutions at their next meeting. Phyllis was thrilled, Aggie remained sane, and Matthew learned that being part of the solution was better than being part of the problem—well, most of the time, anyway. Five weeks later Phyllis shared with her parenting group that she couldn't believe how well things were going and that she wished she had known about family meetings sooner.

Making Changes As a Family

IT IS TEMPTING to use family meetings only for solving problems—after all, they work so well for that purpose. But gathering as a family in a comfortable and predictable way is also a wonderful means to share information, to find out how everyone is feeling, to stay in touch, and to deal *together* with change.

When Brian Harlow sat down with his two children for their weekly family meeting, he was a bit apprehensive; he had some news to share, and he wasn't at all sure how his kids would react. As Brian placed a big bowl of popcorn in the center of the table (and took a large handful himself), he asked Kate, his fourteen-year-old daughter, to start with some compliments.

Kate and nine-year-old Robby talked warmly for a few minutes about their week. Robby had been selected "most valuable player" at his Little League game, and his grin brightened the whole room. Kate had successfully resolved a big argument with a friend at school, and thanked her little brother for feeding Muffin, the dog, so she could go to the movies. As the conversation slowed, both kids turned to their father.

> Gathering as a family in a comfortable and predictable way is also a wonderful means to share information, to find out how everyone is feeling, to stay in touch, and to deal *together* with change.

"You're not saying much, Dad," Kate said. "What's been going on with you?"

"Well," Brian said slowly, "I got a big promotion at work."

"All right!" Robby exclaimed. "Will you make more money? Can we go to Disneyland this summer?"

"That's cool, Dad," Kate chimed in with a smile.

"Yeah, it's cool," Brian said. "I'll make more money, Rob, which should make life a little easier—although I don't know about Disneyland. But there's one catch. You see, the new job is in Florida."

There was a long silence while Kate and Robby digested this bit of information. "Will we be able to get a new house?" Robby asked hopefully. "Maybe one with a swimming pool?"

Brian smiled. "Katie, you're pretty quiet. What's going on for you?"

When Kate looked up at her father, there was an unmistakable quiver in her lower lip. "But Dad, I'll have to leave my school and my friends, and I just got picked to be on the pep squad. What about that? And what about Muffin?" And then the big question. "What about Mom? Does she know?"

Brian explained to his children that their mother knew and approved of the move. Kate and Robby would visit her just as they always had, but they would fly from Florida instead of taking the short bus ride they had now. It seemed, though, that each time Brian answered a question, ten new ones popped up in its place. "Wait a moment," Brian finally said. "Let's write all of this down."

On a large sheet of paper, Brian listed the family's concerns. His children were worried about making new friends, helping to pick a new place to live, packing all of their belongings, finding a new church, being the new kids in school, even moving the dog.

When the family had listed as many concerns as they could think of, Brian listed possible solutions next to each one. Brian would be visiting Florida in a couple of weeks and he agreed to take pictures of possible homes and schools so the kids could help him pick one. The family agreed that they should have a going-away party and that Kate and Robby could each pack one box with their most important belongings to go in the car, so they wouldn't have to wait for the moving van to arrive in Florida. And Brian agreed that they could return, possibly at Christmas, to visit their old home and friends.

"So how are you really feeling?" Brian finally asked.

"Sad," Kate replied. "I'm happy for you, Daddy, but I can't help being sad about leaving."

"I know, honey. What about you, Rob?"

"I'm kinda excited," Rob said thoughtfully. "I mean, isn't Disney World in Florida?"

Even Kate couldn't help giggling. "You know, kids," Brian said, "we'll always be a family, no matter where we go. And I know that with you two to help me, we'll make our new house a real home. It may take time, but you'll make great friends—after all, who could resist such fantastic kids?" And Brian gave each of his children an extra-tight hug.

Family meetings won't magically make problems go away and they do take time and effort, but they are a wonderful and empowering way for single parents and their children to build a new identity as a family, to learn to appreciate one another, and to discover that single-parent homes aren't "broken" homes; they work quite well indeed!

10

Understanding Misbehavior: It Isn't Just Because You're a Single Parent!

ADJUSTING TO SINGLE parenthood takes time. But once you've dealt with the changes and organized your life as best you can, the basic issues of raising children—and dealing with their misbehavior—still remain. "I've worked through most of my feelings," you may be saying, "and my life seems to be running pretty smoothly most of the time. Now how do I handle these children? And what do I do when they misbehave?"

It's important to remember that any problems you may be having with your children are probably pretty normal. There are no perfect kids and no perfect parents, and it's unlikely that your problems and hassles occur just because you're a single parent. Many newly divorced parents believe all of their children's misbehavior is directly related to the divorce, when that may not be the case at all. *All* parents struggle with their children from time to time, and *all* children misbehave. Learning to interpret children's feelings and behavior can be difficult for any parent, but there are clues in everything our children do (and in how we respond). Once you know how to read the clues, dealing with the behavior becomes much easier.

Sandy is a single parent who runs a child care program in her home. She has two children of her own, four-year-old Kyle and six-year-old Joey. Sandy told her parenting group that she needed help. Near tears, she shared that Joey was driving her crazy while she tried to manage the child care program. "He taunts the younger children, hits them, takes their toys, and uses nasty language. He fights with the older boys over the use of the equipment. Joey's not having this trouble at school or at other friends' homes. He only misbehaves with me. He's so bad that I want to stop having the children come right now and give him the attention he needs. I think the day care is too hard for him to handle because I'm a single mom and he doesn't want to share me with so many other kids. He's constantly saying I'm unfair."

Sandy continued to share: She had told Joey she would stop taking care of other children in June. She couldn't stop sooner because of her obligations to the families who counted on her, and because she needed the money to help support her family. She hadn't figured out how she would earn money when she gave up child care, but Joey was her primary concern.

The parenting group facilitator asked, "Do you want to give up your child care business?"

Sandy answered, "No, I love it; but Joey is more important. I want peace and harmony between us, and I worry about his self-esteem."

The facilitator smiled. "Would you be willing to look at some possibilities that could help you continue providing child care, create peace and harmony between you and Joey, and improve his self-esteem?"

Sandy didn't hesitate. "Of course I would!"

"Okay, then," said the facilitator. "Let's look at some basics first, then we'll work on some suggestions. Is it fair that you should have to stop your child care because Joey can't handle it? Could you do this without some hidden resentment?"

Sandy thought a moment. "No, probably not. I just don't know what else to do."

"Who is in control if you do give up your child care, when you don't want to?" the facilitator asked.

"Well, obviously Joey is." Sandy shrugged. "I know that isn't healthy, but I don't know what else to do. He obviously needs my attention."

The facilitator continued, "What message are you sending to Joey by allowing him to manipulate you with his emotions?"

> There are no perfect kids and no perfect parents, and it's unlikely that your problems and hassles occur just because you're a single parent.

Now Sandy smiled wearily. "That he can be a total tyrant—and that's what it feels like to me. I'm so confused. I love him and want to be a good mother, but I will feel resentful if I give in to him and give up a job I love and can do at home. Having a day care program in my home seemed like the perfect way to earn money without having to leave my kids. But the dream has turned into a nightmare. I don't know what to do."

The facilitator turned to the group. "It's time for some brainstorming. Let's see how many ideas we can come up with that could help Sandy and Joey."

The group came up with a long list of ideas Sandy could try. She was invited to choose the one she would feel most comfortable with. Sandy heard so many good ideas, however, that she chose a combination of several of them:

1. Meet with Joey at a calm time and use the Four Steps for Winning Cooperation, which are explained in the following text.

2. Let Joey have some things that he doesn't have to share with anyone.

3. Spend special time alone with Joey (and with Kyle).

4. Give Joey some jobs so he can feel like he is making an important contribution and also can earn some extra money.

5. Get Joey involved in finding solutions to problems so he will feel he belongs and is significant.

6. Reach out for support by talking to someone in a similar situation who can share his or her experience.

Sandy started with the last suggestion. She called Betty from the local child care association and shared her problem. Betty laughed and said, "Am I ever glad I'm over that one! I had the same problem when my kids were younger. I think it's very normal—it's hard for kids to share their moms, even when they aren't single moms. Two things helped me. I wouldn't play the 'no fair' game, so my kids didn't hook me on that one. But I did allow them to have toys that were their own and didn't have to be shared with anyone. The other thing was letting them know how much I enjoyed making a good living while still being with them. It helped them to see the benefits as well as the problems."

Sandy was encouraged—and relieved—to hear that her problem was normal and wasn't happening just because she was a single mom. All kids need attention, but Sandy was giving attention in a way that invited un-healthy manipulation. She realized that she had fallen into the trap of trying to make it up to her kids because they didn't have a father. It was a relief to give up that belief and all the guilt that went with it.

> By reaching out for support, Sandy had experienced the importance of filling her own cup—getting strength and encour-agement—before she could fill Joey's cup and resolve the problem.

By talking to Betty, Sandy felt validated for her desire to make a living that included spending time with her boys. She felt encouraged in her belief that it was a worthwhile endeavor. Betty had made enough money to stay home with her children, and even enough to help put them through college. Betty said, "Of course there were some problems and some hassles, but what job *doesn't* include some problems? The benefits far outweighed them."

By reaching out for support, Sandy had experi-enced the importance of filling her own cup—get-ting strength and encouragement—before she could fill Joey's cup and resolve the problem. She was able to work with Joey on positive solutions because she was able to let go of her misplaced guilt. Now that she was ready, Sandy de-cided to start with the Four Steps for Winning Cooperation.

Sandy was glad to see that Joey was still awake when she got home from her parenting group. Kyle had already fallen asleep. It was a perfect, calm time to try the Four Steps for Winning Cooperation. Sandy started by asking Joey, "Honey, could we have a special talk just between me and you while I'm tuck-ing you into bed?"

"Well, okay," Joey replied.

Sandy continued, "I was wondering if you feel like you aren't important to me when I'm taking care of so many other children?"

Sandy had struck a nerve. Joey replied with some heat, "It's not fair that I have to share all my stuff!"

Now Sandy reflected and validated his feelings. She offered her under-standing—and a story of her own. "I can see how you'd feel that way. I can remember when I was a little girl and my mom made me share all my clothes with my younger sister—even my favorites. I hated it. I can see now that by trying to be fair to all the other kids, I was very unfair to you. I made you share your dinnertime chair, even when you tried to tell me you didn't think it was fair. I'm so sorry I didn't consider your feelings. I'll try to do better from now on, Joey."

Joey felt understood. He was touched by his mother's admission and apology, and he started to cry. "I'm sorry for being so bad." (Children often cry from relief when they feel understood. And when a parent takes responsibility for disrespectful behavior, it frees children to do the same.)

Sandy reassured Joey. "Honey, you aren't bad. We both made some mistakes. I'll bet we can work on some solutions together. First, would you be willing to hear some of my feelings?"

Joey sniffled. "Okay," he said.

Sandy drew Joey close to her. "You are more important to me than any job. And I would really like to keep doing child care so I don't have to go to work outside our home. I like being able to work and be with you at the same time.

THE FOUR STEPS FOR WINNING COOPERATION

1. Get into the child's world and make a guess about what he or she might be feeling. (If you are wrong, guess again.)

2. Show understanding. (Sometimes it helps to describe a time when you felt the same way.)

3. Ask your child if he or she is willing to listen to your feelings. (Children listen better when they have agreed.)

4. Work on a solution together. (The first two steps create a feeling of closeness and trust, so children are willing to listen and to work on solutions in a cooperative manner.)

Would you be willing to help me find some ways that we can do this? I know you have some great ideas that I haven't listened to before. I'd really like to hear them now."

Joey grinned. "Okay!"

Together, Sandy and Joey came up with the following plans: Joey and Sandy would spend fifteen minutes of special time together every day, with no phones, no little brother, and no other children. Joey agreed that Kyle should have the same amount of time and that they could all work together to agree on the times that would be convenient. During a family meeting they would brainstorm suggestions for what each could do while the other was spending special time with Mom.

Joey was enthusiastic about the possibility of helping out and earning some extra money. They agreed that he would earn one dollar every day by making all the lunches for the day care children. He volunteered to take on other jobs, like picking up toys and sweeping the floor. They also decided that no one else could sit in his dinner chair unless he gave permission. They ended their talk by agreeing that in the future if something was bothering them, they would talk about it and work together on solutions that felt respectful to everyone.

Sandy was ecstatic at her next parenting group. "I can't believe how well this stuff works. Joey is now helping and seems to feel great about himself instead of misbehaving. At our family meeting he told Kyle how lucky they are to have a mom who can work at home. When I got Joey involved in problem solving, he had so many good ideas. I'm so glad I got to tell him how much I love him, and that he could really hear me. Thank you all so much!"

Sandy found a way to get out of the win-or-lose struggle. It would not be healthy for Joey to "win" at Sandy's expense, nor for Sandy to "win" at Joey's expense. Control is not an issue when we learn to "win" cooperation *with* our children.

Both Sandy and Joey had an underlying belief that he was being "bad." Children are never bad—but they are often discouraged. And when they are discouraged, they misbehave.

Understanding the Code

MISBEHAVING CHILDREN are using a code to tell us what they're feeling and experiencing. Misbehavior is a coded message that says, "I'm discouraged because I don't believe that I'm important or that I'm loved unconditionally." Children are not consciously aware of these beliefs, nor do they know that their misbehavior is a way of telling us they are discouraged. They don't know that their behavior expresses underlying beliefs; it is not important that they know. It *is* important that parents realize there is a belief behind every behavior, and that their feelings give them clues to understanding the coded language their children are using. These feeling clues and other clues are discussed later in this chapter. For the moment, we need only to understand that there are beliefs behind every behavior (even ours!).

> Control is not an issue when we learn to "win" cooperation *with* our children.

Beliefs Behind Behavior

DEALING WITH THE belief behind the behavior does not mean you *don't* deal with the behavior, but you will be most successful when you are aware of both factors. What happens to us in life is never as important as the decisions and beliefs we create *about* what happens to us. Our behavior is then based on those decisions and beliefs. The decisions and beliefs we form are directly related to the primary goal of all people: our need to find belonging and significance.

The Primary Goal of All People

ALL OF US NEED to belong somewhere, to someone, and to feel significant, worthwhile, and loved. From the moment they first become aware of their surroundings, children are making decisions about whether they belong, whether they are loved, whether they are accepted. Sometimes children decide they don't belong (which might surprise their parents), and they then make unconscious decisions about what they need to do about it. Sometimes those decisions involve misbehavior; sometimes they result in an unwillingness to try at all.

Carter was a sadly neglected little boy; so neglected, in fact, that when his mother's house in a rural town caught fire, his older brother was carried to safety but he was left in his bed to be rescued at the last minute by a diligent fireman. His unmarried mother was pregnant and didn't want him; his grandmother took his older brother but didn't want him. When Carter arrived at Paula's home as a foster child he could barely walk, although he was almost two, and he couldn't talk, except to say "bite-bite" when he was hungry.

A brief four months later, Carter was walking and running, delighting in giving and getting hugs, and chattering constantly. "He called me Mama a week after he arrived," Paula said. What had made the difference? "We just told him over and over that he was special to us and that we loved him."

Is it really that simple? Our children, like all humans, need some very basic things from their parents (besides food, shelter, and clothing). They need to feel accepted, to know they belong, and that they're special and worthy of love just as they are.

From the moment they first become aware of their surroundings, children are making decisions about whether they belong, whether they are loved, whether they're accepted.

"Well, of course I love my kids," we parents say, feeling faintly offended that anyone would question that. Yet, too often we fail to communicate that love in a way that is meaningful to our children. We fail to separate the child from his behavior, for example, leaving him to believe that when he messes up, Mom and Dad don't love him as much. "Bad girl!" we may say. "You'll never amount to anything." Or we reserve our love and encouragement for the times when our child achieves something, letting her believe that love and acceptance must be earned. And setting children up to need approval and acceptance from others is just asking for trouble later down the road.

We must learn, hard as it seems at times, to accept our children just as they are, not as we wish they would be. We can let them know that although there may be room for improvement in certain areas, they don't have to become someone else for us to love them, that our love has no strings and no conditions. We can give them the security of knowing that no matter how rough a situation seems, we will care and will be there. We can choose to let them know that we love them, no matter what.

What Happens When Children Don't Feel the Love and Belonging?

Q. I'm a single parent of a two-year-old boy. My son's father did not want me to have him and is no longer a part of either of our lives (although he does pay child support). Being a single parent is the hardest (and the most rewarding) thing I have ever done. There is nobody to hand him over to and say, "Here, you deal with him for ten minutes; I need a break." And I have needed a break lately. My mother was diagnosed with colon cancer last year. She was in and out of the hospital two or three times. Luckily I work at the hospital where she received her care, so I could spend a lot of time with her. I spent months either at work, at the doctor's with my mother, at my aunt's (where my mother lived), or at home trying to catch up on everything that was not done. Then my mother died.

> We must learn, hard as it seems at times, to accept our children just as they are, not as we wish they would be.

I always swore that I wouldn't hit my kids or yell at them. Well, that's gone out the window! Usually I have infinite patience with my son, but sometimes I'm just exhausted and can't take any more. These are the times that I hate. I get frustrated and don't know what to do. I can't go out because I can't leave him alone. I try to go into the bathroom but he follows me there, too.

One night I just wanted him to go to sleep. He just would not go to sleep; he kept climbing out of bed and coming out to me. I finally put him down on the bed and yelled at him to go to sleep. Well, he hit me in the face and knocked my glasses off. I just got so mad that I hit him back. He was screaming, I was crying. I felt *awful!* I actually went outside and sat on my front step.

I don't want my son to grow up afraid that if he does something wrong, I'm going to hit him. But I also don't want him to think that he can get away with any type of behavior, either. In other words, *help!*

A. Your stress and anguish echo through every word of your letter. You have had far too much to cope with, and it sounds as though you have little in the way of outside support. Your son is only two; all he knows is that he needs to feel belonging and significance, and for reasons he can't understand, he just doesn't right now. So he is using his behavior to send you the message that he doesn't feel good about himself or you. Your frustration and annoyance are clues that the mistaken goal of his behavior is attention—and he'll settle for negative attention if he can't have the positive kind. The problem becomes more intense because you are all he has to turn to—you're a single mom.

Understanding the mistaken goals of misbehavior will help you find ways to cope with his actions and build his sense of connection and belonging. You also need to take the time to nurture and strengthen yourself. You are the foundation on which so much depends right now; do your best to ensure that the foundation is a strong one.

All of us, parents and children alike, are active participants (not victims) in the process of deciding things about ourselves, about others, and about life, and our behavior is based on these decisions. Understanding this process and how your children create their beliefs about life and how they fit into their family is the first step to understanding their behavior. With this understanding, you can encourage your children and provide opportunities for them to change their unhealthy beliefs and behaviors.

All of us seek ways to belong and be important. Sometimes they work—and sometimes they don't. If we think we aren't loved or don't belong, we usually try something to get the love back. Or we hurt others to get revenge when we think they don't love us. Sometimes we even feel like giving up; it seems impossible to do things right, to belong, to be loved and accepted. The things we do when we believe we don't belong and aren't important are often mistaken ways to find the acceptance we need. That is why they are called the mistaken goals of misbehavior.

Children are not aware of these hidden beliefs; they don't sit down and plan a power struggle. But once we understand children's reasons for behaving as they do, we can think of ways to encourage them when they are feeling discouraged—and change their behavior in the process.

The Mistaken Goal Chart (page 126) helps you identify the mistaken goal of your misbehaving child and offers some positive suggestions for encouraging him or her.

Remember that the goals themselves are not wrong; all of us need attention, connection to others, and a sense of personal power. Parents sometimes conclude that children are misbehaving when they ask for attention or when they attempt to gain power, but that is not the case. The problem occurs when they seek "undue" attention or "misguided" power instead of getting attention and using power in constructive ways.

Margaret was a busy attorney with a thriving practice. She was deeply committed to her three-year-old daughter, Samantha; Margaret had spent a great deal of time arranging for Sammy's care when Margaret couldn't be with her. Still, evenings with Sammy often involved more whining and irritating behavior than Margaret would have liked.

> Remember that the goals themselves are not wrong; all of us need attention, connection to others, and a sense of personal power.

When Margaret learned about Positive Discipline parenting skills and the mistaken goals of misbehavior, she understood that some of Sammy's behavior happened because she was a healthy three-year-old girl who was attempting to establish autonomy and initiative—part of her normal developmental process. But Margaret also learned to recognize Sammy's whining as an indication—a clue—that perhaps she had been busier with work than usual. Margaret found that when her own calendar was so full she had little time to spend with her daughter, Sammy responded with the mistaken goal of undue attention. Mother and daughter enjoyed a much smoother relationship—and many more pleasant evenings together—when Margaret built regular time with Sammy into her schedule and gave her attention in *positive* ways.

Sylvia learned a similar lesson. When she found herself engaged in numerous power struggles with her son Nick, she took time to look at her own behavior and realized she was (in the name of expediency) being too bossy and controlling. As soon as she remembered to involve Nick in creating routines, guidelines, and problem solving, he began using his power to contribute instead of to rebel.

Clues That Help You Identify the Mistaken Goal

THE FIRST CLUE in deciphering the code behind misbehavior is to identify the way the misbehavior makes *you* feel. For example, if you are feeling irritated, annoyed, worried, or guilty, then that is a clue that your child's goal is *undue attention.*

The second clue comes from noticing your child's response to your usual ways of dealing with his misbehavior. If your child's mistaken goal is *misguided power,* for example, and you use power to respond, the misbehavior will escalate. The rest of the chart describes the belief behind each mistaken goal and some empowering ways to respond.

There are always several ways to help a child feel she belongs and is significant, and thus to help remove the need for mistaken-goal behavior. However, it is most helpful to keep the secondary coded message in mind. (The primary coded messages is, "I want to belong and feel significant.") The secondary coded message tells you what the child needs for each mistaken goal that will help her achieve the primary goal.

Secondary Coded Messages

The secondary coded message for the mistaken goal of *undue attention* is "Notice me. Involve me usefully." An effective method for helping this child would be to ignore the *undue attention* behavior and redirect the child by giving her a task where she can get attention by being usefully involved.

> Children who seek misguided power are much more likely to switch to cooperation when they can use their personal power to choose instead of to resist being controlled by an adult.

For *misguided power,* the secondary coded message is, "Let me help. Give me choices." One effective way to respond to this mistaken goal is first to admit that you can't *make* the child do something and to let her know you *need* her help. Then give her a choice of two or more ways to help: "Would you like to put this problem on the agenda so the whole family can work on a solution, or would you like to think about it yourself for a day and let me know your ideas for a solution?"

Another possibility is to give her an open choice to use her power in a contributing way: "Anything you can do to help me clean up would be very much appreciated." Children who seek misguided power are much more likely to switch to cooperation when they can use their personal power to choose instead of to resist being controlled by an adult.

For the mistaken goal of *revenge,* the secondary coded message is, "I'm hurting. Validate my feelings." It helps when adults can see past the revengeful behavior and validate the feelings behind it: "My guess is that you are feeling very hurt about something." Name it if you know what it is, or say, "Do you want to tell me about it?" This is often enough to disrupt the misbehavior and put the child in a mood to deal with the problem (perhaps after a little cooling-off time), which may mean to disregard what someone else thinks, to be assertive, or to make amends.

For the mistaken goal of *assumed inadequacy,* the secondary coded message is, "Don't give up on me. Show me a small step." Adults need to find the smallest step the child can do on her own. This may mean doing a step with her until she can do it by herself. Once she has had a small success, she can give up the idea that she is inadequate.

> We are *much* more effective when we deal with the belief behind the behavior (the coded messages) instead of the behavior alone.

When we understand our children's thinking, their beliefs about themselves, about others, and about life, we are in a better position to influence them in positive ways. We are *much* more effective when we deal with the belief behind the behavior (the coded messages) instead of the behavior alone.

Remember Joey and Sandy? Joey felt unimportant and insignificant until Sandy used the Four Steps for Winning Cooperation, which helped Joey come to some new conclusions. As soon as he believed he belonged and was significant, he was open to the encouragement his mom offered by hearing his feelings, sharing hers, and working with him on solutions. Learning to understand the hidden code in Joey's misbehavior gave Sandy the information she needed to help him form different beliefs, give up his misbehavior, and become part of a cooperative team.

Our children's behavior—good, bad, and indifferent—doesn't happen in a vacuum. It is a result of how they're feeling about themselves, about us, and about their place in life. Misbehavior can be annoying and irritating, but understanding these beliefs—and the codes your children use to communicate them to you—may be all you need to solve the problem. Children who feel encouraged, loved, and worthwhile have less need to misbehave. And isn't that what we're really after?

Mistaken Goal Chart

The child's goal is:	If the parent/teacher feels:	And tends to react by:	And if the child's response is:	The belief behind the child's behavior is:	Coded messages	Parent/teacher proactive and empowering responses include:
Undue attention (to keep others busy or to get special service)	Annoyed Irritated Worried Guilty	Reminding Coaxing Doing things for the child he/she could do for him/ herself	Stops temporarily, but later assumes same or another disturbing behavior	I count (belong) only when I'm being noticed or getting special service. I'm only important when I'm keeping you busy with me.	Notice me. Involve me usefully.	"I love you and _____." (Example: I care about you and will spend time with you later."); redirect by assigning a task so child can gain useful attention; avoid special service; plan special time; set up routines; use problem-solving; encourage; use family/class meetings; touch without words; ignore; set up nonverbal signals.
Misguided power (to be boss)	Angry Challenged Threatened Defeated	Fighting Giving in Thinking "You can't get away with it" or "I'll make you" Wanting to be right	Intensifies behavior Defiant compliance Feels he/she's won when parent/teacher is upset Passive power	I belong only when I'm boss, in control, or proving no one can boss me. "You can't make me."	Let me help. Give me choices.	Redirect to positive power by asking for help; offer limited choices; don't fight and don't give in; withdraw from conflict; be firm and kind; act don't talk; decide what you will do; let routines be the boss; leave and calm down; develop mutual respect; set a few reasonable limits; practice follow-through; encourage; use family/ class meetings
Revenge (to get even)	Hurt Disappointed Disbelieving Disgusted	Retaliating Getting even Thinking "How could you do this to me?"	Retaliates Intensifies Escalates the same behavior or chooses another weapon	I don't think I belong so I'll hurt others as I feel hurt. I can't be liked or loved.	I'm hurting; validate my feelings.	Acknowledge hurt feelings; avoid feeling hurt; avoid punishment and retaliation; build trust; use reflective listening; share your feelings; make amends; show you care; act, don't talk; encourage strengths; put kids in same boat; use family/class meetings
Assumed inadequacy (to give up and be left alone)	Despair Hopeless Helpless Inadequate	Giving up Doing for Overhelping	Retreats further Passive No improvement No response	I can't belong beacause I'm not perfect, so I'll convince others not to expect anything of me; I am helpless and unable; it's no use trying because I won't do it right.	Don't give up on me. Show me a small step.	Break task down to small steps; stop all criticism; encourage any positive attempt; have faith in child's abilities; focus on assets; don't pity; don't give up; set up opportunities for success; teach skills/ show how, but don't do for; enjoy the child; build on his/her interests; encourage, encourage, encourage; use family/class meetings.

11

Getting into Your Child's World: Positive Discipline in Action

As parents we have *such* good intentions. We want our children to be well behaved "for their own good." Their ultimate happiness is our main concern, and we "know" they won't be happy if they don't adopt our values and do what is right. We really believe that our lectures, punishments, and shaming will help them to behave better and to adopt our values—the correct ones. We know what we want to teach our children. The trouble is that we seldom take the time to check out what our children are learning. We don't ask them what they are feeling, what they are thinking, and what they are deciding.

Understanding mistaken-goal behavior is just one way to "get into the child's world." There are many other ways, including understanding the long-range results of what we do, understanding your child's personality and developmental process, and using active listening to tune into your child's feelings and beliefs.

Beware of What "Works"

We may be fooled into thinking our methods are working when we punish a child for a certain behavior and the behavior stops. Sometimes, though, we need to *beware of what works*. Suppose you have punished a child for "talking back" and she stops talking back. It may appear that the punishment has worked. What you may not know is that she is feeling hurt and confused; she is thinking that you are unfair and don't really care about her; and she is deciding you can make her stop talking back, but you can't make her do well in school. The long-range effect of what "worked" is revenge. You have just won one battle—and changed the direction of the entire war.

And war it is. Lectures, punishments, and shaming are just a few of the weapons parents use against their children for the "good cause" of helping them behave well and adopt good values. The casualties of this war are discouraged children with low self-esteem, children who haven't been listened to and taken seriously, and who haven't learned to develop their own wisdom and problem-solving skills. These children don't have a sense of belonging and significance. Some of them act out and rebel. Others become "pleasers," finding friends and spouses who will continue to tell them what to do.

Sheila is a single parent who wanted to end the war with her three children. She decided to get some help by attending a parenting class, where she learned about the importance of getting into the child's world. She had an opportunity to practice some of the skills she had learned when she discovered that her son Casey, an eighth-grader, had been suspended from school for calling the teacher names.

When Sheila walked into the den, she found Casey sitting in front of the television set with a belligerent look on his face. Sheila took a deep breath and asked, "Casey, could we talk about the problem you're having at school?"

Casey looked up from his program and, somewhat reluctantly, said, "Yeah, I guess."

Sheila fought back the urge to dive right into the problem and smiled. "I can tell you're not real excited to talk to me about this. I'll bet it's because you are used to hearing lectures from me instead of having us really talk and listen to each other."

Now Sheila had her son's attention. He was obviously surprised to hear his mother admit she lectured. Sheila noticed his interest and continued with a laugh, "I confess. I'm guilty of lecturing and not listening. I really don't want to do that anymore. I'll bet you feel like I don't really care about you when I lecture and scold. The truth is that I care very much. Would you give me another chance so I can show you that talking with each other doesn't always have to include lectures or judgments from me?"

Casey didn't know what to think now. This was new territory. It felt nice to have his mom be so understanding, but he wasn't sure he could trust this new approach. He answered again, hesitantly, "Yeah, I guess."

Sheila relaxed a bit. She said gently, "Tell me what's going on from your point of view. I really want to hear your side of the story."

Casey was still uncertain and he decided to take refuge in his television program. "It's okay, Mom," he said, turning his gaze back to the TV. "I can handle it."

> The casualties of this war are discouraged children with low self-esteem, who haven't been listened to and taken seriously, and who haven't learned to develop their own wisdom and problem-solving skills.

Sheila felt a surge of compassion for her son, and her love for him began giving her clues on how to proceed. She put all of her love for Casey into her voice and said calmly, "I'm sure you can, one way or another. I'd still like to hear your side of what happened."

Casey looked up and met his mother's eyes. There was a pause, and then he blurted out, "Those teachers are jerks. They don't like me." Now there was anger in his voice.

"Could you give me an example of what you mean?" his mother replied. "What do they do to act like jerks and give you the impression that they don't like you?"

This was getting a bit uncomfortable for Casey, and he retreated again. "Don't worry about it. I can handle it." After a moment, he added in a quiet voice, "I've already decided I don't want to get kicked out of school."

Sheila tried not to let her relief show too much. "Frankly, I'm glad that's important to you. *You* are important to me, and I would still like to know what is really going on from your point of view. I have some hunches. I don't know if they're right, but would it be okay with you if I make some guesses? I have more than one guess. You can let me know if I'm off base. Okay?"

Goal Disclosure

SHEILA HAD BEGUN a process developed by Rudolf Dreikurs (*Children: the Challenge*, E. P. Dutton, 1987) called "goal disclosure." During this process an adult makes guesses to discover the child's mistaken goal. When done in a friendly manner, goal disclosure can help a child feel understood. Children, remember, are not consciously aware of their mistaken goal, and awareness is the beginning of change.

As we finish the story of Sheila and Casey you will see how Sheila continues to use the process of goal disclosure. Casey felt encouraged by Sheila's friendly manner. This allowed him to let down his defenses and become curious about her guesses. However, his vocabulary hadn't improved. He said, "Yeah, I guess."

THE FOUR STEPS OF GOAL DISCLOSURE

The four steps of goal disclosure are:

1. Ask the child *why* he or she is behaving in a specific way. Be ready for the usual answer: "I don't know."

2. Ask permission to guess why. Most children will give permission if you have demonstrated friendliness and genuine caring.

3. Ask, "Could it be _____?" regarding each mistaken goal until you get a yes or a recognition reflex. This occurs when a child says no but can't suppress a smile or some other involuntary reaction. (The smile is saying yes while the voice says no.) When you get a recognition reflex, respond by saying, "You say no, but your smile tells me that could be the reason. Would you be willing to work with me on some solutions?"

4. Refer to the last column of the Mistaken Goal Chart (page 126) for some possible solutions and work together to find other possibilities.

Sheila made her first attempt to discover what his mistaken goal might be. "Could it be that getting in trouble with the teachers is a good way to get my attention and make me spend some time with you?"

Casey's answer was prompt. "No way." (This eliminated the mistaken goal of undue attention.)

Sheila said, "Well, let me try another guess. Could it be that you are showing me that no one can boss you around or make you do anything you don't want to do?"

This guess got Sheila an exasperated sigh. "That would be a dumb reason for getting into trouble." (This eliminated the mistaken goal of misguided power.)

Sheila paused for a moment; this was the hard one. "Could it be that you feel hurt and angry at me for divorcing your dad, and getting into trouble is a good way to hurt back?"

Casey caught his breath, and for a brief moment he looked like he had just been caught with his hand in the cookie jar. Then he asked defiantly, "Are you and Dad ever going to get back together?" (Casey's expression and his reply showed Sheila that she had discovered the mistaken goal: revenge.)

Sheila sighed, and sat down next to her son. "Honey, I can see how much this has hurt you—and I'm so sorry. Your Dad and I are not going to get back together. I wish it didn't have to hurt you so much, but I know it does. You don't have to keep it to yourself. You can tell me how angry you are. I will listen."

His mother's understanding had broken down Casey's inhibitions and now he finally said what he felt. "If you hadn't been such a bitch to Dad, you could still be married."

Sheila felt stung and tears came to her eyes. But she realized that to respond by defending herself or by striking back would close the door she and her son had just so painstakingly opened. "Ouch," she said quietly. "That one really hurt. You must really hate me sometimes."

Casey got tears in his own eyes as he struggled with the strong, complex emotions in his heart. He did hate his mom sometimes, but he also loved her a lot. Sheila guessed what he was feeling; she put her arms around him and said, "It's okay, honey. I know you love me, too. It can be a real problem when we both hate and love someone." She laughed, "Sometimes I feel that way about you, too."

The tension slowly flowed out of Casey's body. He didn't realize it, but he had been feeling guilty and confused about his feelings. He hadn't known what to do with all his hurt and anger, but somehow his feelings didn't seem so bad when they were out in the open and he knew his mom sometimes felt the same way.

Sheila continued, "I can't change your feelings and I'm not going to try. Everyone has a right to their feelings. I'd like to talk with you later about some things we could do to solve some of the problems that come up. Would you be willing to do that with me?

Casey grinned. "Yeah, I guess," he said.

During this situation Sheila had used several principles she had learned in her Positive Discipline parenting class.

Create a foundation of love and closeness. Sheila understood the importance of creating a foundation of love and closeness before she could have a positive influence on Casey. Lectures and punishment create distance and hostility, and the result is a negative influence. Most positive parenting tools are effective only after a foundation of love and closeness has been created.

When we use a discipline method that doesn't produce positive results, the first question to ask is, "Are we engaged in a power struggle or a revenge cycle?"

> Lectures and punishment create distance and hostility, and the result is a negative influence.

Sheila had asked herself this question and thought she was in a power struggle with Casey. By taking the time to get into Casey's world, she found out that the goal was not misguided power but revenge because of his hurt feelings about the divorce.

Take responsibility for your part in creating the problem. Sheila took responsibility for her part in creating the problem (lecturing and not listening). Taking responsibility is not the same as blame and guilt. Taking responsibility means gaining insight and awareness of what we create. When we become aware of what we are doing to create a situation, we will also be aware that we can change it by doing something else. This is extremely empowering. Children often will follow our lead when we take responsibility for our part and will be willing to take responsibility for their part. They, too, feel empowered.

EIGHT STEPS FOR GETTING INTO THE CHILD'S WORLD AS A FOUNDATION FOR SOLVING PROBLEMS

- Create a foundation of love and closeness.
- Take responsibility for your part in creating the problem.
- Ask for a chance to try again.
- Ask "curiosity" questions to facilitate deeper listening.
- Understand the belief behind the behavior.
- Validate feelings.
- Allow for a cooling-off period before working on solutions.
- Discussion may be enough.

Ask for a chance to try again. By asking Casey if he will give her another chance to talk with him without a lecture, Sheila was admitting that she had made a mistake and wanted to try again. What a beautiful model for children! They need to discover that mistakes are nothing more than opportunities to learn. They need to know that they can keep learning and keep trying, instead of thinking that mistakes mean failure (so they might as well give up).

Ask "curiosity" questions to facilitate deeper listening. Sheila used effective listening skills to get to deeper levels by asking "what" questions and asking for examples. She avoided the temptation to lecture or moralize. Too often parents *tell* kids what happened, what caused it to happen, how they should feel about it, and what they should do about it. Children feel belonging and significance when we ask, "What happened? What do you think caused that to happen? How do you feel about it? How would you like things to be? What could you do to make that happen?"

Your understanding will increase (and your child can clarify her own thinking) when you ask for examples. It can be very helpful to ask the question: "Is there anything else?" several times. This invites the child to dig deeper (while you listen) and explore any hidden thoughts or feelings that may not have reached the surface yet. However, none of this works if you are not willing to listen and to avoid the temptation to lecture, explain, or defend yourself. Remember, the goal is to get into the child's world.

Understand the belief behind the behavior. Sheila used goal disclosure (by making guesses to reveal the mistaken goal) to help both herself and Casey understand the hidden belief behind his behavior. Casey felt hurt and wanted to hurt back, even though he wasn't aware of it. All too often parents deal with their children's symptoms (their problems and misbehavior) without understanding the cause (their beliefs and feelings). Taking time to understand a child's feelings may make a tremendous difference in your approach to a problem—and in your ability to find a solution.

Validate feelings. Sheila validated Casey's feelings even when he said hurtful things to her. She understood the difference between feelings and actions, and asked Casey to work with her later on possible solutions. Too often we forget that there is a difference between feelings and actions. We try to talk children out of their feelings, or we tell them plainly, "You shouldn't feel that way." Sometimes we try to rescue them or fix things so they won't have to experience their feelings. Neither of these responses helps children choose different behaviors and may actually exacerbate the problem.

> All too often parents deal with their children's symptoms (their problems and misbehavior) without understanding the cause (their beliefs and feelings).

Allow for a cooling-off period before working on solutions. Some people may ask, "But what about the problem of the suspension and talking back to teachers?" Sheila was wise enough to know that simply disclosing the belief behind the behavior in a friendly, accepting manner often is enough to eliminate the misbehavior. When Casey feels better about himself and his mother (a process this conversation helped begin), he will feel less need to get revenge. If the problem occurs again, Sheila has laid a foundation for problem solving that focuses on solutions instead of punishment.

Discussion may be enough. Too often we focus on consequences or solutions and underestimate the power of a friendly discussion that leads to understanding. When children feel listened to, taken seriously, and loved, they may change the belief that motivated their misbehavior. For this reason, we end where we began: *Create a foundation of love and closeness.* It is the most important thing we can do to accomplish all our good intentions.

Creating Closeness—and Change

MARY HAD RAISED six children and had enjoyed being a parent. She had good relationships with all her grown children and looked forward to being a grandmother. She had fantasies that being a grandmother would be even more fun than being a parent because she could enjoy her grandchildren without all the day-to-day hassles. Then her daughter Lori got a divorce and, with her two boys, Cliff, ten, and Jake, six, moved in with Mary.

So much for fantasies. Cliff was a defiant child who became sassy with his grandmother. Because Lori had a full-time job, Mary frequently found herself in the parent role—and it wasn't always a comfortable one. When Mary asked Cliff to do things around the house, he would say, "This isn't my house. Clean it yourself." Mary got phone calls from teachers regarding his misbehavior at school. When she tried to talk to Cliff about it, he would say, "You're not my mom. It's none of your business."

Mary felt deeply hurt. She was trying to do so much for her grandchildren—giving them a home, caring about them and their behavior, trying to teach them responsibility as she had her own children. Mary was a positive, loving person. She could not understand why Cliff would be so negative and hurtful to her.

> Simply disclosing the belief behind the behavior in a friendly, accepting manner often is enough to eliminate the misbehavior.

Mary heard about a single-parenting group at her church and asked Lori if she would attend with her. Lori also was feeling discouraged about Cliff's behavior. They were both afraid Cliff would become a juvenile delinquent if they didn't get help.

At the first meeting, Mary shared how much children and parenting had changed. None of the six children she raised had ever hurt her so much. Of course, she had never had to deal with what she called the "three Ds": divorce, defiance, and drugs. (Mary was afraid drugs would be the next step for Cliff.)

The group leader agreed that times had changed, but pointed out that some things remain constant. One constant is that children still need to feel they are significant and belong. They also want to be treated with dignity and respect, perhaps a new concept for members of an older generation.

One theme of the class was *getting into the child's world* and dealing with the belief behind the behavior. A group member reminded Mary that we usually lash out at the ones we love. It might not look like love, but Cliff must feel safe around her to strike out at her the way she described. Mary felt encouraged and was eager to try out her new insights and information.

At the next class, she shared a wonderful story. During the week, Mary had focused on understanding Cliff's world. When she picked him up after school, she asked him some "what" and "how" questions in a spirit of honest inquiry instead of inquisition. "How are you feeling about school?" she began. When Cliff didn't respond, she continued with sensitivity, "I'll bet it was hard for you to leave your friends and your home and move in with me."

Cliff could feel the energy of her honest caring. He began, slowly, to share with her how angry he was about what was happening to his life. He didn't like being a child of divorce. He didn't like it that his mother seemed to ignore him while she dealt with her own life. He felt like he had no control over what happened to him. After expressing these feelings he apologized for taking them out on Mary. "I know it isn't your fault," he said softly.

Mary responded, "I can only imagine how upsetting this must be for you. I don't know how I would deal with so much chaos in my life. It must really be tough."

Suddenly Cliff felt understood, and this gave him room to move in a different direction. He said, "I'll be okay. I can handle it."

Mary said, "I'll bet you can. I would like to help in any way I can. I'm reading a book about family meetings where family members work together on solutions to problems, share feelings, and plan fun things to do together. Your old family has changed, and now we have a different family. Our family doesn't match society's picture of the ideal family: a mom, a dad, and happy, obedient children. I hope you got that part about obedient children!" she joked. "But I'll bet we can do great things with the family we've got. What do you think?"

Cliff looked hopeful. "Yeah. Maybe."

As the parenting class progressed, Mary shared with the group: "I now have some tools to work with. They've helped me stop overreacting, get centered, and act more appropriately. My relationship with Cliff has really improved. He doesn't even try to hurt my feelings anymore, because I don't take the bait. I just focus on how he must be feeling to act that way. I still ask for his help, and we have to work on what happened at school, but now he feels understood and he's more willing to change his behavior. He helps around the house because he helped plan a chore schedule at the family meeting. We also focus on ways to make our family better. This doesn't mean things are perfect, but they're sure better than they were!"

> Getting into your child's world is about building a relationship of understanding, love, and trust. And that will do you and your children nothing but good on your journey as a family.

"My relationship with my daughter Lori has also improved," Mary continued. "The funny thing was that as Cliff started getting better, Jake started misbehaving for a while. I was glad I had been warned about this and knew that he might start misbehaving when he could not find belonging and significance by being the 'good' child. As we continued using family meetings and the other Positive Discipline parenting tools we had learned in the group, we all found belonging and significance through cooperation instead of competition."

Does getting into the child's world solve every problem? Of course not; nothing works all the time for all people. But it gives parents valuable clues that help us understand why a behavior may be occurring in the first place. And sometimes that can save a lot of energy—and a lot of anger and hurt feelings—down the road. Getting into your child's world is about building a relationship of understanding, love, and trust. And that will do you and your children nothing but good on your journey as a family.

12

Nonpunitive Discipline: Effective Tools for Single Parents

NONPUNITIVE DISCIPLINE: Parents sometimes wonder if such a thing is possible, or even wise. Most of us have absorbed ideas about discipline from our parents and from our society. And most of us have approached discipline with one subtle, basic belief: Children have to suffer or they won't learn anything.

"I have to give my kids a swat once in a while to let them know I mean business," a parent might say. Or, "My children lose all their privileges when they mess up. That's what teaches them not to disobey me." Or, "Punishing my kids teaches them to respect me." The Bible does say, "He who spares his rod hates his son, but he who loves him disciplines him diligently" (Prov. 13:24 *New American Standard* version). Many people interpret this to mean spanking defiant children is mandated by God. However, Biblical scholars tell us the "rod" was a symbol of authority and leadership and was used to *guide* sheep, not to hit them.

> Most of us have approached discipline with one subtle, basic belief: Children have to suffer or they won't learn anything.

Effective discipline is about guidance, not about punishment. Yet, society has thought of punishment and discipline as synonymous for so long that it can be a challenge for parents to accept that they are not the same—and that punishment does not produce the positive, long-range results of helping children develop the characteristics and important life skills that lead to success and happiness in life.

Single parents in particular can find effective discipline a challenge. "Now that I'm alone," they say, "I have to keep a firmer grip on these kids or they'll run wild. You know what they say about kids from broken homes."

Parents often believe in the necessity of controlling their children, failing to realize that total control is not only unwise, it's rarely even possible—especially when children have grown too large to be physically moved and confined. Relying on control and the power of punishment turns parents into policemen, full-time enforcers who set the rules and then watch constantly for violations. But what happens when the policeman isn't around? What happens when children go off with their friends? And what happens when family life becomes a constantly escalating power struggle?

Discipline Is to Teach

TRUE DISCIPLINE IS NOT about punishment or control. The word itself comes from the Latin word *disciplina,* which means "a follower of truth, principle, or a venerated leader" or "to teach." It is the same term from which we get the word *disciple.* And at its best, discipline is about teaching and guiding, helping young people to make wise decisions about their behavior and to accept responsibility for their choices and actions—to choose (or not choose) a certain behavior because they understand its consequences, not because the policeman is lurking around the corner.

> True discipline is not about punishment or control. The word itself comes from the Latin word *disciplina,* which means "a follower of truth, principle, or a venerated leader" or "to teach."

Many parents believe they need to "impose" consequences for misbehavior in the form of punishment. Children learn from their behavior when parents instead help them "explore" the natural consequences of their choices. *Education* comes from the Latin word *educare,* which means "to draw forth." Helping children explore what happened, what caused it to happen, what they learned from what happened, and how they can use this information to solve a problem is "drawing forth" their thinking, perceptions, and learning. Too many parents try to "stuff in" through lectures and punishment and then wonder why their lessons don't *stay* in.

All parents eventually must ask themselves what they believe about discipline. If we believe that *we* are responsible for our children's behavior, that misbehavior deserves to be punished, and that children must suffer in order to learn, we will find ourselves relying on spanking, grounding, humiliation, and all too often, anger. If, however, we believe that the purpose of discipline is to teach children responsibility for their own actions, to find a solution to a problem, and to keep that problem from happening in the future, we will approach discipline—and our children—much differently. But how?

The Perils of Punitive Discipline

THE QUESTION OF how we choose to discipline our children cuts to the heart of what we believe about parenting. Most of us grew up accepting that spanking and punishment were normal, even necessary parts of raising children. And at least in the short term, punishment "seems to work" well enough. But sometimes we need to "beware of what seems to work for the moment" and consider the long-term effects of punitive discipline.

> Sometimes we need to "beware of what seems to work for the moment" and consider the long-term effects of punitive discipline.

ABC television's news show *20/20* took a close look at spanking. Four families who regularly spank their children allowed the television cameras to follow them around and to record their encounters with their misbehaving children. Most parents who viewed that show, including parents who spanked their own children, found it painful to watch. Many agreed that the purpose of the spankings was almost always simply to punish a child for a wrong choice or to vent parental anger and frustration; there was no emphasis on problem solving or on changing future behavior. The spankings alone were supposed to take care of that.

Yet these parents kept having to spank their children regularly. There appeared to be no lasting changes in the undesirable behaviors. Perhaps more important, the show found that spanking and similar punishments produce children who have lower self-esteem, who may accept abusive relationships, and who consider violence an appropriate way to solve problems—results that these parents, who certainly love their children, obviously didn't intend.

Children who live with punitive forms of discipline frequently learn unintended lessons: to misbehave whenever the enforcer isn't around, to get even whenever possible, or to focus on the "mean old parent" rather than on the behavior that got them into trouble. Spanking, in particular, presents several hidden problems. It becomes less and less effective over time and it eventually becomes physically impossible. Is it possible to do things another way?

Preventing Problems

IF DISCIPLINE TRULY IS about teaching and guidance rather than just punishment, a large part of effective discipline will be focused on creating an atmosphere of cooperation, taking into account children's abilities and limitations, and working together to prevent problems before they happen—the sort of discipline we have explored in the preceding chapters. For instance, if behavior in a restaurant or a car is a problem for your child, be sure to teach and explore acceptable behavior before you go.

Exploring means avoiding lectures. It means taking time to ask the child, "What kind of behavior is respectful in the restaurant? How do you think other people feel when children yell or run around? What ideas do you have to make sure we have a good experience at the restaurant?" You might have some fun role-playing ("let's pretend") acceptable and unacceptable behavior with your child before you go. Then involve your child in the task of creating a bag filled with small toys or books or a game to play while waiting for the food to arrive. A little planning on a parent's part (involving the children as much as possible) can make even the longest car trip bearable for everyone: a personal tape player and some story tapes, coloring books and crayons, or a few small, inexpensive new toys can save the day.

Decide What *You* Will Do

IF THE CHILD still misbehaves in a restaurant, quietly take her by the hand and kindly and firmly take her to the car to wait while others in your group finish their meal. This is called "deciding what you will do instead of what you will make the child do." This should also be discussed in advance, so the child will know what to expect. Come prepared with a good book to read while you wait in the car. This discipline teaches the child immediate results of misbehavior—losing the privilege of eating in the restaurant. The loss of a privilege should be used only when it is *directly related* to the misbehavior. (It is a privilege to eat in a restaurant. Every privilege has a responsibility—in this case to behave respectfully. When children refuse to accept the responsibility, they lose the privilege.)

For "deciding what you will do" to be effective, you must be willing to follow through with kindness and firmness at the same time. This often means to "act" (firmly) with "your mouth shut" (kindly). Words (lectures) usually just invite arguments, so avoid them. This discipline method can also be used to avoid dangerous situations. When children misbehave in a car, pull over to the side of the road and read some more of your good book until they let you know they are ready to stop misbehaving.

> Parents who have been willing to make this small sacrifice once or twice have found that they were able to spend many happy hours eating in restaurants and driving in cars with children who could count on their parents to follow through with kind and firm action.

Some parents object, saying that *they* are being punished if they have to leave their unfinished meal and sit in the car with a child, who may be throwing a temper tantrum, or sit by the side of the road reading a book when they have so many other "important" things to do. It does take time and a few sacrifices to effectively teach children. Parents who have been willing to make this small sacrifice once or twice have found that they were able to spend many happy hours eating in restaurants and driving in cars with children who could count on their parents to follow through with kind and firm action.

Know Your Child

SOMETIMES MISBEHAVIOR IS exacerbated by expecting from children what they cannot give. Even the sweetest-natured toddler will become cranky after a full afternoon of errands, especially if nap time has been disrupted—and expecting a young child to refrain from touching the pretty things in a gift shop, for example, is unrealistic. Getting down on a child's level, making eye contact, and explaining why we don't touch, or quietly, kindly, and firmly removing the child, are far more effective than allowing an accident to happen—and trying to cope with it afterward.

It's always helpful to understand a child's (or a teenager's) developmental process, and to know what they are and are not capable of at each age. It helps simply to know your own child; some children enjoy airplane trips and need little preparation or planning, while others are afraid or overly energetic and need much more help finding useful ways to stay busy.

And remember: Pick your battles carefully. Decide which issues are non-negotiable, and which you can compromise on. Every family is different. Some parents insist on church attendance, while it's not important to others; messy rooms push some parents' buttons, while others couldn't care less. *Everything* can become a battle if we let it; be sure you save your energy for the things that really matter.

This is not meant to imply that controlling methods and punishment are acceptable if the battle is important. Most battles can be eliminated when Positive Discipline methods are used. The point is to notice how many battles parents create by trying to control every detail instead of deciding what is really important and then taking the time to get children involved in creating solutions whenever possible. Effective discipline includes knowing how to prevent problems as well as how to handle them when they occur.

Take Time to Teach

IT'S ALMOST ALWAYS better to prevent a problem than to have to react to one. Often problems can be averted by sitting down to talk "with" your children—to explain your point of view, to check your child's understanding, and most important, to teach. Teaching is not only encouraging, it is an effective form of discipline.

For instance, it's important to teach problem-solving skills. Children aren't born knowing how to resolve an argument. Although ignoring sibling rivalry may work if the arguing is intended to get your attention (remember the mistaken goals?), an argument between children may continue indefinitely if children haven't been taught how to solve a problem or how to reach a compromise. And discussing rules in advance isn't nagging or reminding if it's done in a positive, respectful way—which means involving the children in the discussion instead of giving endless lectures.

> Everything can become a battle if we let it; be sure you save your energy for the things that really matter.

A theme we present over and over is how important it is to *involve* your children. Not only does this teach them valuable skills, it also increases their desire to cooperate because they have helped create the rules or solutions. We have explored how important it is to get children involved in finding solutions through family meetings and brainstorming. This is one of the best ways to teach not only appropriate behavior but helpful skills that will last a lifetime. Much of this can be accomplished by involving children in the creation of routine charts.

Routine Charts

WE HAVE ALREADY learned that lectures and punishment invite resistance and rebellion. Yet most single parents use lectures or punishment over and over about morning hassles, bedtime hassles, mealtime hassles, and homework hassles, which can all be prevented by getting children involved in the creation of routine charts. *Getting children involved* is the key.

During a family meeting let your children brainstorm all the things that need to be done at times when you often struggle. Bedtime is a good place to start. Sit down with your children and make a list of all the things that need to be done, and the order in which they should be done. Then bring out poster board, construction paper, markers, magazines, scissors, and glue. Let your children find pictures in magazines to represent each task. If they are old enough, they can take turns writing the items on the poster board, leaving room to paste pictures by each task.

After the routine chart is made, let the children find a place to hang it where it can easily be seen by everyone. The routine chart now becomes "the boss." Instead of telling children what needs to be done next (which is a signal for them to resist and argue), ask them, "What is next on our routine chart?" They love telling you; and they love following the routine they helped create.

Of course, when children spend time with another parent in another home, routines there will be different. You need not worry about this. Children are very flexible and can learn different skills in different situations.

A Word to Noncustodial Parents

"BUT I HARDLY ever see my kids," you may be saying. "Their other parent is responsible for discipline most of the time. Does it really matter what I do? Can I affect my kids when I see them only on weekends?"

Whether you are the custodial parent or not, the way you approach discipline with your children is important. You have the opportunity to create an environment in your own home that nurtures responsibility in your children, regardless of how often you see them. Even one weekend a month in a home that is positive, encouraging, and respectful can have an influence; and it's important that each moment you spend with your children, whether it's a little or a lot, be the best you can make it. Giving some careful thought to how you approach discipline may mean you have to spend less time actually *doing* it—and that leaves more time for fun!

Using Natural and Logical Consequences

EFFECTIVE DISCIPLINE structures a child's environment in such a way that he or she understands—in advance—the consequences of behavior. This will encourage children to use that knowledge in choosing what they will do next time. For example, a natural consequence of failing to get enough sleep is feeling tired the next day. A child who has experienced being tired may be more willing to go to bed when asked—unless, of course, you turn the discussion into a power struggle by lecturing and scolding.

A natural consequence of losing a toy is not having the toy—and learning that painful lesson may be the best way to teach a child to be careful with possessions, especially if you show empathy for the child's feelings of disappointment instead of giving an "I told you so" lecture. Children can learn personal accountability from natural consequences only if parents avoid four traps:

Blaming and Shaming. Children learn best in an environment where they don't feel threatened. Brain research shows that threatening experiences cause children (and adults) to revert to their limbic system, where there are only two messages: fight or flight. How can positive learning take place when the child is focused on fighting (usually in the form of arguing, defending, rebelling) or flight (usually in the form of withdrawal, emotional and/or physical)?

Giving some careful thought to how you approach discipline may mean you have to spend less time actually *doing* it—and that leaves more time for fun!

Parents may think blaming and shaming will motivate a child to stop the behavior, but even when it does, the price is a defeated child who develops low self-esteem. Blame and shame take the focus away from the behavior and the opportunity to learn from a poor choice. Instead the child will focus on anger at you for your verbal abuse, or defending herself, or (worst of all) may believe she is truly a "bad" person.

TRAPS THAT DEFEAT POSITIVE EFFECTS OF NATURAL CONSEQUENCES

- Blaming and shaming
- Adding punishment
- Fixing or rescuing
- Not showing empathy

Adding Punishment. Most parents have good intentions when they use punishment. They think punishment will stop misbehavior. And it usually does—for a while. However, parents often fail to understand the long-range results of punishment: resentment, rebellion, revenge, retreat into sneakiness or low self-esteem, or retaliation by misusing power over a younger sibling or anyone smaller or less powerful. Punishment teaches children more about getting even, avoiding detection, or hurting others than it does about the consequences of their choices.

> Punishment teaches children more about getting even, avoiding detection, or hurting others than it does about the consequences of their choices.

Fixing or Rescuing. Children don't learn the consequences of their choices when parents take care of everything or bail them out. Children learn when parents help them explore what happened, what caused it to happen, what they learned, and what ideas they have to fix the problem or to avoid it in the future. Punishment is one ineffective extreme. Fixing or rescuing is the other ineffective extreme. Helping children learn from their choices is the true meaning of logical consequences. And children learn best when adults offer empathy but refrain from interfering.

Not Showing Empathy. Parents can show empathy without falling into any of the first three traps by saying, "I can see how unhappy you must feel." Period! Most children already feel bad when they make a poor choice. It does not help to blame, shame, punish, fix, or rescue—all of which take the focus away from the behavior. It does help to support the child in exploring her feelings about the consequences and to validate those feelings. When children feel support, they are able to avoid "fight or flight" reactions and use their brain cortex for reasoning and learning. The most effective learning takes place in a safe and encouraging environment.

Logical Consequences

SOMETIMES A BEHAVIOR has no natural consequence, or the natural consequence is unacceptable (the natural consequence of playing in the street, for instance). In that case, a parent can substitute a *logical* consequence. A logical consequence of failing to pick up toys could be losing the privilege of using those toys for a few days. As discussed previously, the loss of a privilege should be related to not accepting the responsibility (in this case, taking care of toys).

When taking a privilege away, it is important to follow with: "Let me know when you are ready to accept the responsibility so you can again enjoy the privilege." When children promise to accept the responsibility but don't follow through, the privilege can remain removed until you and the child can create a workable plan.

Involving Children in the Creation of Plans, Consequences, and Solutions

USING NATURAL AND LOGICAL consequences is an effective way for parents to involve children in the process of discipline, by focusing on future behavior, by talking with children about the results—good or bad—of the choices they make, and by setting up ahead of time consequences that are reasonable, respectful, and related to the behavior.

For instance, when a child is constantly late for dinner, a parent can tell that child respectfully and kindly that dinner will be served at 6:00; if she chooses not to be home and ready to eat, the next meal served will be breakfast. A parent can ask the child how she feels about this arrangement or what she thinks might help her to come home on time. And if the child chooses to arrive late, the parent can then follow through with the agreed-upon consequence with love, dignity, and firmness—and without anger and yelling.

If a child becomes upset when you follow through with an agreed-upon consequence, show empathy. You might follow up by helping her explore what happened and figure out a better plan. You might also invite her to put the problem on the family meeting agenda so everyone in the family (even if that is only two people) can have fun brainstorming for possible solutions. This type of discipline teaches children the skills of personal accountability so important for success in today's world.

Children can learn personal accountability from logical consequences only if parents avoid three traps:

Using consequences that are not *related*, *respectful*, and *reasonable*. Many parents "ground" children or take away privileges—punishments that have

> # TRAPS THAT DEFEAT POSITIVE EFFECTS OF LOGICAL CONSEQUENCES
>
> Using consequences that are not *related, respectful,* and *reasonable.*
> Not having children help decide on logical consequences in advance, or at least letting children know beforehand what the logical consequence will be.
> Not being *kind* and *firm* while enforcing consequences.

nothing to do with the misbehavior. It is not related to take a child's bike away because he didn't do his homework; it is also disrespectful and unreasonable and may invite more misbehavior later on. It would be much more effective to work with the child to create a plan that would help him get his homework done. It might be reasonable to remove toys when children avoid the responsibility of taking care of them, but it would be disrespectful to use blame and shame instead of kindness and firmness while doing so.

Children can come up with creative solutions to problems when given the opportunity, and their ideas on effective consequences may include things that matter to them—things you might never have thought of.

Not having children help decide on logical consequences in advance, or at least letting children know beforehand what the logical consequence will be. It is important to involve children as much as possible in the process of setting up consequences. After all, they're much more motivated to obey a rule when they've had a voice in making it. Children can come up with creative solutions to problems when given the opportunity (see chapter 9 on family meetings), and their ideas on effective consequences may include things that matter to them—things you might never have thought of.

Not being *kind* and *firm* while enforcing consequences. Kindness and firmness create a supportive atmosphere where positive learning can take place. Most problems created by parents are due to too much kindness without firmness (permissiveness) or too much firmness without kindness (excessive control). Kindness shows respect for the child and firmness shows respect for what needs to be done.

Children often push our buttons and we revert to our limbic systems where our only options are fight or flight. Is it any wonder that our children respond in kind.

We need to take some deep breaths or some positive time out until we can access our cortex and be kind and firm at the same time.

What could be a logical consequence is always turned into a punishment when it is not enforced with kindness and firmness at the same time—or when it is carried out with anger, lecturing, or blaming.

Important Things to Remember About Consequences

MANY PARENTS LOVE the idea of giving up punishment and using logical consequences. However, there are two things to keep in mind when using logical consequences. First, there is a fine line between logical consequences and punishment. Many parents use punishment in the name of logical consequences, but the disguise is not a good one and children know the difference. They will be discouraged by punishment—no matter what it is called. Only if parents use true logical consequences will children be empowered to accept the personal accountability that fosters self-esteem.

> Many parents use punishment in the name of logical consequences, but the disguise is not a good one and children know the difference.

Second, avoid thinking that logical consequences are the solution to every problem. We propose many nonpunitive discipline methods throughout this book. Our favorite is family meetings where everyone in the family works together to brainstorm logical consequences and work on solutions to problems. Another favorite is kind and firm follow-through.

Remember, too, to pay attention to that time-honored maxim of parents everywhere when following through on consequences: "Say what you mean, and mean what you say." Don't tell your whining five-year-old that if she's not in the car this minute, you'll leave for grandma's house without her. She knows as well as you do that grandma lives in the next state and you're not about to leave her standing on the driveway alone. Such empty threats teach children that they only need to listen to about half of what their parents say—not a good way to build trust. Be sure that you're willing and able to follow through *before* you decide on a consequence. (The opposite applies, too: If you've made a promise to your children, do your best to keep it!)

Decide What You Will Do— and Follow Through

ONCE A CONSEQUENCE has been decided upon, with or without the children, it is important to follow through. Of course this follow-through should be done with dignity and respect. Notice that this does not include punishment, lectures, blame, or shame. When deciding what you will do, be sure your actions are respectfully related to the behavior, and that when you follow through you do so kindly *and* firmly.

> When deciding what you will do, be sure your actions are respectfully related to the behavior, and that when you follow through you do so kindly *and* firmly.

Bill Hadley had told his kids many times that it was their responsibility to pick up their toys. One day when he had straightened up the family room for the third time in an afternoon, he sat them down and told them that from now on if they did not pick up their toys, he would—and the toys would go right into a box on the high shelf to be given to Goodwill in a week.

Bill decided to keep the toys in a box for a week because everyone makes mistakes. If the kids felt bad about losing a toy he had picked up, he would say, "Show me you can take care of your toys for a week, and I'll let you try again with the toy you want to keep." He explained the new rule and made sure everyone was in agreement. But Bill was realistic; he expected some problems—and they showed up right on schedule.

The first week he was annoyed to see how many things the kids left lying around. Because Dad was following through and putting the toys on the high shelf, it became obvious that the children didn't particularly care if the toys went to Goodwill. Bill was wise enough to know that his children's lack of concern was his problem, not theirs; apparently he had given them too many toys that they didn't appreciate. He made a decision not to buy any more toys for his children unless they wanted them enough to save their money and contribute to the purchase.

Still, the Goodwill box filled up fast. It was, the family accidentally discovered, a marvelous way of cleaning out unwanted and outgrown toys! After a while, all that remained were toys the children used and wanted to keep. When they were left lying around, all Bill had to say was, "Do you want to pick your toys up or do you want me to do it?" By now the kids realized that their dad would stick to the logical consequence and give the toys away if they didn't pick them up, so they would scramble to take care of the things they wanted. Did Bill actually take toys his children wanted to Goodwill? Only once—which was enough to teach his children the consequence of choosing not to pick them up.

Was Bill a "mean" father? Bill Hadley was a responsible father who used a logical consequence (by deciding what he would do and following through) for something that had been discussed with his kids in advance.

What Is Follow-Through?

FOLLOW-THROUGH MAY SEEM similar to logical consequences. The important difference is that logical consequences allow children to experience the results of their choices. Follow-through requires that parents decide what *they* will or won't do in response to a child's choices. Follow-through is appropriate only when a parent is present to carry out his or her decision.

When children are young, follow-through is simple. When you say something, mean it. When you mean it, follow through with kindness and firmness. Or, as Rudolf Dreikurs used to say, "Shut your mouth and act." To demonstrate the use of follow-through with young children we will describe two scenes. Scene I describes a mother using typical, punitive discipline. Scene II portrays another mother using follow-though for the same behavior.

SCENE I: It is bedtime. Five-year-old Jennifer is sitting on the floor coloring. Her mother cheerfully says, "It's time to put your crayons away now, honey, and get ready for bed."

Jennifer keeps coloring. Mom's voice gets a little tight. "Did you hear me, Jennifer? It's time to get ready for bed. Put your crayons away."

Jennifer keeps coloring. In a very tight voice Mom says, "Jennifer! I'm going to count to three. If you haven't started putting your crayons away, you are going to get a spanking."

Jennifer keeps coloring. Mom starts to count. When she reaches three, she starts toward Jennifer. Jennifer scrambles to pick up her crayons. Mom spanks her anyway and drags her to her room. Jennifer cries. Mom pours a little salt on the wound by saying, "It serves you right. Why don't you listen to me when I tell you to do something? You can just go to bed without a story now!"

Jennifer gets into bed and screams for fifteen minutes before falling asleep. Mom wishes for retroactive birth control.

SCENE II: It is bedtime. Five-year-old Becky is sitting on the floor coloring. Her mother cheerfully says, "It's time to put your crayons away now, honey, and get ready for bed."

Becky keeps coloring. Mom quietly walks over to Becky, reaches down, and takes her hand. Becky tries to pull her hand away and says, "Let me just finish this page."

Mom does not say a word. She gives Becky a kind but knowing glance and firmly but gently pulls her up from the floor. Becky starts to complain. Mom says, "Do you want to pick out your bedtime story or do you want me to?"

Becky says in a pouting voice, "I want to."

Mom says, "Fine. Call me as soon as you are ready for bed and I'll come and read as much as I can before eight o'clock. The longer you take to get ready for bed, the less time we'll have for reading."

Becky knows Mom means what she says, so she gets ready as fast as she can. When Mom finishes reading she tells Becky, "You didn't pick the crayons up tonight. In the morning you can pick them up before kindergarten or I will pick them up and put them on the high shelf."

If Becky does not pick up the crayons, Mom will follow through on what she said. Becky and her mom have already agreed that when any toys go on the high shelf, Becky must demonstrate she is ready to have them back by picking up her toys responsibly for at least two days.

Follow-through is more effective with older kids when they are involved in some preliminary preparation. As soon as they are old enough to be involved in decision making, we suggest Four Steps for Effective Follow-Through, as shown in the following example.

Fifteen-year-old Karen had accepted the job of keeping the kitchen clean. She rarely did it unless Jim, her dad, scolded and threatened to ground her for a week if it wasn't done.

After one particularly heated argument, Jim realized that his method wasn't working too well and decided to try follow-through, which he had learned about in a parenting class. He asked Karen if she would be willing to work together on a solution so they could end their power struggle over the kitchen. Karen agreed reluctantly; she was expecting a lecture and wasn't sure what this new approach might mean. She was surprised when her dad

FOUR STEPS FOR EFFECTIVE FOLLOW-THROUGH

- Have a friendly discussion during which everyone gets to voice their feelings and thoughts about the issue.

- Brainstorm for possible solutions and choose one on which both adult and child agree.

- Agree on a specific time deadline (to the minute).

- Simply follow through by holding the child accountable for keeping the agreement.

said sincerely, "Karen, I would really like to hear what is going on for you regarding the kitchen. Do you think it's too big a job for you, or unfair, or are you too busy?"

Karen fidgeted and said, "No, Dad. I know I should do it. I always mean to. I just get busy and forget."

Jim said, "I have a hunch that something else might be involved, too. I have been pretty bossy about telling you what to do and very insulting to you when you don't jump to my commands on schedule. Could it be that you are showing me that I can't make you if you don't want to?"

Karen grinned sheepishly. Jim laughed and said, "I thought so. I remember feeling the same way, and I don't blame you. In fact, when I think about it, I have to admire your spunk in refusing to be treated that way. I really want to stop being bossy and insulting. Are you willing to work with me on ways to treat each other respectfully?"

Karen said, "Sounds good to me, Dad."

Jim paused for a moment. "How about brainstorming with me on some solutions to the kitchen problem? I have one suggestion. We could both get extra jobs so we could earn enough money to hire a maid."

Karen laughed and said, "We could just let it go and eat pizza every night."

Jim added, "We could try and con your friends into doing it."

Karen was quiet for a moment. "Or I could just do it. I know I agreed to, and I don't do much else to help."

Jim said, "Well, that's the solution I would prefer, if you're really willing and don't feel forced by a bossy Dad. Would you be willing to agree to a specific deadline for when it will be done? Then I won't say a word unless it is not done by the deadline."

Karen said, "How about Sunday night?"

Jim shook his head and smiled. "I could enjoy the weekend a lot more if the kitchen was clean before Saturday."

Karen sighed. "Okay, I'll do it by Friday."

Jim asked, "What time Friday?"

"Da-aad! I'll do it by Friday."

"It will be easier for me to keep my mouth shut and not nag if the deadline is very specific."

"Okay, okay. How about six o'clock Friday evening?"

"Sounds good to me, kiddo."

It is now 6:00 P.M. the next Friday. The kitchen is a maze of dirty dishes and leftover food, and Karen is chatting happily on the phone. Jim is not surprised; he expected this. He is ready to follow through.

When Karen hangs up the phone, Jim places his hand on her shoulder and says, "Karen, it's 6:00 and the kitchen is not cleaned."

Karen says, "Aw, Dad, I had to talk to Shannon about homework. I'll do it later."

Jim says simply, "What was our agreement?"

Karen squirms and there is a hint of irritation in her voice. "Come on Dad. Don't be so uptight. I'll do it right after I call Shannon back."

Jim simply smiles, gives his daughter a knowing grin, and points to his watch. Karen's lower lip juts out. "Okay, okay. I'm going. Talk about uptight!"

Jim decides to ignore both the insult and Karen's obvious annoyance and says, "Thanks, Karen. I really appreciate your willingness to keep your agreement."

Some parents say, "My son or daughter wouldn't give in that easily." We disagree. When we follow the Four Steps for Effective Follow-Through and avoid the following Four Traps That Defeat Effective Follow-Through, kids do cooperate, even when they don't especially want to.

FOUR TRAPS THAT DEFEAT EFFECTIVE FOLLOW-THROUGH

- Wanting kids to have the same priorities as adults.
- Judging and criticizing instead of sticking to the issue.
- Not getting agreements (noncoerced) in advance that include a specific time deadline. (This step is not necessary for children too young to make an agreement.)
- Not maintaining dignity and respect for the child and for yourself.

If you reread the example of Karen and her father, you will see that Jim did not expect Karen to be excited about cleaning the kitchen. When Jim thought about it he could name many things that were a priority for Karen—things like zits; how to pay for a car when she gets her license; getting a job to pay for insurance and gas; how much homework to do without being called a nerd; what to do about drugs, sex, and college; worrying about whether she'll have a date or what her friends think of her. Cleaning the kitchen was not in the top one hundred. However, it is still important for Karen to contribute to the family in meaningful ways.

Notice that Jim avoided judgments and criticism and stuck to the issue of the agreement. The more Karen talked, the less her dad had to say. He simply gave her a knowing grin and pointed to his watch. This was effective because Karen knew she had agreed to the deadline. Jim maintained dignity and respect for both his daughter and himself throughout the follow-through process.

Some people object to follow-through. They say, "We don't want to have to remind our kids to keep their agreements. We expect them to be responsible without any reminders from us."

> Follow-through takes less energy and is much more loving—and productive—than scolding, lecturing, and punishing.

We have three questions for these people: Have you noticed how responsible your kids are about keeping agreements that are important to them? Do you think cleaning the kitchen or mowing the lawn is really important to them? When you don't take time to remind them with dignity and respect, do you spend time scolding, lecturing, and punishing them for not keeping their agreements? Even if it is not important to them, it is important to have them do it anyway to teach responsibility, mutual respect, and shared contribution. Follow-through takes less energy and is much more loving—and productive—than scolding, lecturing, and punishing.

Adults are not using their common sense when they expect children to use their free will to follow adult priorities. Young people are very good at using their free will to follow their own priorities! Follow-through is a respectful way to help kids live up to appropriate adult expectations.

Once we understand that kids have their own priorities but still need to follow some of ours, follow-through can make parenting pleasurable, magical, and fun. We can see the things kids do as cute, adorable, and normal instead of lazy, inconsiderate, and irresponsible.

Follow-through helps parents be proactive and thoughtful instead of reactive and inconsiderate. Follow-through helps us empower kids by respecting who they are while teaching them the importance of making a contribution to the family. In the following example, another mom offers a different slant on follow-through.

Carmen Ruiz had tried nagging her seventeen-year-old daughter, Nita, about the cereal bowls she left in her room. She would find as many as seven bowls in Nita's room, coated with hardened cereal that made them very difficult to wash. And it wasn't unusual for the rest of the family to have to search high and low for a clean bowl when they needed one.

One day when Carmen was scolding Nita for being so inconsiderate, Nita said, "I'm sorry, Mom. It's just that I'm so busy with school, my job, homework, and dance lessons. I need some time for my friends and some fun. I just keep forgetting about the bowls."

Carmen suddenly realized the truth of what Nita was saying. Nita was an extremely busy teenager with a lot of pressure in her life. Her mom remembered all the little errands Nita routinely did for her, her generally cheerful attitude, and her responsibility in balancing all the demands on her time.

> Consequences, follow-through, and other forms of nonpunitve discipline are effective ways to help children learn the life skills they need to feel good about themselves, while teaching them to be contributing members of society through personal accountability.

Carmen sighed, then smiled. "Honey, you are right. You do have a lot going on in your life, and you are doing a darn good job keeping up with it all. I'm really very proud of you. I'm going to quit nagging you about these silly bowls. I'll tell you what—when I notice them, I'll just take them to the kitchen and put them in water to soak for a while. It would make me feel good to do that for you as a reminder to both of us about how much I love you."

Nita looked at her mom with genuine surprise and gratitude. "Gee thanks, Mom. I'll try harder, but I really do appreciate your understanding and support."

Carmen felt much better. It was much easier to just pick up the bowls than to nag and get upset about it.

In other circumstances it might be inappropriate for Carmen to do too much for her daughter. However, in this case Nita was not taking advantage. She was being a very responsible teenager in most areas of her life.

Positive Time Out

TIME OUT IS used in a negative manner by most parents. "Go to your room, young lady, and think about what you did!" So what does the "young lady" think about while sitting in her room? It's our guess that she's not thinking about what she did, but about what her parent just did, or how she can get even, or how she can avoid getting caught next time.

When parents remember that "children do better when they feel better," and that the purpose of discipline is "to teach," positive time out will make more sense. Positive time out is designed to help children learn the valuable life skill of calming down until they can think rationally, and then do better.

Positive time out is most effective if children help create a "feel-good place." Then when a child is engaging in some kind of misbehavior, you might ask, "Would it help you to go to your feel-good place for awhile?" Children are more likely to go to positive time out if they have helped create it, if they see it as helpful to them, and when parents realize it is only one of many possible discipline tools.

We have presented several alternatives to punitive discipline or permissiveness. These nonpunitive methods help change behavior while maintaining dignity and respect for all concerned. Consequences, follow-through, and other forms of nonpunitve discipline are effective ways to help children learn the life skills they need to feel good about themselves, while teaching them to be contributing members of society through personal accountability.

13

Beyond Single Parenthood: Taking Care of You

T HE FIRST MONTHS, even years, of single parenthood can be a busy
time. Raising children alone, especially when you're new at it, requires a
great deal of your time and energy. Eventually, though, the dust settles a bit
and life relaxes into a routine. And at some point a single parent may begin to
say, "But what about me? Don't I have needs, too?"

Sometimes being a single parent seems to be all about the parent part. Our
children are our main priority—providing for them, helping them grow and
flourish, keeping their lives on an even keel. What we sometimes fail to realize
is that to be healthy, effective parents, we must first
be healthy, effective human beings—and that can
feel like a tall order. Where, you may wonder, do I
find the time and energy to "get a life"?

Social life often seems to revolve around couples. When you're not part of one it's easy to feel
lonely, different, set apart. If you were part of a couple for a long time, it may be difficult to adjust to
being on your own; much of your identity can be
tied to your partner and your old way of life.
Hitting the singles scene may be far too intimidating—and too much work.

Single parents may also find themselves with jobs and roles they had never
anticipated. Figuring out the income tax may terrify a single mother whose ex-
husband always did that, while dealing with a daughter's clothing and hairstyling

> Social life often
> seems to revolve
> around couples. When
> you're not part of one
> it's easy to feel lonely,
> different, set apart.

may baffle a single dad. Lifestyles may have changed dramatically. Adults who never really worried about money may suddenly find themselves scrambling to get by, unable to enjoy activities and pleasures they took for granted before. And all single parents inevitably find themselves longing for just a little free time, independence, and adult conversation.

Can you meet the demands of single parenthood, do all the jobs required of you, and still find time for a healthy adult life? Not only *can* you—you must! Taking care of yourself is one of the most important jobs you have.

Finding the Courage to Change

TAKING CARE OF YOURSELF can take many different forms. For Carolyn, it meant making some sweeping and traumatic changes in her life. Carolyn had been married for fifteen years, and she had two beautiful children, Paul and Cheryl. During Carolyn's marriage, her husband had made all of the decisions about finances and business. Steve was a loyal husband and a kind man, but there was never any doubt about who was in command. Other than working very hard in her home and in the PTA during her children's school years, Carolyn never held a job during her marriage.

Gradually Carolyn realized she'd lost *herself* in her marriage. She was her husband's wife and her children's mother, but she wasn't sure *Carolyn* even existed. She began to feel that these familiar roles were no longer enough for her. She felt stifled. Paul and Cheryl were well into their teens and were busy with friends and school activities; Steve was busy with work and seemed uninterested in Carolyn—except to find out what she was cooking for dinner.

Carolyn suggested counseling to Steve, who wasn't interested. She tried hobbies and clubs. She tried to join Steve in his activities, with only limited success. He barely tolerated her attempts to join him on the golf course and she just couldn't get the hang of tennis. Nothing seemed to make any difference.

Carolyn decided that she had to take charge of her own life. When she announced to her husband that she wanted a divorce, he retorted, "If you want a divorce, *you'll* have to move out." He believed she would never leave. Carolyn surprised him (and herself) by taking some of their savings, finding a small apartment, and moving out.

Carolyn hadn't worked in fifteen years—at least, she hadn't received a salary! She had only a high school education. She hadn't taken any college courses or developed any marketable skills, and she knew she couldn't make a living organizing school bake sales, carnivals, and other activities. It was a terrifying situation, but her sense of opportunity and freedom was heady and she was determined to make her life better.

The first year was the most difficult. At times her fear was so great that she felt completely defeated. Sometimes she was tempted to return to her old life. But she kept remembering her restlessness before her divorce and her determination to take care of herself. She knew she couldn't go back. She found a job in a department store and by working twice as hard as anyone else, earned a promotion to department manager. After two years, her divorce was final and her children chose to come and live with her.

Carolyn never looked back. She did her best to help Paul and Cheryl adjust, accepting their anger and hurt (and later, their support) with understanding. Although she experienced both grief and guilt, she worked through, and learned from, her emotions.

> Change can be a catalyst to help us develop new courage and creativity.

Steve, however, was so full of anger and resentment that he spent thousands of dollars fighting both the divorce and the custody agreement. He was furious when his children chose to live with their mother instead of with him. Long after Carolyn had begun to thrive in her new life, Steve continued to wallow in bitterness.

Are sweeping changes—such as divorce—always necessary to teach us to take care of ourselves? No, of course not. But change can be a catalyst to help us develop new courage and creativity. We always have opportunities to turn negative experiences into positive ones. If we are to be creative, we must be willing to take care of ourselves—an important ingredient of self-esteem.

Self-Esteem? What Self-Esteem?

SELF-ESTEEM IS THE PICTURE we have of ourselves, the sum of the decisions we've made about who we are, what we're capable of, what others think of us, and whether we're "good enough." Everyone has self-esteem, but not everyone's self-esteem is healthy. As we've said before, feelings of self-worth can come and go. Sometimes the events and circumstances that make us single parents also leave gaping wounds in our opinion of ourselves. Healthy self-esteem doesn't mean you always feel on top of the world. Healthy self-esteem can be measured by your ability to deal with the ups and downs of life. Feeling "down" is a normal part of life. Staying down is an indicator of unhealthy self-esteem.

Single parents may be struggling with feelings of rejection and hurt because a partner has left them, or they may be feeling guilty because they themselves chose to leave. Just being different from those around you—being an unmarried woman who chose to adopt a child, for example—can cause you to feel isolated and alone. A single parent may feel anxious, incapable of raising whole, healthy children, and all too aware of the mistakes he or she made in the past.

Everyone is occasionally haunted by feelings of inadequacy and failure, but single parents sometimes find that those feelings are constant companions. The result can be a sense of hopelessness, lack of confidence, and deep discouragement. Allowing those attitudes to take root in your heart will affect how you approach your life, how you behave, what you accomplish—or whether you attempt anything at all.

> Healthy self-esteem doesn't mean you always feel on top of the world. Healthy self-esteem can be measured by your ability to deal with the ups and downs of life.

Children, too, can suffer in the aftermath of a death, divorce, or perceived abandonment. Because their world is centered on themselves and their own perceptions, children often believe that their parents' problems are the result of something they have said or done or wished—no matter how many times we tell them differently.

A child's thinking is often "magical." If a child was angry at Mom and Mom suddenly disappeared from his life, it *must* have been his fault. Children who sense tension between their parents sometimes increase their misbehavior in an attempt to keep their parents busy and involved with them—and in the process, to keep them together. "Failure" in the form of death or divorce is devastating, and children often blame themselves. Rebuilding your children's self-esteem and sense of worth may seem like a huge task when your own is heavily damaged. How do we go about healing self-esteem? Where do we begin?

Healing Your Self-Esteem

"MAYBE SOME PEOPLE CAN HEAL," you may say, "but I can't help the way I feel." You may not quite believe that feelings can be changed (and it may seem far easier to stay stuck where you are). However, it's important that you begin to examine your beliefs and attitudes about yourself and others and to change the ones that are keeping you from healing and growing. Remember that your children adopt many of your attitudes—fear, guilt, or depression—and though natural and unavoidable for a while, these will affect your entire family.

> Remember that your children adopt many of your attitudes—fear, guilt, and depression—and though natural and unavoidable for a while, these will affect your entire family.

Everyone agrees that children must have a healthy sense of self-esteem; believing in themselves and in their intrinsic worth is what gives them the courage to try new things, to take risks, to handle challenges, and to resist peer pressure. What we need to remember is that much of that sense of worth is learned from parents. Children learn to respect and accept who they are when their parents show them how—by doing it themselves.

The first step in healing your self-esteem is to realize that you are worthwhile and entitled to dignity and respect just the way you are. That doesn't mean there aren't areas you'd like to improve—all of us struggle to work through different aspects of our personalities and poor habits. But you don't have to finish the work (in other words, you don't have to be perfect) to be a lovable and valuable human being.

There are a number of things you can do that will help you not only to heal your own self-esteem but to build that of your children. Begin with yourself. It takes time and patience, but eventually you *and* your children will find that you're able to pursue life with confidence and hope.

Learn to separate the person from the actions. The fact that you've made mistakes and "messed up" does not mean you're a bad person. We are usually

STEPS TO HEALING YOUR SELF-ESTEEM

- Learn to separate the person from the actions.
- Beware of labels and self-defeating beliefs.
- Learn to "hold on to yourself."
- Begin to affirm yourself.
- Don't be afraid to change when it feels right to you.
- Learn to value the moment.

our own worst critics; we're quick to dismiss ourselves as worthless when we feel we've made wrong choices. But our worth as human beings is not defined by what we do; it rests on who we are, and all of us deserve dignity and respect. Rudolf Dreikurs spoke often of having the "courage to be imperfect." That means recognizing that all of us—parents and children alike—make mistakes, and expecting perfection will only lead to disappointment.

Mistakes, as we have said, are wonderful opportunities to learn; life becomes much easier when we treat errors that way. When you make a mistake, learn to forgive yourself, dust yourself off, and try again.

Beware of labels and self-defeating beliefs. Most of us believe the messages about who we are and what we are capable of that we have heard over and over again. Often they become so much a part of the way we view ourselves and our world that we are unaware of the influence they have over us. Our children, too, will believe what we say about them. When we tell a child (by words or actions) that she is bad, lazy, or stupid, she believes us. Oh, she may still argue with us. But a little voice inside tells her that if Mom (who knows everything) says she's stupid, she really must be stupid. And before long, she becomes a discouraged child who no longer tries because she believes success just isn't possible.

> When you make a mistake, learn to forgive yourself, dust yourself off, and try again.

Happily, the reverse is also true. As we've discovered, encouragement, looking for positives, and sharing compliments and appreciation will enable us and our children to see ourselves as capable and worthwhile human beings (especially when we also receive opportunities to experience our competence).

This world of ours often leads us to value superficial things. If you watch much television, you'll quickly learn that worthwhile people are beautiful, intelligent, athletic, wealthy, popular, talented—all sorts of things we and our children may not be. Learning to find and to appreciate the positive qualities in ourselves and our children will keep all of us centered and secure.

> Learning to find and to appreciate the positive qualities in ourselves and our children will keep all of us centered and secure.

Sometimes old ways of viewing yourself may be incorrect. Grant, for instance, had suffered more than the usual growing pains during his teen years. For an unbearably long time he hadn't grown much at all and remained much shorter than his peers. When he finally did shoot up, he suffered knee and foot problems. For the first part of his high school career, he was too small for sports; for the last part, he was in too much pain. Somewhere along the line Grant began to believe that he just wasn't athletic—and never would be.

Grant got an opportunity to change his picture of himself when he met Cara. An avid skier and golfer, Cara wanted a companion who could share

BEWARE OF THE THREE QUESTIONS OF ETERNAL TORMENT:

- "Did I do the right thing?"

- "Am I doing the right thing?"

- "Will I do the right thing?"

Make the best choices you can and go forward, one step at a time!

those activities with her, and she was a patient teacher. Grant harbored serious doubts as they planned their first skiing vacation—but he was amazed to discover that skiing came easily to him. So, it turned out, did a number of other sports. Grant began to see himself differently. He was still an excellent accountant, but he was also good at sports. His self-esteem improved dramatically— and his high school memories lost some of their sting.

Learn to "hold on to yourself." There is an old joke: "I'm going to be assertive today—if it's all right with you." We may smile at the idea, but the truth is that assertiveness often turns into aggressiveness when people mistakenly stand up *to* someone else instead of standing up *for* themselves. When you stand up for yourself, people can't help but admire you, even if they don't agree with you. When you stand up to someone else, that person often feels the need to defend, to withdraw, or to retaliate. Healthy individuals eventually learn to hold on to themselves, to decide what they will do, and to accept the responsibility for their own happiness.

Ingrid and her son, Ivan, had always been a family of two. Ingrid had chosen to have Ivan, even after his father abandoned her, and had never regretted her decision. She enjoyed her work and had a circle of close friends, but Ivan was the center of her world. As Ivan grew into adolescence, though, Ingrid began to have a difficult time. Ivan was becoming an adult and wanted the right to make his own decisions. He argued with Ingrid; he argued with his friends. And he spent long hours locked in his bedroom, listening to loud music.

When Ivan withdrew, Ingrid thought obsessively about what he was doing, what had happened, and what he was feeling. She either felt depressed and guilty about her inability to "fix" Ivan's feelings or she became angry and tried to argue him into his old, close relationship with her.

Seeing a therapist helped Ingrid learn to hold on to herself, to realize that she was not responsible for Ivan's feelings—and could not fix or control them. She could, however, decide what she would do. She learned to tell Ivan with genuine caring, "I can see that you need some time to yourself. I want to help you, but you'll have to let me know how. I'll be around if you want to talk." Then she would do something to nurture herself: go for a walk, settle down with a good book, or get together with a friend.

Ingrid's relationship with her son did not magically become smoother overnight; Ivan was in the midst of an individuation and maturing process and would undoubtedly make his own mistakes. (For more information on living with teens, see *Positive Discipline for Teenagers* by Jane Nelsen and Lynn Lott—Prima Publishing, 1987). Ingrid realized that she was better able to support and understand her son's emotions when she wasn't ensnared in them herself. Holding on to herself did not cause Ingrid to care less; it enabled her to encourage Ivan while remaining calm herself.

Most of us believe there are only two ways to have a relationship. Either we are *dependent* and fuse ourselves with another's feelings and needs or we are *independent* and remain stubbornly apart. The healthiest relationships are *interdependent* and allow us to be separate, whole human beings who choose to be connected by trust and love to others. Learning to hold on to yourself without pushing others away takes time and practice, but it will help you gain serenity, self-confidence, and true self-esteem.

> The healthiest relationships are *interdependent* and allow us to be separate, whole human beings who choose to be connected by trust and love to others.

Begin to affirm yourself. Affirmations—statements we repeat to ourselves until we make them a permanent part of our thinking—are powerful encouragement. To be effective, an affirmation needs to be something we can really believe or are willing to act as if we believe.

Fred was a single dad; he was also a recovering alcoholic. When Fred was abusing alcohol, his children learned to be extremely demanding to get what they wanted—and it usually worked. When Fred went into recovery, he expected everything to miraculously change, but the kids didn't stop being demanding. Fred knew that giving in to them only made matters worse, but he didn't know what else to do. (For more information on healing from addiction, see *Parenting in Recovery,* by Jane Nelsen, Lynn Lott, and Riki Intner—Prima Publishing, 1996.) The nagging and whining began the moment he hit the front door after work, and Fred was almost at his wits' end. He was starting to think the effort wasn't worth it; perhaps a drink would help him cope.

One day Fred picked up the phone and called his Alcoholics Anonymous sponsor. "I'm losing hope," he said sadly.

His sponsor chuckled and replied, "I remember feeling that way. But, Fred, it will pass. Not only that; you have to expect a miracle."

Fred snorted. "What do you mean, 'expect a miracle'?"

AFFIRMATIONS THAT HAVE HELPED PARENTS HEAL THEIR SELF-ESTEEM:

- "Expect a miracle."
- "Work for progress, not perfection."
- "I'm a worthwhile person in spite of my flaws and imperfections."
- "One day at a time; one step at a time."
- "This too will pass."
- "It's good to be a learner."
- "I'm not a bad parent; I'm just unskilled and skills can be acquired."
- "I like the person I'm becoming."

His sponsor explained. "Some things are out of your control but that doesn't mean they won't get better. Your attitude and expectations make a difference. Try telling yourself to expect a miracle every time you walk in the front door, or when your kids start making their demands, and see what happens."

Fred was doubtful, but he didn't want to start drinking again. And he began to notice that the more he told himself to expect a miracle, the less he noticed his kids' demands and the less he was affected by them. He started seeing his children as miracles. He began to feel more loving toward them and began suggesting that they sit down and tell him about their day or that they all go out and play catch together before they started dinner. He and his children began to listen to one another, to talk more, and to complain less. Fred was surprised that such a simple step could have such powerful results.

As a single parent you may be giving yourself many negative, discouraging messages. Listen sometime to the conversations you have with yourself in front of the bathroom mirror or while you're driving. Do you focus on positive, hopeful things? Or are you reliving old battles, probing old wounds, and criticizing yourself for old mistakes? Sometimes it's easier simply to start a new habit of repeating affirmations than to change an old way of thinking. You probably know already what you need to hear and believe. Repeating these affirmations often during the day is a way to give yourself positive, encouraging messages.

Don't be afraid to change when it feels right to you. Often there are habits in our lives—ways of thinking and behaving—that get us into trouble. Learning to look for the positive and to accept our own worth apart from our mistakes are important, but so is developing the courage to change.

Change of any sort is one of the most difficult and uncomfortable aspects of human life and most of us resist it as long as we can. After all, a cozy rut or a bad habit may not be getting us anywhere, but it's familiar; we know what to expect even when we don't like it.

> Change of any sort is one of the most difficult and uncomfortable aspects of human life and most of us resist it as long as we can.

Bart felt stuck in a rut but was reluctant to change. He kept using the excuse: "This is just the way I am." One day his counselor asked, "What do you think might happen if you acted as the person you want to be instead of who you think you are?" Bart had an epiphany when he heard this. He realized he didn't have to stay stuck—that this was his life and that he could change it.

You will know when it's time to make a change. Begin with *small* changes that you can make with success. For instance, if you want to be less critical, you can begin to comment on the positive traits of coworkers, family, and children. Success in meeting that goal will encourage you to tackle the next one—when you're ready.

Some changes feel so risky that we hesitate to make them even when we believe we should. Moving to a new city can be a frightening prospect for us and for our children; changing jobs, going back to school, finding a counselor, beginning a new relationship or ending an old one are all big changes that require courage, and most people feel insecure at first. Having a support network—people you trust and can talk to—will help. So will success; making changes that work is the best encouragement of all!

Learn to value the moment. It is all too easy, especially when we're in pain, to focus all of our energy on what happened yesterday, or on what we want to happen tomorrow. However, our entire lives take place in the present. Each moment that we live is the only moment we have to enjoy; so if our attention is always directed behind us or ahead of us, we will never truly enjoy now and may miss much of what is happening in the world around us—and in our children's hearts and lives.

> Making changes that work is the best encouragement of all!

Learn to practice mindfulness. When you feel your thoughts running out of control into the future, or when you find yourself stuck in a past experience (again!), take a moment to breathe deeply several times and center yourself. Many people find that prayer, simple forms of meditation, or other ways of slowing down and connecting with "now" help them to relax and be at peace. When we can stay firmly rooted in the present, we will be able to enjoy so much more of life and our children, and we will be more completely open to life's possibilities.

Filling Your Pitcher

IN MOST SINGLE-PARENT HOMES there is one person who consistently seems to be overlooked and neglected: the parent! Single parents usually find themselves balancing work, domestic duties, child care, and goodness knows what else. Most report that they feel guilty taking any time out for themselves, especially if it's just for fun.

But it's important to remember that we don't do our best work as parents when we're stressed out, tired, and frustrated. Imagine for a moment a beautiful crystal pitcher. The water inside represents the amount of emotional energy you bring to each event throughout your day. Your children need your help getting ready in the morning—out goes a drop. Work is hectic and the traffic coming home is horrendous—out flows a large splash. Your friends, your partner, and your children need your time and attention—and the pitcher is empty. And that is usually when the *real* crisis occurs. Where will you find the energy to deal with what you face? How will you refill your pitcher?

Each of us needs occasional downtime, moments when we relax and get recharged. Parents are valuable people, too; your children will learn to respect and value themselves (and you) if you show them that you respect and value yourself.

Begin by budgeting time each week (see chapter 5) for your own activities and learning to treat yourself as a priority. You may discover that you approach parenting and work responsibilities with more energy and less resentment if you give yourself half an hour each evening after the kids are in bed to read a good book or soak in a hot bath—rather than ironing or cleaning the bathroom. Sure, a few household chores may have to wait, but they'll be done (eventually) by a more cheerful person.

> Whatever it is that makes you feel energized and alive, make sure you find time to do it on a regular basis. It is not selfishness; it is wisdom.

Nurture your own creativity and uniqueness. Give yourself the freedom to do what you enjoy, whether it's gardening, tinkering with an old motorcycle, doing crafts or home decorating projects, or playing a musical instrument. Set up a baby-sitting co-op with neighborhood parents and take one evening each week to go out to a movie, sing in a choir, play softball, or take dancing lessons. Whatever it is that makes you feel energized and alive, make sure you find time to do it on a regular basis. It is not selfishness; it is wisdom.

Remember, too, that you have a body, a mind, and a spirit, and it is essential to nurture each of these parts. It *is* important to pay attention to what you eat, to get enough sleep, and to get regular exercise. In fact, exercise is one of the most effective antidepressants we know!

Keeping your mind active and engaged will make life much more enjoyable, too. Give yourself permission to explore, to be curious, and to be a learner. You will find life much more interesting—and you don't need to spend large amounts of time or money. Nurturing your spirit in ways that have meaning to you is one of the best ways to keep your pitcher brimming. Nevertheless, change—including good change—can feel uncomfortable at first, as Nadine discovered.

Just Do It!

NADINE HAD BEEN on her own for three years. She was a devoted mother to her two sons, a conscientious employee, and a regular churchgoer. Her apartment was usually clean, the bills were paid, and the kids never ran out of clean underwear. But, Nadine realized one day, she was bone tired and she wasn't having any fun.

Nadine mentioned her feelings to a good friend at work. "You used to love country-western dancing," her friend replied. "Why don't you start doing that again?"

Nadine was shocked. "I couldn't go alone. Besides, what would I do with the boys?"

"I'll watch them. And you can watch my two another time when I want to go out." Nadine was clearly tempted, and her friend grinned at her. "Look, they have free lessons on Tuesday night at that new place downtown. Tomorrow's Tuesday; bring the boys over after dinner and just go!"

And Nadine did, though her palms were sweaty and her stomach was full of butterflies as she drove downtown the next night. Walking into the noisy dance hall was one of the hardest things she'd ever done. But once the music began, there wasn't time to be nervous. The room was full of people—some in couples, some alone—and Nadine found herself smiling as they all learned the steps together. She discovered that she loved line dancing, which didn't even require a partner; and after a few Tuesdays had gone by, she found that her new friends included several prospective dance partners.

Nadine's coworkers (and her children) soon noticed that she had a new spring in her step and a much brighter smile. And Nadine discovered that the minor irritations of life didn't bother her the way they once had. After all, there was always Tuesday to look forward to!

Repairing and maintaining your self-esteem take time and patience. But doing that will make you a more contented parent, and a much healthier role model for your children.

Make Room for Growth

IT MAY BE HARD to believe, but many single adults find that learning to live on their own opens doors and reveals possibilities they hadn't anticipated.

The day may come when a single mom sits down for an evening cup of tea after a busy, productive day and finds herself thinking unexpectedly, *I'm really happy.* Or a single dad may stand gazing down at a sleeping child and find himself basking in a warm glow he had never noticed before.

It is often change that breaks down the walls we've built for ourselves and helps us to become aware of all that is possible. Even if you did not choose to become a single parent, you may find yourself one day with a new circle of friends, with a new job or career goal, with abilities and talents you'd never acknowledged or explored before. It can be fun to have a whole closet to oneself, never to have the toilet seat left up (or down!), to be able to choose brilliant turquoise paint or fuschia carpeting without asking anyone's permission.

> Even if you did not choose to become a single parent, you may find yourself one day with a new circle of friends, with a new job or career goal, with abilities and talents you'd never acknowledged or explored before.

Sometimes, though, children don't react well to a single parent's newfound sense of peace and enjoyment. If Mom likes her new life too much, isn't that being disloyal to Dad? If Dad is too happy, does that mean he hates Mom? Are children being disloyal to one parent if they enjoy life with the other?

You can give yourself permission to enjoy the positive parts of your life as you discover them—and there will be more and more as time passes. You can also give your children permission to take their own time adjusting by not making yourself overly responsible for their feelings, and you can help them to realize that each of us is responsible for his or her own happiness. Again, sensitivity to feelings—both your own and your children's—and a little patience will help you arrive at the day when life feels good to *all* of you.

Dealing with Loneliness

REACHING THE POINT where life feels good can seem a long way off, and it is a rare single parent who has never struggled with feelings of isolation and loneliness. Evenings can be hard. What do you do when the children are finally asleep, the dishes and chores are done, and the house falls silent? It would be wonderful to have someone to talk to, but it's too late for the telephone. A movie would be fun, but how do you take the baby-sitter home without having to haul the children out of bed? Many single parents know how it feels to settle down for the evening with only the television for company and the depressing feeling that none of their friends (most of whom may be married) has any idea what being a single parent is really like.

All people feel alone occasionally, whether they're single or married. But somehow loneliness seems to be a much more pressing problem when you're a single parent. Dealing with loneliness begins with examining your expectations. Sometimes, because society seems to be geared to couples, we feel incomplete without a partner. No matter how much we might otherwise enjoy what we are doing, if we're doing it alone it just can't be fun. Can it?

COPING WITH LONELINESS

There are some positive steps you can take to combat the feeling of loneliness.

- Build a network of friends and make time to be with them. Simply having someone to talk to when you're feeling blue can make all the difference in the world.

- When you're feeling cheerful, start a list of things you'd like to do, books you'd like to read, projects you'd like to begin. Then, when loneliness strikes, get out your list and get going. Having something constructive to focus your energy on can be a wonderful way to dissipate the blues.

- Get involved with people—even if you don't feel like it. There are many organizations and groups in your community that need volunteers, and many businesses encourage and allow time for employees to get involved. Spend an hour a week vol-

Most of us learn eventually that being with the wrong person can be worse than being alone. Many single parents forget how lonely they felt in their marriages. Often they did not have time to feel the loneliness because they were so busy dealing with the problems. Amazingly enough, being alone can be a good thing. It can force us to develop our own strengths. Being alone can—if we let it—give us opportunities to explore within ourselves, and to develop new ideas and abilities.

Making It on Your Own

ALL TOO OFTEN, Chris found being single an overwhelming experience. She had been married for eighteen years, and her divorce had been unexpected

unteering at a hospital or a senior citizens' home. Tutor a student or mentor a young mother. Being involved in the lives of others will give you a new perspective on your own.

- Take time to nurture yourself. Yes, it works here, too!
- Learn to be yourself, by yourself. It's tempting when you're single to believe that things would be better if only you had a partner to share your life. And it's undeniably difficult when there is no one to hold you, touch you, or comfort you. But peace and contentment are things we all must find within ourselves, difficult as that may be. No one can "make" us happy. If you can find the strength and energy to be truly comfortable alone, you'll be far better able to build a healthy relationship when someone special does wander into your life.
- Ask for help if you need it. If you find feelings of loneliness and depression are too strong to handle alone, look for a therapist, pastor, or support group to help you.

and painful. Both she and her children, Keith and Debbie, had gone through many difficult adjustments, and Chris often felt terribly alone and hopelessly inadequate. Chris had purchased a small new house for her and the children.

Watching it being built filled her with hope but moving in seemed to mean one project after another. Her ex-husband had been the handy one; Chris hardly knew one end of a hammer from the other and had never been encouraged to learn. Still, settling into the new home gave Chris and the kids something to do together, something that was fresh and special and *theirs*.

> Although change and growth can be painful at times, the person you are afterward couldn't have come about any other way—someone who is an inspiration and a joy to everyone.

One detail of the house was a constant annoyance, however. Chris had wanted a ceiling fan in the family room but couldn't afford to put one in right away. She had requested that the builder wire it for her, and he had—but he'd left a bare lightbulb right in the center of the ceiling to complete the circuit. The glare of that ugly bare bulb bothered Chris every time she turned it on.

Chris found a perfect ceiling fan on sale at the hardware store several months later. Her brother offered to come and install it for her, but he was busy and weeks went by while the fan sat in its box in a corner. At last a Saturday night arrived when the kids were with their dad and Chris, lonely and bored, had had enough. Her eye fell on the fan in its box.

How hard can this be, anyway? she thought, as she ripped the box open.

It took hours, and Chris wanted to quit more than once. The instructions were in fractured English that she had trouble understanding, and the fan was large and hard to assemble alone. Her tools were inadequate. She had to make two calls to a neighbor to ask how to connect wires and where to find the circuit breaker. She almost fell off the ladder twice.

But when she flipped the switch and saw the fan's blades actually begin to turn, she felt a surge of elation and accomplishment she'd never experienced before. It worked! Even more miraculous, she had done it *herself*! It was such fun to watch Keith's and Debbie's faces the next day when she showed them what she'd done.

It didn't seem all that important to anyone else, but for Chris it was a new beginning. She discovered that not only could she do things she hadn't thought possible, she actually enjoyed working with her hands. She became a one-woman home-improvement operation. She painted jungle animals on the walls of the kids' bathroom. She acquired a drill and installed extra shelves in the bedroom closets. She planted roses and was thrilled when she cut the first blooms for her house; she joined a garden club to learn more about gardening and met a wonderful new group of friends.

Best of all, Chris, Keith, and Debbie spent a weekend together building a front patio. They carried bags of sand, smoothed it, and placed paving stones on it. They put together inexpensive garden furniture and hung up a bird feeder and wind chimes. And they planted a rainbow of brightly colored flowers.

Chris and her children shared a pizza on the patio when it was finished, smiling happily at one another over the pepperoni. And suddenly Chris realized it was going to be okay. It wasn't what she'd planned for herself and her children, and it wasn't exactly what she'd wanted—but it was going to be okay. In fact, life was starting to feel *good* again. And that was the best accomplishment of all.

You may find that defining your identity as a single parent also defines your role as a human being. Although change and growth can be painful at times, the person you are afterward couldn't have come about any other way—someone who is an inspiration and a joy to everyone. Keep your eyes and your mind open, try to enjoy the journey (bumps, wrong turns, and all), and watch what happens.

14

Unmarried with Children: Social Life and Significant Others

DAVE HAD HAD a wonderful night. He'd been out dancing with an old friend from college and he'd had more fun than he could remember in several years. As he whistled his way through the next morning, he realized that his daughter was not her usual cheerful self. Her lower lip protruded, her eyes wouldn't meet her father's, and Dave could have sworn he heard her muttering when his back was turned.

"Okay, Rachel," he finally said. "You've seemed unhappy all morning. Do you want to tell me what's bothering you?"

There was a long moment of silence; then, rather sullenly, "I don't like you going out, Dad."

Dave sighed, exasperated; they'd been through this before. And Rachel had made several "get acquainted" dinners positively miserable for Dave's helpless friends. He looked at his daughter's bowed head and felt a wave of both sympathy and frustration. He could understand her feelings, but he did his best to be a good father. Wasn't he entitled to have a life of his own sometimes?

Life for single parents can be a lonely thing. Living (and parenting) alone can be like living in a fortress; the longer we stay in it, the harder it may be to come out. It can be hard to meet people, scary to trust, tricky to overcome lingering feelings of hurt, rejection, or guilt.

And, that's not all. The logistic problems can be overwhelming. How do you squeeze time for dinner and a movie out of a week that already contains work, housework, and time with your children? What about money? And child care?

> Living (and parenting) alone can be like living in a fortress; the longer we stay in it, the harder it may be to come out.

Single parents do need lives of their own, and eventually most do find themselves ready to tackle the dating game. Unfortunately, like Dave, many single parents also find that their children aren't exactly thrilled with the concept. And when children are feeling insecure, they often show it by inventing new and creative forms of misbehavior.

But Why Do My Kids Act This Way?

IT'S REALLY NOT HARD to understand why so many children find their single parents' social lives threatening. A child's entire world is built around his relationship with his parents, and their relationship with each other. When those parents are no longer together, for whatever reason, and life, security, and belonging depend on one parent, the world can become a fragile and unstable place. We may tell our children "I love you and I would never choose to leave you," but for a child whose world revolves around one solitary adult, those words may provide little comfort.

It's normal for a child to cling to her parent and feel a sense of ownership, and to be jealous of anything that deflects that parent's attention. Many single parents have had the experience of introducing their sons and daughters to a new friend and being met with either indifference or outright hostility. Then again, some children go to the opposite extreme, trying relentlessly to find a new mommy or daddy, someone to fill the void in their own and their parents' lives. Either reaction can make parents and their partners terribly uncomfortable.

Does that mean you give up the entire idea? Or that you go out only when your children aren't around? It is easy for single parents to choose one extreme or the other—being totally insensitive to the feelings of their children, or over-reacting to children's demands and allowing themselves to be manipulated to unhealthy extremes. How can single parents ease the transition into new relationships for both themselves and their children?

So You Want to Have a Life: Helping Children Adjust

MONICA HAD JUST MET an interesting, exciting man. Her enthusiasm and happiness were obvious when she told thirteen-year-old Jesse and nine-year-old Samantha that she was planning to go with her new friend to an out-of-town concert. She was startled and a little angry when Jesse announced, in an authoritative tone, "You can't go out of town with this guy."

Monica knew it would not be helpful to tackle this subject while she and Jesse were upset, so she said only, "We'll talk about this later." That evening, she went into Jesse's room, where he was doing his homework, turned down the stereo a little, and said, "Are you ready to have a little talk with me now?"

Jesse looked up at his mother, then returned his gaze to his book. "I guess so," was all he said.

> It's normal for a child to cling to her parent and feel a sense of ownership, and to be jealous of anything that deflects that parent's attention.

Monica took a deep breath and began. "Honey, first I need to tell you that I'm the mom, and it is not okay for you to tell me what I can or can't do. But second, I really value your opinion and want to hear your thoughts and feelings. Do you want to tell me why you don't want me to go to this concert with my new friend?"

Jesse looked directly into his mother's eyes. "You don't know this man very well, Mom. How do you know you can trust him?"

Her son's evident concern and love touched Monica's heart. "Jesse, that is a very good point. I *don't* know him very well. I have a good feeling about him, but I don't know him yet. Would it make you feel better if we went with another couple who I do know? Come to think of it, that would make me feel better!"

Jesse nodded. "I think that would be very smart, Mom."

USING CONFLICT TO ESTABLISH CLOSENESS AND TRUST

- Postpone discussion of sensitive issues until there has been a cooling-off period and both you and your child are calm.
- Respectfully establish firm parent-child boundaries.
- Let children know that you value their opinion and are willing to consider their feelings.
- When appropriate, incorporate your child's opinion into a plan that works for both of you.

Monica added, "And how would you like it if I invite him over for dinner first, so we can all get to know him a little better? After all, I know I can trust your opinion."

Jesse sat up a little straighter and said, "If you want to."

Monica used a conflict with her son as an opportunity to build closeness. First she waited for a "cooling off" period instead of trying to deal with the problem when emotions were high. Then she kindly and firmly established the boundaries between parent and child: She acknowledged her son's feelings but let him know that it was not appropriate for him to tell her what she could or could not do. Next she told Jesse that she valued his opinion and then demonstrated the truth of that statement by incorporating his opinion into a plan. Finally, through this interaction, she taught Jesse how to express his opinions in ways that are respectful and helpful. What could have been a major conflict became an opportunity to enrich her relationship with her son. Unsolicited advice, however, is not always so helpful.

Dating with an Audience

MOST SINGLE PARENTS are the objects of a great deal of advice—both solicited and unsolicited—on the subject of dating. Everyone, from family to friends to ex-partners, has an opinion: "The sooner you get remarried, the better—your kids need a whole family." "Don't rush into anything—you don't want to make another mistake!" "Always bring your dates home. You need to find out from the beginning whether they're good with your kids." "Don't let your children meet your dates unless the relationship is serious. Too many people coming in and out of their lives is upsetting and they'll be hurt if you break up with someone they've become attached to." "Keep your private life away from your children—you don't want to give them ideas." "Enjoy your sexuality while you can. And it will teach your kids not to have hang-ups."

> Each parent must trust her own wisdom and knowledge of herself and her children to decide what is comfortable, what feels right, and what balances the needs and feelings of both adults and children.

Where on earth does the truth lie? Adult relationships are rarely simple and they seem to be even less so when children are involved. Dating too soon, while a child is grieving the loss of one parent, can cause unnecessary pain. Not dating at all can cause both parent and child to doubt that relationships are healthy or necessary. In the end, each parent must trust her own wisdom and knowledge of herself and her children to decide what is comfortable, what feels right, and what balances the needs and feelings of both adults and children. The answer will probably be different in each family but there are several things to keep in mind.

Work Toward Understanding

Q. I am a single mom with two children, six and nine years old. Lately I've been seeing a really wonderful man. This is the first good relationship I've had since my marriage ended and I don't want to lose it, but I'm worried about my kids. My boyfriend and I are sleeping together, but I only stay with him when my children are at their dad's house, and he never stays with me. My kids call me every night at the same time to tell me "good night," and they let me know they worry about where I am. I've been telling them that sometimes I'm just too tired to drive all the way home from my boyfriend's house so I sleep in the guest room, but I think my oldest has his doubts about that. Should I tell them the truth?

A. The fact that you feel the need to disguise what is happening with your boyfriend is a clue that you aren't entirely comfortable with your choices—and your children can sense your anxiety. Only you can decide whether to tell your children how important this new relationship is to you, and decide how much they need to know about it, but it is always wise to pay attention to the messages your own emotions are sending you. Finding ways to let your boyfriend and your children get to know one another better may help. It is also important to spend time alone with them and to consider carefully what it is you believe about relationships—and what you want your children to learn.

Frequently children in single-parent homes have experienced many changes in their short lives. Perhaps the most helpful thing you can do is make an effort to understand how your children are *feeling* about your adult relationships. If you can see that your children may be afraid of losing your time and attention, that they worry about you, that they feel threatened

HELPING YOUR CHILD ADJUST TO A NEW RELATIONSHIP

- Take time to listen to your child without defensiveness or explanations and use active listening so she feels understood.
- Ask your child if she would now be willing to listen to you.
- Don't engage in conduct you are ashamed of or feel compelled to keep hidden.
- Make sure your actions match your words.
- Do some problem solving to find solutions that work for everyone concerned.
- Above all, be patient.

or replaced or jealous, then you can deal honestly with their feelings, letting them know you understand and using emotional honesty to help them understand you.

Remember Dave? He discussed with a group of single friends at lunch one day his frustration over Rachel's resistance to his social life. These friends were able to give him a number of helpful suggestions, ideas all single parents might want to keep in mind:

Take time to listen to your child without defensiveness or explanations and use active listening so she feels understood. Whether or not you agree with them, your child's perceptions have a lot to do with how she behaves. Once a child knows her parent understands and accepts her feelings, she may have less need to demonstrate them with troubling behavior.

> Be sure you conduct your relationships in a way you wouldn't mind your children conducting theirs.

Ask your child if she would now be willing to listen to you. Children are usually more open when they have agreed to listen and when they feel listened to themselves. Your child may need to see that having friends is just as important to you as it is to her. You may choose to explain what a particular relationship means to you and what is—or is not—happening. Be honest; it will save untold trouble later on. But be aware, too, that it's important not to talk too much; the young people in your home don't need to know the intimate details of your relationships.

Remember that you are always your child's most important role model. "Do as I say, not as I do" doesn't hold much water these days, especially with teenagers. Be sure you conduct your relationships in a way you wouldn't mind your children conducting theirs.

Don't engage in conduct you are ashamed of or feel compelled to keep hidden. Some single parents develop an unhealthy pattern of secrecy (with the rationalization that their children don't need to know all the details) when the truth is that they are doing something they aren't proud of.

Your own instincts and inner wisdom will tell you what you need—if you are willing to listen. Single adults often begin unhealthy relationships (and ignore their own misgivings) because having *someone* seems better than being alone and lonely. Most eventually realize that there are worse things than being alone; violating their own moral and ethical principles is one of them. If you are uneasy with any aspect of an adult relationship, it may be better to take your time.

For example, some parents are comfortable having a friend spend the night while their children are in the same house. Others choose not to sleep together, or to do so only when children are with the other parent. Whatever you decide to do, be sure you feel comfortable with your actions. If you find you must lie or bend the truth to explain a relationship to your children or friends, that relationship may not be a healthy one for you—or at least, not yet.

> If you are seeing someone who is a regular part of your life, include him or her in a family meeting with your children and have everyone share in the compliments, brainstorming, choosing of solutions, and planning special activities.

Make sure your actions match your words. When you tell your children, "You're important to me," but somehow never make room in your life for special time with them, children don't feel important at all and may react with resentment and hostility. If your significant other is included in everything, your children may feel pushed out. Be sure you spend time with your children alone, whether it's doing special things, talking, or just hanging out.

Do some problem solving to find solutions that work for everyone concerned. Plan ways for you and your children to have time together, time alone, and time with friends. If you are seeing someone who is a regular part of your life, include him or her in a family meeting with your children and have everyone share in the compliments, brainstorming, choosing of solutions, and planning special activities (see chapter 9). You will learn a great deal about your significant other by seeing how he or she functions in a family meeting setting.

However, it is important to give your partner several chances. It takes time for children and adults to learn the skills for participating respectfully in family meetings. Use whatever doesn't go perfectly (and we have never seen a "perfect" family meeting) as an opportunity for discussion and learning. A willingness to learn is much more important than perfection.

Above all, be patient. It takes time to adjust to change, to new relationships, and to new ideas. Most children eventually figure out that a parent who is happy and interested in life is a whole lot easier to get along with than one who's depressed and isolated.

Single Parents and Sexuality

THERE IT IS: the *s* word. In a world where teens (even preteens) experiment with sex, where sex is used to sell everything from beer to cosmetics to coffee, and where the consequences of unsafe sex can be so devastating, it's not surprising that single parents are often unsure how to feel, what to think, and how to proceed with a relationship. Is there a "right" way or a "wrong" way? Although intimate relationships are outside the scope of this book, there are a couple of ideas that may help you make healthy decisions about life as a single adult— particularly a single parent with a young audience watching your every move.

Kathleen was thirty-eight when her husband died of cancer. The final stages of his illness had been traumatic for the entire family. Their grief was strong, and sometimes it felt as though the grieving would never end. For the first year, it was easy for Kathleen to lose herself in her children and her work—staying busy eased the pain.

"For a long, long time," she told a friend over lunch one day, "I never even thought about sex. Oh, sometimes I missed being held and loved. Doug and I had such a good relationship. But I just felt so sad and empty that the idea of having sex never crossed my mind. I'm not unattractive and I suppose I could have gone out occasionally. I guess I was just numb.

"But all of a sudden," Kathleen continued with some embarrassment, "it seems to be all I think about. If I go to a movie or read a novel, the sexy parts really affect me. I'm starting to think I'm obsessed. What am I supposed to do? Is there something wrong with me?"

Many single parents, male and female, can identify with Kathleen. The death of a spouse or the emotional upheaval associated with a divorce can kill sexual feelings for months, sometimes years, even in a person who has enjoyed an active sex life with a beloved partner. Other things seem much more important: making sure the children are adjusting, dealing with job stress, all of those pressures we're so familiar with. Sooner or later, however, frozen feelings begin to thaw. Having a physical relationship with someone not only begins to seem possible, it may seem necessary!

Remember that sexuality is a normal part of adult life and sexual feelings are perfectly healthy. You are the only person who can decide whether you want your relationships to include sex and how you will handle that, but it is normal to feel the desire for human touch and contact.

Remember that your children will form their own decisions about what is right and wrong by watching you. What they observe in your relationship with a new partner may be very different from what they observed in the last stages  of your marriage, and it may be wise to check their perceptions and feelings occasionally. Even when they like your new friend, children may believe that kissing, holding hands, or other forms of touching are disloyal to the missing parent. Open communication, active listening, sensitivity, and a little patience will help you work through these issues together.

Remember, too, that you are highly vulnerable in the aftermath of a death or divorce, or when you've been alone for a long period of time. All too often, single adults suffer from a low sense of self-worth and become involved in a relationship they're not ready for (or that they're ashamed of later) because having someone want their company is so intoxicating. It is easy to become involved romantically (and sexually) with a sympathetic friend, an attorney, a counselor, or a casual acquaintance when you've been alone or when you've been hurt. It's undoubtedly easier said than done, but try to be patient and gentle with yourself, and don't be afraid to move slowly.

Self-Respect Leads to Mutual Respect

WHEN SINGLE PARENTS feel lonely and insecure, they may be more concerned about being wanted than considering what *they* want. In other words, they may ask, "Does this person want me?" instead of "Do I want this person?" Too many tragic relationships are created because people don't value themselves and their own healthy needs and desires. Wanting to be loved by "just anyone" is not a healthy need or desire. Wanting to be loved by someone you respect is a very healthy need and desire.

It may be a cliché, but it is undeniably true: Healthy people are far more likely to have healthy relationships. Only when you have learned to value and nurture yourself are you able to create an *interdependent* relationship with a partner, one in which you can both hold on to yourself and enjoy real intimacy with another. The more comfortable and whole you feel *alone* (because you value yourself), the better your choices are likely to be when you begin to date.

As much as possible, try not to think of everyone you meet as a potential mate. Most single adults feel a bit desperate at times, particularly if they've been alone for a while or if close friends or an ex-spouse are marrying or finding romance. Sometimes we evaluate coworkers, fellow students, neighbors, or people we meet at church solely on the basis of their attractiveness or suitability as a partner. Judging people this way can cause us to disregard people who might prove to be wonderful friends, part of the support network that all single parents need. If you are taking time to nurture yourself and getting involved in things you enjoy, the chances are good that you will meet people who can become wonderful friends or, perhaps, more than friends.

> The more comfortable and whole you feel *alone* (because you value yourself), the better your choices are likely to be when you begin to date.

What About the Kids?

BUT, YOU MAY BE WONDERING, *what if I do meet someone I want to become involved with? Is there a right way—or a wrong way—to handle that relationship with my children? If I become sexually active, will they assume that's okay for them, too? I'd like to have an adult relationship, but I'm not sure I'm comfortable with my kids having one!*

Sorting out relationships and how children will react to them can be difficult. Randy had been separated from his wife, Mary, for only one month when he met Leigh. Sparks flew when Leigh and Randy were together—they felt an immediate passion for each other and soon were spending all of their free time together. Randy was eager to introduce Leigh to his seven-year-old daughter, Sarah, who was coming for her weekend visit with her dad. He knew Sarah was still struggling with her parents' decision to separate, but he felt sure she'd love Leigh, and he thought the coming weekend would be a great time for them to get acquainted.

The weekend, however, did not go smoothly. Randy was so infatuated that he couldn't seem to keep his hands off of his girlfriend. As Sarah watched her dad and Leigh giggling and teasing, she felt more and more embarrassed; her dad certainly had never acted this way with her mom. Randy invited Leigh to spend the night without a second thought, and Sarah grew more uncomfortable by the minute. When her dad tucked her into bed, he said with a grin, "Isn't Leigh great, honey?" Sarah nodded silently, blinking back confused, angry tears.

When Sarah woke up the next morning, she forgot all about Leigh—until she skipped into her dad's bedroom to say good morning and found him making love to Leigh. Sarah's words died in her throat. Confused and frightened, she ran back to her room crying. She called her mother and pleaded with her to come pick her up early.

Sarah came home from her dad's house feeling both neglected and confused by Randy's behavior with Leigh. Sarah's mother was angry and immediately called her attorney to ask that Sarah's visits with her father be restricted.

A judge later determined that Sarah needed time to adjust to her parents' divorce and it was in her best interests that her visits with her father occur only if he had no guests—and that she shouldn't visit overnight for six months.

Randy's enthusiasm for his new love was understandable, but he forgot to consider Sarah's feelings. This does not mean that children should rule the household and that parents should never do anything that their children don't like. However, if Randy had considered Sarah's vulnerability, he might have moved with more caution, allowing Sarah time to adjust at her own pace. Sarah might never have liked Leigh, even if her father had been less demonstrative; it's hard for most children to watch someone take the place of their mother or father. However, children can learn to accept other adults in their lives, in time, when parents are considerate and respectful of both their own needs and the needs of their children.

> Children can learn to accept other adults in their lives, in time, when parents are considerate and respectful of both their own needs and the needs of their children.

Like it or not, the way you conduct your relationships and intimate life has a direct effect on your children. It may also be wise to remember that several studies tell us a sobering fact: The risk of child abuse increases significantly when single parents invite an unrelated adult to live with them. It may not seem fair, but single parents may be faced with a choice between their own immediate happiness (or pleasure) and the well-being of their children. Exercising caution and restraint may be difficult, even painful—but the benefits for both you and your children may prove to be well worth the effort.

But Can You Keep Everyone Happy?

EVEN WHEN A RELATIONSHIP is healthy, working out the details can be difficult for everyone concerned. Janet collapsed into a chair at her single parents' group one evening with a sigh. The group facilitator laughed. "Looks like you might have a problem, Janet," she said.

Janet sighed again. "I don't know whether having a boyfriend is worth the trouble." Then she laughed. "What a dumb term for a forty-five-year-old man, but 'significant other'? Anyway, my daughter Jessica loves Steve. When he comes to visit, Jessica is all over us, wanting our attention and interrupting everything we try to do. I told her I wanted to spend time alone with Steve, but she says he's her boyfriend and she wants time alone with him, too. In fact, she wants him to be her daddy.

"What should I do? Steve and I are in an exclusive relationship but I'm afraid to let Jessica get too attached to him because I don't know if we'll get married. I don't want her to be hurt if we end the relationship. And occasionally I'd like some time alone with Steve. Do we always have to go out to be alone?"

A number of heads nodded vigorously as Janet finished; others had had the same problem.

"Why don't we see if we can come up with some solutions to Janet's problem?" the facilitator asked. It wasn't hard for the group, with their variety of experiences, to offer some suggestions. Janet heard several ideas she wanted to try. When Janet arrived at the next week's meeting she told her friends what had happened.

"Steve and I decided to have a family meeting with Jessica (even though I felt a little awkward including an 'outsider' in a 'family' meeting). I took some time to tell Jessica how much I appreciated her help around the house that week. Then each of us got a chance to say what we felt and what we wanted from our relationships. It was interesting—I learned some things about both Steve and Jessica that I might never have known otherwise. Then we decided to brainstorm some ideas about how we could spend our time so that no one felt left out.

"We planned some things that Jessica and I would do alone together—she wanted to go for ice cream after school and maybe to the park—and we talked about some things that Steve and I planned to do on our own. Then we agreed that when Steve comes over to our house, he and Jessica will spend ten minutes alone together, maybe to read a story or play a game.

"We agreed that after Jessica's time with Steve we will all have dinner together. Then Jessica will leave us to have some time alone. She said it would help her if she could have a friend over. I'd never thought of that. We also agreed that Jessica would be allowed to interrupt us three times. After all, she needs to know that I'm not too busy for her. Our agreements seem to be working pretty well so far, and it feels more comfortable for all of us now when Steve comes over. And if it stops working, we'll just discuss it again at the next family meeting."

Jessica was willing to cooperate with her mother and her boyfriend because she felt a sense of belonging and significance through her involvement—and because she felt loved. Making sure the message of love gets through is so very important, yet in the midst of busy lives and new relationships it's often harder to do than we think.

Dealing with the Belief Behind the Behavior

AS DISCUSSED IN chapter 10, behavior never happens in a vacuum—there are always beliefs and feelings behind it. Sometimes parents try to tackle behavior head-on by lecturing and controlling, but Anne, a single mother with a new love in her life, found a special way of getting past her young son's behavior to the belief behind it.

Anne was nervous about bringing Richard home to meet her sons, but he was a wonderful man and she was fairly sure her boys would like him. Jeff, her older son, accepted Richard with enthusiasm, but Jonathan, her little one, reacted with outright hostility.

PUTTING THE PIECES TOGETHER

Janet's experience incorporates the principles of effective parenting:

- Children need to know they matter to you, and that they still have access to you even when you are busy or with someone else. If the access isn't planned, they will take it anyway with constant demands for attention. Also, when kids help plan the number of interruptions they can have, they seldom use their total allotment. Involvement invites cooperation.

- Children feel they belong and are significant when they are included in problem solving or planning sessions. And when they feel they belong, they are less likely to feel discouraged—and less likely to misbehave.

- When a difficult situation arises, decide what you will do instead of what you will make your children do. Trying to make children do something often invites power struggles. Letting children know your expectations in advance gives them an opportunity to choose their responses—and to experience the consequences of their choices. It is important to follow through with kindness and firmness. Firmness requires action; kindness requires eliminating lectures and put-downs.

"We don't need you here," he said to the startled Richard. Then he disappeared into his room with a resounding thud of the door.

Anne was surprised and embarrassed, but she realized that Jonathan was probably afraid—afraid of changing their life together, afraid that if Mom loved someone new she would love him less, afraid that nothing would be right anymore.

One evening, after dinner had been eaten and all the evening's work finished, Anne sat down with Jonathan. "Would you like to hear a story?" she asked. "This one is about our family."

As the little boy snuggled against her side, Anne smiled at Jeff, who was sitting across the room, and lit a tall candle.

"These candles represent our family," she told the boys. "This tall one is for me," she said pointing to the candle she'd just lit. "This flame represents my love."

"It's bright," Jonathan said, entranced by the flickering flame.

"It is," his mother agreed. "That's because I have so much love in me." Anne picked up a smaller candle and lit it with the flame from her own. "This candle is your big brother, Jeff. When he was born, I gave him all my love. But look—I still have all my love left."

She put Jeff's candle in a holder and picked up a smaller one. "This candle is you, Jonathan."

"It's red," the little boy said delightedly. "That's my favorite color!"

Anne smiled and ruffled his hair, and lit his little red candle from her tall one. "When you were born, I gave you all my love. Jeff still has all my love, and I still have all my love left." The candles' flames danced brilliantly. "See all the bright love we have in this family?"

Then Anne picked up another tall candle and used the flame from her own to light it. "Now I am giving my love to Richard." Anne pointed to the two smaller candles where the flames still glowed with radiance, and said to Jonathan, "You still have all my love, Jeff still has all my love, and I still have all my love left. That's the way love works. The more you give away, the more you have. Every candle we add to our family just brings more love into our home. Richard is someone new and it will take you some time to get to know him. But I have plenty of love for all of you."

> Facing the changes that occur in a family can be a complicated process, but it can also be an opportunity to build a truly special and lasting relationship with your children and to teach them understanding and coping skills they will have for a lifetime.

Anne and the boys were quiet for a moment, watching the flames and letting the message sink in. Then Jonathan gave his mom a big hug and went off to get ready for bed.

There would still be problems to be solved and adjustments to be made. There undoubtedly would be rough spots ahead. But understanding that his mother had plenty of love to share made Jonathan feel far less vulnerable, and increased the chances that he could eventually accept a new person in his family.

Facing the changes that occur in a family can be a complicated process, but it can also be an opportunity to build a truly special and lasting relationship with your children and to teach them understanding and coping skills they will have for a lifetime. If it seems to take more time than you would like, try to be patient. Your children may believe you are their only lifeline and they may be reluctant to release you to a life—and relationships—of your own.

Have faith that with time your children can handle the challenge and become better people because of the skills they develop in the process. You will all be healthier in the long run if your life balances the well-being of your children with your own happiness and contentment. Learn to listen with your heart as well as your head, and eventually that balance will come.

15

Your Child's Other Parent: After the Divorce

ALTHOUGH THERE ARE many reasons adults raise children alone, the vast majority of single parents have endured a divorce. That means that for most single parents, an important—and often stressful—part of parenting is coping with their child's other parent.

How do you get along now that you're not married? How do you handle visitation, custody, and new relationships in either household? What do you do if you simply can't stand each other? What if your child's other parent never visits, never calls, doesn't care? What if he or she never contributes to your children's support? And what do you tell your children?

Coping with Divorce

DIVORCE IS A highly traumatic event in anyone's life. Even for those who believe that leaving their marriage is the best choice they can make for themselves and their children, divorce is still traumatic. It involves not only a sweeping change of the family structure, but new homes, new jobs, new living conditions, new lives. Most divorcing parents realize that children have the best chance of emerging from divorce whole and healthy when their parents can build an amicable relationship, when children can love and spend time with both parents, and when they are spared open hostility between two people they love. However, most divorcing parents are so caught up in their personal pain and anger that they often overlook the effect their behavior will have on their children.

Newly divorced parents frequently are trying to meet their children's physical and emotional needs at a time when major decisions must be made and their own resources are at low ebb. Adults who are in the throes of a divorce  frequently suffer from depression and anxiety, both of which make them less responsive to their children's needs—and which, in turn, may create discouraged, frightened children who misbehave in a misguided attempt to reach their parents. Is it any wonder that both adults and children suffer in the aftermath of divorce?

"Build an amicable relationship" sounds good. But whatever the reasons you divorced, your inevitably tangled emotions can make it all but impossible. "You don't know my ex-wife," mutters one man. "I'm willing to try," chimes in a woman, "but my ex-husband does everything he can to hurt me."

Most parents love their children and worry about the effects a divorce will have on them (when they are thinking rationally). Most are aware that open hostility, negative and critical remarks about the absent parent (even when they're true), and manipulative actions and comments can be devastating to children. Yet sometimes the temptation to strike back is irresistible. Many times parents feel the only way to keep their children's love is to compete—to show more love, buy more gifts, do more for the child than the other parent. Children, bewildered, hurting, and often blaming themselves, can become the most potent weapons between warring parents—and the ultimate victims.

Divorced Parents Remain Connected (One Way or Another)

WHEN YOU SHARE a child with someone, that person may be a part of your life for years, like it or not. Overcoming hurt, anger, disappointment, jealousy, guilt, and regret enough to carry on a civil relationship with that person can seem impossible. Yes, too many parents disappear, don't care, don't pay support. But some parents wish they could be involved in their children's lives and wish they could find a new way to relate to their ex-spouse.

Is it really possible? Can divorced parents share their children's lives? Can they show up at school programs, high school graduations, or weddings without having to sit at opposite ends of the room? Can they discuss problems at school, illness, or financial arrangements without fighting the same old battles? Is it possible for wounded adults to put their children first?

Not always, perhaps; after all, we're human, we have our own needs, and we do make mistakes. But building a working relationship after divorce is possible, and both children and adults are invariably better off for it.

> When you share a child with someone, that person may be a part of your life for years, like it or not.

Building a Working Partnership

DIVORCE IS NOT the end of parenting. It marks a change in direction, but the opportunity remains to raise children who know they have two parents who love them. Healing, forgiveness, and rebuilding an old relationship in a new form takes time, maturity, and a great deal of commitment—when those things are possible at all—and unfortunately, all stories don't have happy endings. Facing hurts and old memories is painful and that pain doesn't fade as quickly as we might wish. Still, our children's emotional health and well-being remain the best reasons to work at making things different. But how?

It simply isn't true that parents who couldn't get along as marriage partners cannot work together as coparents. They can. But working together as coparents means breaking the old patterns of relating to one another and learning new ones. It means putting your children's welfare first—ahead of your hurt, your anger, and other emotions. It means cooperating with the other parent about raising the children no matter how you may feel about each other. It means sharing an interest in your children's activities and feelings, sharing responsibility for your children's care, respecting the other parent's rights and privacy, and developing ways to communicate about the children's needs and problems. It also means accepting the difficult truth that you probably can't change your ex-spouse or the way he or she chooses to run a household.

A Word About Fathers

THERE ARE MANY dedicated single fathers, both custodial and noncustodial, who devote endless time, energy, and resources to their children. Those fathers share both the frustrations and joys of watching their children grow and develop, and they deserve to be acknowledged and encouraged. Statistics, however, tell us some sobering facts. More than a quarter of all children under the age of eighteen live in single-parent homes—and the overwhelming majority of those single parents are mothers. Sadly, statistics also tell us that almost half of all divorced fathers fail to see their children regularly and two-thirds fail to support them adequately. The results for children, economically and emotionally, are devastating.

American culture over the years has tended to minimize the importance of fathers. We have traditionally viewed raising children, especially young ones, as women's work. Though that perception is changing, it remains true that changing diapers, spoon feeding strained vegetables, and walking the floor with a crying infant are not perceived as masculine endeavors.

Fathers often become more involved as their children grow older, but consistency and regular participation in the rhythms and rituals of everyday life are important from the beginning. Fathers play crucial roles in the emotional, moral, and intellectual development of their children, and the absence of fathers creates a void.

> If you are a father, you have a critical part to play in your children's life—and no one can play that particular part but you.

Do children need their mothers? Absolutely. Can stepfathers and close family friends help fill the gap and provide positive male role models? Certainly. Yet the bottom line remains unchanged: No one can truly replace a child's father. And even when a child, a teenager, a young adult, has not seen his or her father for years, the yearning may remain. Sometimes a sense of betrayal and abandonment remains as well, and that can cripple a child's trust or willingness to risk marriage and parenthood himself.

If you are a father, you have a critical part to play in your children's life—and no one can play that particular part but you. If you've been absent from your children's lives, it's never too late to begin. Yes, you may encounter resistance from your children's mother and, possibly, from your children themselves. Taking the time to learn effective communication skills and Positive Discipline parenting principles will help you respond. There are also a growing number of support groups and Internet sites for single fathers. Ask for help if you need it; be willing to practice patience. But there may never again be as good a time as now.

The Noncustodial Parent

IN AN IDEAL WORLD, children enjoy the active love and involvement of both parents. If you are a noncustodial parent, it may be difficult for you to participate regularly in your children's lives. If you live at a distance, your contact with your children may be limited to occasional summer and holiday visits. Noncustodial parents often report that they lose their sense of family connection without the daily routine of living together. Time with children and emotional connection are closely related; one reason noncustodial parents sometimes fail to pay child support is that they no  longer feel an emotional bond with children they may see only rarely. Noncustodial parents (especially mothers) sometimes believe that society looks down on them for not having their children with them; they may feel defensive and ashamed, not a climate that encourages closeness and understanding.

Still, children benefit when both parents remain connected and involved, and there are many ways to be a vital part of their lives. Regular phone calls are a wonderful way to stay in touch. Letters and cards can be kept, re-read, and treasured. Even the fax machine and e-mail can come in handy. One father gave his children a fax machine for Christmas and regularly sends notes, drawings, cartoons, and messages from wherever he happens to be.

STAYING CONNECTED: SUGGESTIONS FOR NONCUSTODIAL PARENTS

- Make regular phone calls. Even if you live in the same town, a quick call to say good night and hear the day's happenings will help you and your child feel connected. If contact with your ex is a problem, arrange to call at a specific time and ask that your child be allowed to answer the phone.

- Remember holidays, birthdays, and special events. If you can't be present, send cards, e-mail, or faxes.

- Send a double-entry journal back and forth to record events, thoughts, and feelings.

- Share yourself with your children. Take time to share your personal history, hobbies, and skills.

- When you are with your children, have family meetings and use Positive Discipline parenting skills to build trust and closeness. Never use your time with your children to manipulate their behavior; for instance, don't say, "If you don't behave, I won't pick you up next weekend."

- Have faith. Children sense your attitude and will feel the energy of your love even when you can't be with them all the time.

If you travel without your children or live far away from them, sending a "treasure box" filled with shells, leaves, rocks, or small souvenirs from the places you visit can let them know that they are always in your thoughts and close to your heart. Try sending a double-entry journal back and forth, recording your activities and thoughts and leaving room for your children to record theirs. Anything that keeps you tuned in and in touch is well worth the effort it takes.

It is sometimes difficult to feel like a parent when you don't have custody of your children. Sometimes their feelings and behavior can be harder to deal with when your time together is limited; and you may feel that an occasional weekend is hardly worth the effort. If you don't have a lot of time together, work at improving the *quality* of the time you do spend. Do simple things, but do them together. Share *yourself* with your children; teach them your skills, involve them in your hobbies and interests, show them who you are and what you do, and let them be a part of your life. The best solution is probably the hardest to find: a balance of continuity and consistency, love and attention.

Try to end each visitation on a positive note. Children often fear that their noncustodial parent won't want to see them again if they misbehave, and parents sometimes use that threat to motivate children to behave properly. Your children are less likely to feel rejected if you resolve any differences *before* they leave. Making family meetings a part of the time you spend together can help.

If it's at all possible, try to work *with* your child's other parent at raising your children. Show that you are interested in child care decisions, school events, religious training. Offer your opinions without criticizing those of your former mate. You might try giving the other parent a copy of this book, attending the same parenting class (perhaps at different times!), or finding other ways to create a consistent environment for the children you love.

Try to remember, even when the going is tough, that your children started life with two parents and you are one of them, an irreplaceable part of who they are. Children are able to sense the energy of honest love and caring and will know that you are committed to them even when you aren't able to spend a lot of time together. Continuing to be involved after a divorce can be difficult, even painful, for both mothers and fathers, yet it may be the greatest gift you ever give your children.

How *Does* Divorce Affect Children?

MOST DIVORCED PARENTS have heard the horror stories about children who are so damaged by their parents' divorces that they never develop self-confidence, self-esteem, or healthy relationships of their own. Recently several states have considered legislation that would end no-fault divorce on the grounds that, while divorcing adults no longer fight about who is to blame for a marriage's demise, they frequently turn child support, custody, and visitation into battlegrounds—with serious consequences for children. Is it possible for parents to end a relationship without damaging their children—and each other?

> Try to remember, even when the going is tough, that your children started life with two parents and you are one of them, an irreplaceable part of who they are.

A University of Nebraska study recently found that children's adjustment and their emotional health are far more dependent on the intensity of their parents' conflicts, custodial parents' parenting skills, involvement of noncustodial parents, economic hardships, and stressful life changes than they are on divorce itself. The good news is that all of these critical factors are issues that caring, committed parents can do something about.

Divorce *does* affect children. Yet when parents watch their own words and attitude, get help for themselves when they need it, and consider the impact of their actions on their children, the damage can be minimized. Although children of divorced parents can and do grow up to be capable, confident, happy people, it is helpful for parents to remember a few things.

Divorce feels entirely different for children than it does for parents. Children base their entire world on their family structure. When that structure collapses, the child's world is temporarily without supports. Children have a different sense of time than adults; they do not understand that the chaos is

UNDERSTANDING THE EFFECTS OF DIVORCE ON CHILDREN

- Divorce feels entirely different for children than it does for parents.
- Divorce affects children differently at different ages.
- Effective communication skills will help you get into your child's world and understand her feelings and worries.

temporary. What they do know is that they are dependent on the family and that the family has now fallen apart.

Children often feel helpless. They can't prevent the divorce, fix it, or rescue Mom or Dad. No one gives priority to their wishes, concerns, and fears. Children may feel intense loneliness. Divorce is an acutely painful, long-remembered experience that children may endure with the uncomfortable feeling that they are alone in the world.

Divorce affects children differently at different ages. Anthony E. Wolf, Ph.D., has found that children wrestle with a variety of issues, depending on their own developmental process (*"Why Did You Have to Get a Divorce—and When Can I Get a Hamster?" A Guide to Parenting Through Divorce,* Noonday, 1998). When children are younger than two years of age, their parents' separation appears to affect their sense of trust and attachment. From the ages two to five, they suffer most from the stress associated with change and loss.

By the age of six, children are old enough to worry, and frequently experience anxiety about where they will live, what will happen to them, and how they will cope with their own sense of conflicting loyalties. Teens' complex needs for both independence and connection are disrupted when their parents divorce, which may escalate rebellion and conflict with both parents.

Effective communication skills will help you get into your child's world and understand her feelings and worries. Most parents have difficulty accepting the truth that they cannot guarantee that their children will not feel pain, nor are there magic words and actions that will take away the suffering. If you refrain from either blaming your ex-partner or defending yourself and simply *listen,* your inner wisdom and love for your child will let you know how to help. Avoiding the traps of postdivorce parenting and establishing a respectful coparenting relationship (when possible) with your child's other parent will help, too.

The Absent Parent

Q. My husband left me when I was three months pregnant with our second child. Our oldest was barely three at the time and doesn't remember her father.

Their father isn't a part of our lives at all; in fact, I haven't heard from him in a couple of years. Both children are in elementary school now and have been asking lots of questions about their father. I think they feel depressed because they don't have a dad and their friends do. How can I help them deal with this?

A. Because children are egocentric for most of their early years (seeing themselves as the center of their own universe), they sometimes believe a parent's absence is somehow their fault. Children are also gifted observers but poor interpreters; they can see that other children have dads and can only wonder why they do not.

The same skills that work so well in other settings will help you here, too. Use active listening to learn about your children's feelings and to validate those feelings. Use emotional honesty to share with them the simple truths of what happened between you and their father. Remain "askable"; let them know it's okay to want to know more. Do your best not to take their feelings and longings personally; their grief about not knowing their father does not mean they do not love and appreciate you. And have faith in your children's ability to deal with this challenge. Effective parents don't try to protect their children from all pain but do help them learn to deal with it.

It is normal for a child to show curiosity about a missing parent. He may feel angry at that parent for disappearing. And he needs to understand that the parent did not leave because the child was "bad." He may idealize the parent he does not know personally. Fantasy can seem much better than reality.

Encouragement, lots of listening, and a willingness to deal honestly with the differences between your family and the traditional picture of a "normal" one will help your child make sense of a sometimes confusing and disappointing world. And yes, one loving, committed parent truly is enough.

Avoiding the Pitfalls of Postdivorce Parenting

NO ONE CAN tell you exactly how to build a working partnership with your children's other parent; it takes trial and error, effort and commitment. There are, however, a few pitfalls to mark and avoid.

Respect your child's need to love and spend time with the other parent. Children are amazing. They have the ability to see their parents' faults and

AVOIDING THE PITFALLS OF POSTDIVORCE PARENTING

- Respect your child's need to love and spend time with the other parent.
- Resist the temptation to use your children as spies.
- Accept that you cannot control your child's other parent.
- Don't invite manipulation by criticizing your "ex" or rescuing your child.

flaws clearly and yet to love them anyway. They may know, for instance, that Dad often breaks his promises, or that Mom is flaky and unreliable. Still, they also know that their parents are part of who *they* are; attacking your child's other parent or interfering in the relationship they have with each other hurts the child—and may damage her respect for you. Most children want to go on loving both parents despite those parents' opinions of each other—and often despite neglect, broken promises, and human failure.

Parents can be insecure and vulnerable in the aftermath of a divorce and it may be tempting to influence a child's loyalty by demeaning the other parent, or by being possessive and controlling. It helps to remember that wanting to see and spend time with the other parent doesn't mean your child is betraying you or that he doesn't love you. Children usually find it far easier to love several adults than to be forced to choose between two.

Our feelings are easily hurt when circumstances require us to give up time with our children, even for a weekend. Unfortunately, children often wind up afraid to love Mom when they're with Dad and afraid to love Dad when they're with Mom, afraid to let either parent know that they enjoy being with the other. Life becomes a balancing act, trying to keep both parents happy and secure—and the ultimate loser will be the child.

Sometimes, too, a noncustodial parent who wants to be involved in a child's life is shut out by an insecure custodial parent. Not only does the child lose the opportunity for a life with two active parents but the custodial parent may lose a valuable source of support, help, and advice.

Occasionally the noncustodial parent fights for the children's loyalty by being the "good" parent, providing special treats and outings every time they are together. This makes life difficult both for the children, who need order and daily routines, and for the custodial parent, who may resent being the one responsible for day-to-day discipline and maintenance. (It eventually becomes difficult for the "good" parent also, because children will learn to expect special treats all the time.)

Remember that it is normal for children to want their parents to be together—and that they try sometimes to engineer a reconciliation. Frustrating and embarrassing as these efforts may be for you, you can recognize your children's feelings with compassion and understanding while still being honest about your situation (see chapter 4).

Resist the temptation to use your children as spies. It is difficult not to be curious about what goes on in the other parent's home. For instance, when an ex-partner begins a new relationship, you may find yourself struggling with hurt, bitterness, anger, or rejection. The idea that your ex is out there enjoying love and romance with someone new can be like a grain of sand in your shoe—a constant irritation.

Temptation arises when we realize our children know exactly what is going on at our ex-partner's house and all we need to do is ask one little question. . . .

Eddie came home from his mom's house one morning and announced that he and Mom had had a wonderful evening with Jerry, Mom's new boyfriend.

"We went out for pizza," Eddie said, "and then we played a game together." Then he added innocently, "And then Jerry spent the night with us." Dad, hurting, jealous, and a little bit angry, said, "Oh yeah? And where did he sleep?"

It doesn't matter how Eddie answers. As we've mentioned, children have incredibly sensitive antennae where their parents' feelings and motives are concerned, and by the time Dad's question had registered, Eddie was already weighing the consequences of his answer—and squirming inside. The only way he could avoid betraying his mother while satisfying his father's curiosity was to lie or say, "I don't know."

Children caught between two parents live with conflicting loyalties, loving both, wanting to protect the one who's hurting, wanting to avoid conflict.

Even if the relationship between ex-spouses is friendly, there are inevitable differences in life in the two households, and the knowledge that our children might be sources of "inside information" is dangerously tempting.

But employing our children as spies is a risky business. Most children want to be free to love both parents and to participate fully in both homes—to have two families. Being used by Mom as a weapon against Dad, or by Dad as a spy in Mom's house is painful and uncomfortable, and children often resort to keeping the two halves of their family as separate as possible, not talking to one parent about what the other is doing for fear of causing hurt or anger. And "don't talk" rules, wherever they come from, can be emotionally devastating.

> Most children want to be free to love both parents and to participate fully in both homes—to have two families.

What's a single parent to do? Perhaps the best thing is to develop your own antennae, to become aware and tuned in to your child's feelings, and then to be willing to work respectfully with those feelings. When you can understand the whole situation and the feelings of everyone involved, you can at least talk together—and possibly reach an understanding that allows healing to take place.

Beth was driving her young son, Mark, home from school one afternoon. Mark's father had just told her he planned to take Mark with him to visit his new girlfriend and her children in Arizona for Christmas. Christmas was only a month away, but Mark had yet to mention the trip to his mom, and Beth's instincts told her that she needed to help him talk about it. Although Beth wasn't at all sure she was happy about the prospect of spending Christmas alone while her only son was with his father, she knew she had to make it safe for Mark to go and to enjoy his time with his dad.

"You'll probably have a wonderful time with Dad and Carol at Christmas," Beth said conversationally as they pulled away from the school. Mark turned to her with shock written all over his face. "You *know* about that?" he asked. And as Beth watched, his shoulders sagged in obvious relief.

Beth's inner wisdom gave her the clues she needed to make sense of Mark's reaction. "Were you afraid to tell me about your trip because you were afraid it would hurt my feelings?" she asked. Mark nodded, still shy about saying too much.

Beth was then able to explain how she did feel. "How would you feel if your best friend suddenly had a new friend and didn't want to play with you ever again?" Mark knew the answer right away. "I'd feel bad," he said simply.

"Well," Beth continued quietly, "I still feel a little hurt that your Dad doesn't want to be with me anymore. But I understand that you love him and really like Carol, and that you're looking forward to your trip. I want you to be happy, buddy."

It took time, but Mark began to realize that his mom could accept his feelings even though her own were different. Gradually he began to talk freely about his other home and new family. It wasn't always easy for Beth to hear; but she was genuinely glad that Mark felt comfortable being honest with her and that he no longer felt that he had to hide part of his life from her. As long as she could see that he was content and thriving, she knew there was little in the other home she needed to be concerned about—and no need to use Mark as a spy.

Careful attention to the verbal and nonverbal clues your children give—without prying—will also tell you when you *do* need to know what's going on in the other parent's house, and you can deal with that situation if it arises.

> Careful attention to the verbal and nonverbal clues your children give—without prying—will also tell you when you *do* need to know what's going on in the other parent's house, and you can deal with that situation if it arises.

Building an honest relationship of love and closeness and keeping the lines of communication open are the best ways to make sure your children are doing well.

Accept that you cannot control your child's other parent. Susan's two daughters were up and dressed early Saturday morning. Their dad was coming to spend the day with them. They barely watched Saturday-morning cartoons—their ears were tuned for the sound of the doorbell and they got up frequently to look down the street. Susan watched helplessly as the clock ticked on, the cartoons ended, and lunchtime came and went. She watched her daughters' smiles and excitement fade, watched their heads droop. She didn't know what to say to them so she bustled busily around the house, stopping occasionally to pat their heads or hug them while having angry mental conversations with their father.

It was midafternoon when Robert, the girls' dad, finally arrived, looking more than a little guilty. Susan, her daughters' disappointment fresh in her mind, attacked him the moment the door opened.

"Where *were* you?" she shouted. "Didn't you know the girls were waiting for you? Why didn't you call? You've *always* been like this! If you can't keep your promises to your kids, maybe you shouldn't have *any* visitation."

"I'd promised to take my girlfriend and her kids to lunch. I forgot all about it. Quit nagging me!" Robert felt defensive and ashamed and hid it beneath a cloak of anger, shouting just as loudly as Susan. As their parents argued over their heads, the two girls stood looking at their shoes and fidgeting with their clothing, silently wishing they could be somewhere else, far away from the shouting and the disappointment.

Married couples raising children disagree occasionally, or have differing opinions on parenting. But somehow when couples divorce, those differences seem to be magnified. It is hard not to want to control what happens in the other parent's house or to force the other parent to change somehow. And it is difficult to accept the reality that such changes are almost impossible to make.

> The only life a single parent can control is his own. Trying to manipulate the other parent or to force changes in attitudes and methods is likely to produce only resentment and anger—a loaded situation for the child caught in the middle.

"But my ex-wife is so permissive—she spoils those kids rotten," one dad may say. "My kids' dad is too strict. I hate to send them there because he's so hard on them," a mom responds. "My ex-husband never sees the kids." "My children's mom only cares about her boyfriend." "His house is a pigsty." "She lets them watch too much TV." Is there any way to resolve all these differences?

Susan may have been justified in her anger over the girls' disappointment. However, she may have hurt them just as much by her reaction. Robert may have made an honest mistake but was inconsiderate in not thinking about how his daughters might be feeling. In either case, neither has much chance of changing the other, especially by shouting and arguing—and the children are the ones who really suffer.

Effective communication can help a great deal. Still, the only life a single parent can control is his own. Trying to manipulate the other parent or to force changes in attitudes and methods is likely to produce only resentment and anger—a loaded situation for the child caught in the middle.

It is undeniably painful for a child to deal with the disappointment an irresponsible parent causes. Still, all of us must learn to handle disappointments and to accept reality, and you can help by focusing on the child's feelings rather than on the other parent's failures. Work on making your own home a secure and healthy place. When necessary, talk with your children—without blaming—about why you do things differently than their other parent. When conflicts and disappointments arise, acknowledge their feelings and explain your own. Sometimes a family meeting can help you find solutions to a problem.

Don't invite manipulation by criticizing your ex or rescuing your child. Peggy was just getting ready to take a shower when the phone rang. "Mom?" said a hushed little voice. "Mom, I *miss* you. I don't want to be at Dad's. Please come and get me!"

Peggy could hear the tears in six-year-old Paul's voice, and his whisper told her that his Dad didn't know he was calling. Peggy took a deep, slow breath and fought back the almost overpowering urge to drive immediately to her ex-husband's house. "Honey," she said with all the love she could muster, "what's going on?"

Now Paul was crying openly. "I just don't want to be here. I want you! Mom, don't make me stay here."

Peggy groped for the right words. "Paul, sweetie, I know you're sad. I can hear how hard this is for you. I miss you, too. I'm sending you a big hug through the phone—can you feel it?"

There was a muffled sniffle on the other end of the line. "Uh-huh," he said. Then Peggy asked, "Paul, where's your Dad? Can you get him for me?"

By the time her ex-husband picked up the phone, Peggy had regained her composure. "Paul just called me, Ben. He's pretty upset and lonely. I think it would help if you sat down and had a talk with him." Peggy heard Ben take a deep breath; then he thanked her for calling and offered to have Paul call the next morning.

> Children thrive, however, when their parents can take responsibility for their own feelings and actions, put children's needs first, and work toward a mutually respectful coparenting relationship—even if it can no longer be a loving one.

Peggy hung up the phone feeling desolate and lonely herself, yet she believed that she had done the right thing. As angry as she sometimes was at Ben, she knew that he was a good and dedicated father who took his role as a parent seriously. She wanted their son to feel close to both of them—and she didn't want Paul to learn that he could play one parent against the other, even with genuine feelings. As time passed, his parents' decision to work together rather than to fight for Paul's affection would allow Paul to love and respect them both.

It is tempting—sometimes overwhelmingly so—to want to intervene in a child's relationship with his other parent. Children often do not know what they need; at other times, their parents' desire to attack each other exacerbates the children's already divided loyalties and makes it possible for them to manipulate situations—and their parents. It is difficult to curb your tongue, to refrain from criticism and attacks on the other parent. But encouraging respect and closeness with both parents (in the absence of actual abuse or neglect) can only benefit you and your children in the long term.

It is probably unrealistic to expect that divorcing adults will never argue, say an unkind word, or put their children in the middle. Healing and adjusting to change take time, and as we have said so often, all of us make mistakes. Children thrive, however, when their parents can take responsibility for their own feelings and actions, put children's needs first, and work toward a mutually respectful coparenting relationship—even if it can no longer be a loving one.

16

Creating a Respectful Coparenting Relationship

As we discovered in the last chapter, former mates *can* work together, but no one ever said it would be easy. A legal divorce is not enough—an "emotional divorce" is necessary before you can really change the old patterns of relating to your former spouse and begin to build a working, coparenting relationship. Unfortunately, an emotional divorce—which includes recovery and healing from the trauma of separation—can take time. Learning to nurture and care for yourself will help you move from intimacy to a parenting partnership (see chapter 13 for suggestions)—but the process is rarely painless.

Adults who have experienced a divorce grieve, just as do adults who have lost a mate to death. Sometimes it seems the grieving process takes longer when you are dealing with guilt or rejection and the "lost" person is still out there. You must learn to cope with seeing him or her, let go of your vision of a "whole" family, and if you share children, find a way to have regular contact without continual pain and anger.

Healing Takes Time

There are a number of events that can trigger a relapse in the emotional healing process. Things such as signing the papers, having the divorce become final, celebrating holidays alone, or watching a former spouse remarry, buy a new home, or have a new child can cause the old wounds to reopen, for both you and your children. Healing takes place in stages, but with each completed stage you move closer to true wholeness.

> A legal divorce is not enough—an "emotional divorce" is necessary before you can really change the old patterns of relating to your former spouse and begin to build a working, coparenting relationship.

The house was quiet as Barbara washed her face and got ready for bed. She opened the windows to let in the cool evening breeze, and checked the doors before going into ten-year-old Abigail's room to tuck her in. When Barbara got close to the bed, however, muffled sniffling sounds let her know that her daughter wasn't asleep after all.

"What's wrong, Abby?" Barbara asked gently, settling herself on the edge of the bed and stroking her daughter's hair. "I thought you were asleep. Do we need to have a cuddle and a talk?"

"Oh, Mom." Abby sighed and sat up. "I want to talk to you, but I don't know how."

"Well, honey," Barbara responded, "whatever it is, I'd like to help. Why don't you just tell me what's going on?"

There was a long pause. Barbara could feel her daughter gathering her courage. Finally, out came the news.

"Dad's getting married, Mom. Next month, to Joan. I get to be a brides-maid with Cassie, Joan's daughter, and we get to go on the honeymoon and everything. I mean, it'll be fun and I'm happy for Dad. And I really like Joan and Cassie a lot and I've always wanted a sister. We're going to get a new house and Cassie and I will have our own rooms. But Mom, it'll never be just Dad and me now—someone else will always be there. Everything's going to change. And if I want to spend more time with Dad and Joan, you'll be all alone and I hate that. Maybe you should get married, too. Oh, Mo-om!" Abigail, overwhelmed, sniffled again, laying her head on her mom's shoulder.

Barbara was stunned. She didn't know how to respond. She was glad Dan had found someone as considerate and respectful as Joan, and part of her was genuinely happy for them. The other part, though, felt as though it had just been kicked in the stomach—hard. She took a long, deep breath. The divorce had not been her choice and it had taken a long time to adjust to life on her own.

"Mom?" Abigail asked, "are you okay?"

Barbara shook herself back to reality and looked into her daughter's face. "Yes, I'm okay. It just feels odd to think of your dad marrying someone else—I guess it still hurts a little. That surprises me. I knew your dad and Joan would marry one of these days and I didn't think I'd mind. But I know you really like Joan and Cassie and they've been great to you. If you decide you want to start spending more time at your dad's house, you know I will miss you, but I'm sure we can work it out.

"As for leaving me alone, Abby," Barbara continued, giving her daughter a squeeze, "I appreciate your love and concern, but taking care of me is *my* job, not yours. You'll always be my precious little girl, no matter where you happen to be. And you know I really enjoy my life these days. I have good friends and I love my work. I'd like to get married some day but not anytime soon. I'm just fine, sweetie," Barbara said quietly. "Now, you'd better get some sleep. Feel better?"

Abigail answered her mother with a wan smile and a hug, then burrowed down into the covers. Barbara lay awake a long time that night, thinking and remembering, and a few tears squeezed their way out. She realized that it was going to be harder than she'd thought to watch Dan remarry, and to see Abby become part of a family in which she had no place. She knew she would be hearing a lot of wedding talk, and that she would probably have to help with the bridesmaid's dress, which she might not enjoy much.

But Barbara also realized that just as she'd adjusted to Dan's leaving, she would adjust to his remarriage. And she'd been honest with Abby: She *did* like her life these days and she never would have believed that was possible even a year ago.

"I'm going to make it," she told herself before she dropped off to sleep. "It's going to be different and I may have to grit my teeth a little, but I'm going to make it."

Being able to accept her ex-husband's remarriage, even though it was painful, meant the chances were good that Barbara would eventually be able to build a different sort of relationship with Dan, one in which they were working partners in raising their daughter. Slowly but surely their old relationship was turning into something new, something that would eventually help their family to heal and change.

What About the "Old" Family?

IT CAN TAKE TIME to learn new patterns and responses. Ex-partners are sometimes bewildered to find themselves addressing each other as "honey" or "dear" out of sheer habit, and other habits can linger as well. Other members of the "old" family—grandparents, aunts, uncles, cousins—struggle to adjust to a divorce, too, and wonder how they will fit into the new arrangements. Family members sometimes take sides, and a divorcing parent may cut children off from contact with the family of the former spouse.

> Grandparents and other family members can be an important link between children and their history, and can provide a sense of permanence and continuity when everything else seems to have been shaken.

It may be difficult—after all, it hurts to be excluded from "family" events—but try to keep in mind that your children will probably still consider themselves part of the "old" family and will still want to see Grandma and Grandpa, Aunt Kate and Uncle Bill.

What's more, those extended-family members may provide valuable support and relief for you, especially when everyone has begun to heal. Grandparents and other family members can be an important link between children and their history, and can provide a sense of permanence and continuity when everything else seems to have been shaken. It may be well worth the effort to keep those relationships alive and strong.

Communicating Effectively

PERHAPS THE SINGLE MOST positive thing ex-partners can do to build a working relationship after divorce is to learn to communicate effectively. You can choose to communicate calmly even if your ex-spouse doesn't. Emotional honesty (see chapter 4) does not require expertise from two people—one is enough. You can share what you think, what you feel, and what you want. The key is not expecting your ex-partner to think the same, feel the same, or to give you what you want. Expressing yourself honestly is an important key to healthy self-esteem and healthy relationships. The next step is to decide what *you* will do (and to follow through), even when you can't control what someone else will do.

Some divorced parents find it helpful to view their new relationship as a sort of partnership in the business of raising children. It is possible to work through the details of visitation and to share information on sports activities, school, illnesses, and special events without referring to the emotional issues surrounding the end of a marriage.

> You can share what you think, what you feel, and what you want. The key is not expecting your ex-partner to think the same, feel the same, or to give you what you want.

Think for a moment about the relationships you may have in your workplace. You probably don't love everyone you work with—in fact, you may not even like some of your coworkers. Still, most people understand that personal feelings complicate working relationships and can choose to practice respect and simple courtesy. Your relationship with your ex can function the same way. Keep your emotions in check, follow through on agreements, and concentrate on getting the job done.

Former spouses can learn to be accepting and considerate of each other's feelings and to avoid actions they know will cause conflict. They can talk about parenting ideas; as we've suggested, they can even agree to take parenting classes in order to develop similar approaches. It is sometimes helpful—or even necessary—to have the help of a good counselor or mediator. Children deserve the chance to know and love both parents—and it is up to parents to make it possible. If your ex-spouse refuses to participate in a respectful relationship, it will help you and your child if you don't take it personally. Realize that your ex-spouse's choices are about him or her, not about you. You will save yourself and your children a lot of pain and grief if you don't retaliate.

Where Do We Begin? Moving Toward Coparenting

IN HER EXCELLENT BOOK, *Mom's House, Dad's House: Making Two Homes for Your Child* (Fireside/Simon & Schuster, 1980, revised 1997), Isolina Ricci

WHAT IS A PARENTING PLAN?
ISSUES TO CONSIDER

At some point in the legal process, you should consider the following issues and try to reach agreement with your child's other parent:

- Visitation schedules (overnights, midweek visits, summers, holidays, and special events)
- Custody: legal and/or physical
- Responsibility: Who will make which decisions?
- Education, college, and expenses
- Medical and dental care and insurance
- Mental health care
- Other insurance: life insurance or car insurance (for teens)
- Child care (be sure to include pick-up and drop-off instructions)

suggests approaching divorce as the *reorganization* of a family, not its destruction, with the goal being "two homes with no fighting." It's good advice—but sometimes easier said than done. Parents must tackle the challenges of separating legally before they can begin to build a new sort of relationship. Unfortunately, the mechanics and legalities of divorce often create strong emotions—and a great deal of confusion.

The legal issues of support and visitation are beyond the scope of this book; however, a few general facts on these subjects included here may be helpful. Many jurisdictions now require divorcing adults to attend classes on how their decision will affect their children. Many also encourage parents to agree on a "parenting plan," a document that states clearly each person's responsibilities and rights. We encourage divorcing parents to consider this idea; having an agreed-upon structure can save everyone a great deal of conflict and heartache.

Although some parents choose to write such a document themselves, others find it impossible without the help of professionals. Your inner wisdom will

- Religious training
- Parenting education
- Contact with extended family (visits with grandparents and other family members)
- Moving: Can either parent move out of town and take the children?
- Activities (sports, dance, music, and so on): Who will pay? Drive? Attend?
- Transportation
- Access to school and other records
- Tax consequences: Who gets the deduction?
- How will changes in schedules be handled?
- How will disagreements be resolved?

tell you how you need to proceed. Most people find the legal system and the terminology of divorce intimidating (and even depressing); don't be afraid to ask for help if you feel you need it.

The law generally states that parents cannot be compelled to visit their children but that they do have a legal obligation to provide support. If you are not receiving the child support your children are entitled to, you should make every effort to have the support provisions of your divorce decree enforced or modified; it is in both your own and your children's best interests. The least expensive place to enforce child support provisions is through the district attorney's office for the county where the support order was filed.

The law also acknowledges that children do best with continuous and frequent contact with both parents. Only if evidence exists proving that visitation would actually harm a child will the courts restrict a parent's right to visitation. If you have serious disputes with your children's other parent about custody, support, or visitation, a possible solution lies in mediation by an objective third party. Divorce mediation is now a recognized specialty;

your local family-law court can give you referrals to trained mediators in your community.

Making It Work: Creating Two Healthy Families for Your Children

AS STATED EARLIER, coparenting—creating two homes and two families for children—sometimes isn't possible. Your child's other parent may not be interested or available, or perhaps you've tried and it just didn't work. Coparenting isn't necessary; children can grow up healthy and happy with just one loving parent. But building a respectful working relationship with your ex-partner can benefit both you and your child. Here are some ideas to consider.

Offer respect and dignity. "But I *don't* respect my ex!" you may say. "I don't even like her!" Remember, there is a difference between feelings and actions; you can dislike someone and still choose to treat her with courtesy and respect. You cannot make your ex return the favor, but even one respectful partner makes a difference.

Create structure and keep agreements. Creating a parenting plan will help you and your ex (and your children) know what to expect, which can help you

BUILDING A COPARENTING RELATIONSHIP

- Offer respect and dignity.
- Create structure and keep agreements.
- Be wary of legal battles.
- Show appreciation when appropriate.
- Work together to ease transitions.
- Share information.
- Honor your history.

avoid a great deal of confusion and conflict. Whether or not you have a written document in hand, be aware that consistency and predictability help everyone work together smoothly.

Most parents (and children) find it much easier to handle the back-and-forth of shared custody and visitation when there is a schedule in place and everyone can plan accordingly. Although unexpected changes of plan are inevitable, do your best to be consistent and to keep the agreements you make. When you cannot, let your child's other parent know in advance and work together to make new arrangements.

Be wary of legal battles. Sometimes legal action is unavoidable, but court often is not the best place to solve problems. Legal battles have a tendency to last longer than anyone expected; attorneys are expensive. And it is difficult to remain calm and respectful in the stressful, adversarial setting of the courtroom.

It isn't always possible, but try to work out differences without threatening suit. Consider employing a mediator, a pastor, or a counselor to help you find solutions. Court battles usually escalate the anger and hostility between ex-partners—and cause children anxiety and pain.

> Most parents (and children) find it much easier to handle the back-and-forth of shared custody and visitation when there is a schedule in place and everyone can plan accordingly.

Show appreciation when appropriate. "My daughter's father and I went through a pretty messy divorce," one mother reports, "so it took me a long time to be open to parenting together. One thing that made a huge difference was that he paid—without my even asking—to send her to a wonderful ballet program for the summer. I could never have afforded it. It wasn't easy for me to do, but I called and thanked him. Our relationship has gotten easier since then."

Raising children can be simpler when two people share the tasks and responsibilities. If your ex does something helpful or considerate, take the time to show appreciation. If actually calling is too difficult, a friendly note of thanks is enough. All of us like to feel appreciated; saying thank you creates an atmosphere of respect.

Work together to ease transitions. Many single parents report that their children's mood and behavior change when the children return from their other parent's house. Many children find it difficult to go back and forth but the process can be made smoother with parents' help. You and your ex may have very different approaches to parenting; your children will learn to adjust if each of you is willing to be kind and firm about the rules in your own home. (Remember, you can't control the rules in your ex's home!) Children sometimes test well-known boundaries to reassure themselves each time they change homes; your Positive Discipline parenting skills and lots of patience will help you all adjust.

> You and your ex may have very different approaches to parenting; your children will learn to adjust if each of you is willing to be kind and firm about the rules in your own home.

Some single parents find it helps to use routine charts to simplify the packing and unpacking, especially when books, homework assignments, and clothing must travel back and forth. Be patient with "forgotten" items but avoid rescuing or lecturing: With practice, children learn to be responsible about keeping track of what belongs where.

It is also helpful to allow children to have their own personal space in each home. If a separate room isn't possible, try to provide drawers, shelves, and storage containers so that a child can organize her possessions. (It may be wise to provide duplicate blankies, teddies, and other security objects for toddlers and preschoolers!)

Share information. Information about your child's activities, health, and progress can be a valuable tool to help both parents stay connected—or it can become a weapon in the war for a child's affection. The Golden Rule works well here; try to let your child's other parent know the things that you would want to know in his or her place. Remember, your child will benefit from the active love and involvement of both of you. Inform your ex-partner about school conferences, soccer games, and illnesses; he or she may or may not be involved but you will know you have offered respect and courtesy. If you cannot talk calmly with your child's other parent, use e-mail or voice mail to share information.

Honor your history. Many divorcing adults have experienced it: the urge to burn the photo albums and love letters, to dispose of the wedding ring and mementos, to erase all record of their failed marriage. One woman even left her wedding dress hanging in the bedroom closet when she moved out, a silent rebuke to the husband who divorced her. But many parents find that the passage of time leads them to regret these acts. The marriage may have ended, but a child's need for a heritage goes on.

Annie knew something was wrong the moment Christian, her eight-year-old son, walked in the door. She got up from the couch, where she'd been studying, and walked over to give her son a hug. "Did you have a good time with your Dad, Chris?" she asked.

Christian shook his head. Then, chin quivering, he looked up at his mother. "Dad's going out of town again, Mom. We were supposed to go to the ball game this weekend but now we can't. He says he's sorry—he just has to work." Christian wrestled with his feelings for a moment, then exploded. "He doesn't love me, Mom. I hate him! His old *job* is always more important than I am. I'm just going to stay with you from now on."

Annie's mind produced a dozen responses and lectures, ranging from angry sympathy for her son to defense of his dad. Annie knew Carl loved Christian; she also knew that part of the reason Carl worked so much was to provide for him. She gazed at her son's bowed head, felt his hurt, and made a decision.

"I'll tell you what," she said with a hug, "meet me here on the couch after dinner and I'll show you something important."

Christian looked both defensive and curious as he settled down next to his mom after the dinner dishes had been put away. "What is it, Mom?" he asked.

"Well, you told me that your dad doesn't love you. I can prove that you're wrong," Annie said quietly, reaching for a photo album. She had spent the afternoon going through boxes in the garage, searching for the albums containing photos from Christian's infancy and toddlerhood. She hadn't looked at them in several years, but now seemed like the right moment.

The Golden Rule works well here; try to let your child's other parent know the things that you would want to know in his or her place.

Together, mother and son turned the pages. There was Carl, proudly holding up his newborn son. "He held you before I did, Chris," Annie said. There were pictures of Carl and Christian playing, laughing together, tickling, and curled up asleep. There were pictures of Christian with the tiny set of tools his dad had made for him, working in the garage with Carl. Christian didn't say much, but he looked hungrily at the pictures. Finally he pointed to one of his mom and dad holding him up between them.

"Can I have this one, Mom?" he asked softly.

When they'd reached the end of the albums, Annie took something out of her pocket and offered it to her son. Christian held up a gold locket, with a date engraved on the back. "Open it, Chris," his mom said.

Inside the locket, a young man and woman smiled at each other. "This was your father's wedding gift to me. I want you to keep it, honey, so you can remember that you have two parents who loved each other once and were so happy when they had a baby boy. We may not be together now, but one thing hasn't changed. We both love you, Christian."

Christian looked at the locket, then at his mom. "Thanks, Mom," he said. "Can I call my Dad?"

Annie knew that her son would be disappointed with both of his parents from time to time, and that all three of them would make mistakes. But she recognized that knowing his own history would help Christian adjust to the changes that had happened to his family. Regardless of what lay ahead, he would always know where he had come from.

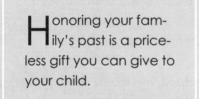
Honoring your family's past is a priceless gift you can give to your child.

Even if you no longer love your child's other parent, you can make an effort to help your child appreciate the good times you did share and to understand his special place in the world. Honoring your family's past is a priceless gift you can give to your child.

Even the best coparenting relationships have difficult moments. You will not always agree, and it takes effort and patience to keep the lines of communication open. Children benefit, however, when they can share life with both parents, in two happy homes.

When Children "Work the System"

SOONER OR LATER, in single-parent households the world over, it happens. It is the ultimate threat against a single parent, and children figure it out with alarming speed. "I want to go live with my dad (or my mom)," they say. "I don't want to live with you anymore." It is a rare parent who can hear those words without feeling hurt and alarm.

Why do kids say that? (And most do, eventually.) Children are intelligent people and they do what works—and threatening to leave works so well because single parents love their children and often feel insecure, especially when the situation is new. Remember the mistaken goals of misbehavior? A child who threatens to go live with his other parent may be acting out of a desire for revenge. He may feel hurt for some reason and may want to strike back at the nearest available person who cares—his parent. Or he may be threatening to leave as part of a power struggle. Kids often play one parent against the other to get something they want, even when their parents are married; and the ploy becomes far more effective when those parents are separated. Or the need may be real—a child may have compelling reasons for wanting to live with his other parent. It may even be your child's way of telling you that he just needs to spend more time with his other parent.

> Kids often play one parent against the other to get something they want, even when their parents are married; and the ploy becomes far more effective when those parents are separated.

How can you tell what's really going on? A quick review of the Mistaken Goal Chart (page 126) will help. If you can figure out how *you* feel when your child threatens to leave, you'll have an important clue to what's really going on. Using active listening and emotional honesty to talk through the problem will help you and your child resolve it peacefully. Try not to overreact. In fact, many times when a parent refuses to take the bait and responds by saying simply (and without anger or sarcasm), "Well, that may be something we should talk about," the threat loses some of its magic and a child retreats from it.

Melinda's initial response was to feel hurt when her thirteen-year-old daughter Megan announced, "I want to go live with Dad." Then she remembered the discussion on this very subject that had taken place two weeks ago in her single-parenting class. She calmly said, "I would really like to discuss this with you later this evening."

Megan shot back, "You aren't going to change my mind."

Melinda said, "My goal is not to change your mind but to really hear and respect your thoughts and feelings; and I know I will do a better job of that in a few hours. How about 7:30 tonight?"

Megan agreed sullenly.

At 7:30 Melinda sat down at the kitchen table with Megan and began the conversation by saying, "I'm ready to listen to what is going on for you."

Megan sighed and said, "I just want to go live with Dad."

Melinda said, "I understand that, and I'm not saying you can't. I would like to know what is behind it. Why do you want to go live with your Dad?"

"I just do, that's why," Megan said.

Melinda said, "Megan, I have a hunch you feel hurt about something. I have tried to think what I might have done to hurt your feelings, but I don't have a clue. Is there something you aren't telling me?"

Megan started to cry. "I just miss my Dad. Angela's Dad is taking her camping this summer and I hardly ever see my Dad. He's never been to my piano recitals or anything. I just hate never having two parents!"

Melinda put her arms around Megan. "Oh, Megan," she said, "I'm so sorry. I know how tough this can be. I know how much you love your Dad. And the truth is, I can see why you would want to be with him just as much as with me. At least I hope you still want to be with me, too."

Megan admitted, "I do, but I just hate it that you and Dad got a divorce."

Melinda said, "I know, Megan. Sometimes I hate it, too. Life gives us some tough lessons to learn, but I know you and I can get through this and also enjoy all the good stuff in life. I'll make a deal with you. You can try living with your Dad for a while. And if you change your mind and want to come back and live with me, that's okay. What you can't do is change your mind every time things get tough. You have two changes coming, so think about them carefully."

Megan was surprised. She asked, "Do you mean you wouldn't be mad at me if I lived with Dad for a while?"

Melinda said softly, "I would miss you terribly, but I wouldn't be mad."

Megan called her father and did decide to try living with him. After a year she decided to come back and live with her mother. Many single parents would not want to consider the option of letting their children make choices about where they live, but it worked for Melinda. Several factors made it a workable option for her:

> Everything does not require "fixing" or resolution. Often it is enough just to have a sensitive discussion in which children can become more aware of their feelings and express them.

1. Initially she was wise enough to wait for a cooling-off period before discussing such a "hot" issue.

2. Melinda knew (from her single-parenting class and the discussion of mistaken goals) that Megan probably wasn't aware that hurt feelings were motivating her actions. She had covered up her hurt feelings with anger—a common practice for many people. Her confusion led to hostility; she struck back at the handiest person—her mom. Melinda's goal was to help her sort out her feelings and come to some kind of resolution.

3. Melinda was willing to be more concerned about her daughter's feelings than her own. (Actually she used her feelings to give her a clue that Megan might be feeling hurt even if it didn't "make sense" to either of them initially.)

4. Melinda was willing to respect Megan's ability to make some decisions but declared limits so Megan would make her decisions thoughtfully instead of reactively.

Many parents don't even consider the wishes of their children and instead fight over children as though the parents' wishes were all that counted. Melinda encouraged Megan to love both parents instead of feeling she was disloyal if she wanted to be with both.

Melinda allowed Megan choices. In some situations just allowing a child to air feelings is enough. Everything does not require "fixing" or resolution. Often it is enough just to have a sensitive discussion in which children can become more aware of their feelings and express them. This can start a process of healing and/or natural resolution.

If you and your child's other parent decide to include your child in making decisions about visitation or living arrangements, don't invite manipulation; be sure you set limits on the choices. Children sometimes want to change visitation arrangements temporarily because of special events or needs. Some parents find that allowing older children to work out changes directly with the parent involved works quite well. The

> If your child is lucky enough to have the love and active involvement of his other parent, that person will be a part of your life as long as you share your child.

better your ability to communicate with your child's other parent, the smoother such changes will be.

"I Need You Both!"

WHEN PARENTS CONSIDER the thoughts and wishes of their children, they'll know that sometimes both parents are needed in the same place at the same time. If your child is lucky enough to have the love and active involvement of his other parent, that person will be a part of your life as long as you share your child. Your child will want to see both of you at school programs, Little League games, Scout meetings, graduations, weddings—all of the important events and celebrations of life. Investing the time and energy to make your relationship with your child's other parent a positive and healthy one (even if it can't be a loving one) will spare you and your children a great deal of pain and may lay the foundation for a happier, healthier life for all of you.

17

Celebrating
Your Family

SEVERAL YEARS AGO, curious researchers conducted a survey to determine how adults viewed families. They asked adults of differing ethnic and economic backgrounds to define a "normal" family. Despite the changes in our society—and often despite their own experience—most adults answered that a "normal" family consists of a mother and father who have never divorced or been remarried and a couple of children. And, interestingly enough, the mother in this "normal" family does not work outside the home!

The researchers then decided to determine how many American families fit this description. They found that less than 10 percent do.

Does this mean that single parents and their children are not "normal"? No—but the research does tell us that our long-held beliefs about what makes a family healthy sometimes get in the way of appreciating the families we *have* (whatever their shape or size). Attitude may not be everything, but it is vitally important. One of the most important tasks single parents face is learning not only to accept but to celebrate the family they have.

> Attitude may not be everything, but it is vitally important. One of the most important tasks single parents face is learning not only to accept but to celebrate the family they have.

If you have read this far, you are probably beginning to realize that single-parent homes can be wonderful places to grow up. They aren't "broken" homes, and their children aren't doomed to failure and disappointment. Single-parent families take some getting used to, but they can be peaceful, secure, loving homes for the adults and young people who share them.

Recognizing the Worth of Your Single-Parent Family

THE FIRST—and possibly the most important—thing you can do for your single-parent family is simply to recognize its worth and uniqueness. Both as individuals and as a family, you and your children have strengths, abilities, and perceptions that no one else has. Your family may not look or function quite like the one next door (or the ones you see each week on television), but it is just as valuable.

It's often easier to focus on what's wrong than on what's right, but there is much that is positive about single-parent families. As we've said before, there is less chance of disagreement and conflict over parenting approaches, and many single parents report that they enjoy more time with their children, as well as the ability to be more spontaneous.

Remember, it may take time before we can find the blessings in single parenthood, but there are a number of ways to widen our vision and to turn what might seem negative into positive opportunities.

What's So Special About Our Family?

HUMAN BEINGS ARE wonderful creatures. Each of us is unique, possessing a special combination of qualities, insights, and abilities that no one else has. And because each of us is so special, the families we make are special as well. Our expectations shape our reality; as a single parent, you may dwell on the things that are difficult, or that appear to be different than what you see in "traditional" families. But as life settles down a bit, you'll be able to use your own wisdom and creativity to make some changes—perhaps not in the facts of your existence but in how you perceive them and what you make of them.

One day soon (perhaps at a family meeting), take some time with your children, grab a big sheet of paper, and start thinking, talking, and writing down the things that make your family special. "We're not special at all," you may be saying. "We're just ordinary people trying to get by." But you'll find, if you take the time and energy to explore it, that there are some wonderful things that set your family apart.

> And because each of us is so special, the families we make are special as well.

What you discover may surprise you. There may be a special atmosphere of warmth and acceptance in your home, or a feeling of drive and enthusiasm. Each child has interests—baseball, music, ballet, video games, reading—that make him or her come alive. You have your own abilities and talents. Your family may have funny pets or shared interests (such as your church, camping, biking, or gardening) that give you a sense of identity. Your home, your neighborhood, everything about you—even the uncomfortable parts—make you different and special.

Once you've filled your sheet of paper, spend some time together cutting out pictures from old magazines that illustrate the things you've written down. Then post your "family portrait" in a prominent place and add to it as inspiration strikes you. You may even find that there is a family motto or saying that will make a perfect title. Setting time aside to discover as a family what makes you special will help give all of you a sense of unity and appreciation for what you have—and it will help you to see that your family's differences may be its greatest strengths.

Building New Traditions

A GREAT DEAL of a family's identity and specialness lies in its traditions—the ways we spend our special times, the celebrations and rituals we build into our lives together. For single parents, holidays can be an especially difficult time. Time with children often must be divided between parents, and for a single parent alone on a holiday or birthday, life can seem pretty bleak.

Many times the family traditions and celebrations we've relied on in the past don't feel "right" when we're single. Holidays are stressful for just about all families these days, and they seem especially so for families complicated by divorce, death, or remarriage. Which set of parents do you spend the day with?

How many turkey dinners will you have to eat? Whose children will be with which parents? Sometimes it seems that no matter how you choose to spend those special days, someone's feelings are bound to be hurt and someone is going to feel left out. Add to all of the preceding a liberal helping of financial stress and it's no wonder that single parents may find the prospect of holidays a depressing one.

> Setting time aside to discover as a family what makes you special will help give all of you a sense of unity and appreciation for what you have—and it will help you to see that your family's differences may be its greatest strengths.

There are a few things you can do to put the joy back in holidays and family occasions.

Adjust your expectations to fit your situation. Most of us still believe that family celebrations should resemble a Norman Rockwell painting. You know the one—Dad carves the huge, succulent turkey on a table set with beautiful things while the family, rosy-cheeked and smiling, sits in happy anticipation. There are no arguments, no tired whining children, no bitter memories. Unfortunately, reality is seldom like that, even for the happiest of families. Perhaps the best way to approach family traditions is to accept what is and to make it the best it can be for everyone concerned. *Different* doesn't mean "worse."

Don't be afraid to improvise or to do things differently. It's hard not to fall for the "but we've always done it that way" approach, but don't be afraid to change what you do to fit who you are. If your children won't be with you on

PUTTING THE JOY BACK IN HOLIDAYS

- Adjust your expectations to fit your situation.
- Don't be afraid to improvise or to do things differently.
- Ask your family what matters most to them, then build your celebration around the answers.
- Try to resist the pressure to give an abundance of gifts.

the actual holiday, plan a special celebration for a day when you are together. There's nothing magical about the calendar—what matters is taking the time to create special moments together.

At first glance some of your old traditions may appear to be in tatters. If half of your cherished Christmas ornaments went with your ex-spouse, spend a day with your children making new ones. Bits of ribbon and construction paper, old Christmas cards, blown-out eggshells, photographs, and a little imagination will not only fill the empty spaces on your tree, they will create treasures you and your family will cherish for years to come—and some wonderful memories to go along with them.

> There's nothing magical about the calendar—what matters is taking the time to create special moments together.

Ask your family what matters most to them, then build your celebration around the answers. It can be interesting to ask children which traditions mean the most to them. You may discover that no one particularly cares about the extravagant desserts you've been laboring over for years, but that everyone would enjoy time spent playing a game or watching a special movie together. Don't be afraid to keep things simple—you may find that the best part of your special day is a walk together in the park after dinner.

Your local bookstore or library is a good place to look for ideas—there are a number of excellent books on creating family celebrations. Whatever you and your family decide, spending time making special memories will help you build a sense of belonging, completeness, and joy.

Try to resist the pressure to give an abundance of gifts. Don't confuse love with showers of presents. No one will enjoy a holiday if you're going to spend the ensuing months worrying about how to pay the bills. Remember that even two-parent families have children who say, "Is this all?" after they have opened a mountain of gifts. Instead of feeling guilty that you can't provide enough gifts, take this opportunity to teach your children other possibilities.

You might want to give each child one special gift and use whatever money remains in your budget to help someone else, perhaps to "adopt" a family together. Amazing as it sometimes seems, there are always people who are struggling more than we are. Finding a way to help someone else can both restore your perspective on what holidays are really about and provide your children with valuable opportunities to share and to give.

New Ways to Celebrate

FINDING NEW WAYS to celebrate holidays and to bind a single-parent family together can take courage. Ellen was dreading the prospect of Thanksgiving. Not only was it the first holiday since her divorce, but her two children would be spending the weekend with their father and grandparents, eating the usual turkey dinner with all of the family—except Ellen. The idea of sitting alone in her empty apartment brought tears to her eyes, but she wasn't sure what to do about it.

She was reading a magazine article about the Pacific Coast when an idea struck her, and she picked up the phone and made reservations before she could change her mind. That evening, Ellen and her children sat down together to make some plans.

"You two know that you'll be spending Thanksgiving with your dad and your grandparents this year, don't you?" Ellen asked. The children nodded, unsure how their mom was going to react.

Ellen smiled. "I still want to have a celebration with you even though we won't be together on Thanksgiving itself, so I thought we could have a special meal together on Wednesday, just us. What do you think?"

> Finding a way to help someone else can both restore your perspective on what holidays are really about and provide your children with valuable opportunities to share and to give.

Enthusiastic smiles greeted the suggestion, and Ellen and her children organized a wonderful Thanksgiving together. The kids decided that because they'd be having turkey at their grandmother's house, they'd prefer cheeseburgers with Mom. Ellen laughed and agreed. Together they made a centerpiece with candles and Indian corn, talking while they worked about what the holiday meant. When their own Thanksgiving arrived, they set the table with the best dishes, lit the candles, and turned out the lights.

In the soft glow of the candles, Ellen took her children's hands and asked what each of them was thankful for. It took some time to think—it had been a difficult year for everyone—but each member of the family had at least one thing to be genuinely thankful for.

Then Benny, the youngest, asked uncertainly, "Can we say what we're not thankful for?" Ellen nodded at her son.

"I'm not thankful for the divorce," Benny said quietly, "but I'm glad we still love each other." More than one tear fell around the table that evening, but it was a time for healing and understanding as well, and Ellen knew as she hugged her children good night that their special Thanksgiving had been a good idea.

The next day, after Ellen had dropped her excited children off at their father's, she packed a suitcase and drove off to the coastal town where she'd made reservations at a small bed and breakfast inn. It wasn't easy being alone, especially when everyone else seemed to be part of a couple or a family. Still, she found she enjoyed the peace and quiet, and having time to read a book and walk along the beach—and being somewhere new and interesting took the sting out of her rearranged holiday. In fact, she decided to take the children with her next year—her turn—for Thanksgiving at the beach. It was a beautiful spot, Ellen thought. Why not try something new?

Creating Special Moments

THE MOMENTS THAT make us a family needn't be saved just for holidays and special occasions. Special "together" moments can happen every day—and it's important that we make time for them in our busy lives.

A neighbor looking in the window of Brad's house might think life there was a bit unusual. Brad comes home each night to three hungry children. There is usually laundry to do, homework to supervise, and all the odds and ends that make up domestic life to take care of.

But Brad's approach is a little different. He walks in the front door, takes off his shoes, and stretches out on the carpet. "Where are my kids?" he shouts. "Where are all my children?"

And from wherever they happen to be, in the yard or in the house, Brad's children come running to throw themselves on their father's stomach, tickling, giggling, and shouting. For a while, it's a free-for-all. Then, when the laughter has subsided, Brad

> Special "together" moments can happen every day—and it's important that we make time for them in our busy lives.

and his children talk about what has happened that day, how they're all feeling, and what lies ahead for the evening. It may seem like a silly ritual to the

neighbors, but for Brad's family it's a wonderful way to stay in touch, and to make some time for laughter. Then they all tackle dinner and the chores together.

Special moments can be built around any activity that the family enjoys. Regular family meetings not only provide time to solve problems, they build a sense of family and wholeness as each person participates and shares. Family meetings also teach that the single-parent family *works,* and they provide a time for listening, talking, and just having fun.

Creating special moments for your family may include such things as taking turns reading aloud from a book each evening before bed (a double blessing, because reading to children is one of the best ways to encourage healthy brain development and school readiness), taking a weekend bike ride, having a picnic or a baseball game, or simply hanging out together. These times need not be perfect—in fact, they probably won't be. But the more often they happen, the more solid a foundation your family will become for all of its members. The special moments you spend with your children need not cost a lot of money or be major events—time spent simply *being* together is the most important thing.

> One of the most valuable things parents can give their children is memories of times shared.

One of the most valuable things parents can give their children is memories of times shared. These precious memories are the roots from which the family tree grows. And for single parents, special moments are a way to bind the family together, to heal, and to bring joy.

The Power of Ritual

THERE DOESN'T SEEM to be much time in modern life for rituals. In fact, most of us aren't really sure what the word *ritual* means. Yet the weaving of ritual into our everyday existence can bring with it a richness and sense of celebration that can make our lives joyful, at least most of the time.

Rituals are those familiar repeated events that become part of the structure of our lives. Sometimes they simply happen on their own, but sometimes we can plan them, create them, and use them to gather and bind our family together. One familiar—and extremely effective—example is the bedtime ritual. Getting children to bed, especially young children, can become a nightly struggle that everyone in the family dreads. Developing a ritual (we call some of them "routines") allows children to feel secure and cozy, and makes the entire process much easier.

Rituals can help us mark and celebrate the transitions and landmarks in our lives. They can help us heal, and give us a way to express sorrow or joy. Most of us are familiar with birthday rituals—the cake, the candles, the familiar song—but there is more you can do that will make the occasion special. You may choose to take the birthday child out for a special "just us" lunch. Perhaps the birthday person will get to choose the dinner menu and eat from a special plate. There may be an old, cherished decoration that always goes on the cake. One mom wraps small coins and a lucky charm in wax paper and puts them in the frosting between cake layers. The person who receives the lucky charm gets to make a special wish. If your child is adopted, celebrating the day he or she came to live with you can be a wonderful way to cement the bond between you.

If your children have lost a parent or a sibling through death, you may want to begin a special ritual of "remembering" on the anniversary of his or her death. You may choose to plant a tree or a rose, to look through old picture albums, or simply to share favorite memories over a special meal. Especially in those first difficult years, such rituals give your entire family an opportunity to share their sorrow, to remember, and to heal.

Rituals are a powerful way to bind a family together. Be sure, though, that you consider the uniqueness and situation of your family when planning

> Rituals can help us mark and celebrate the transitions and landmarks in our lives.

these special celebrations of life. Though inherited or traditional celebrations can be wonderful events in the life of a family, doing something just because it's expected may create a sense of obligation and boredom rather than the spirit of identity and joy you're looking for. Make an effort to fit your rituals into your real life as a family; make them personal and special. Incorporating ritual into everyday life can give your entire family a chance to touch, to hope, and to celebrate.

Letting the Message of Love Get Through

IT'S ALL TOO EASY for parents—all parents—to get caught up in the rush of daily life. We're busy *doing*, dealing with problems, listening, talking, keeping our families together. Sometimes we forget to take the time (or we're not sure how) to remind our children that we love them. Sometimes we overlook the ways they try to say that they love us.

There is a beautiful story about a child's love circulating on the Internet. We share it here with our thanks to its unknown source.

Some time ago, a father got angry at his three-year-old daughter for wasting a roll of gold wrapping paper. Money was tight and he had become infuriated when the child tried to decorate a box to put under the tree.

Nevertheless, the little girl brought the gift to her father the next morning and said, "This is for you, Daddy." He was embarrassed by his earlier overreaction, but his anger flared again when he found that the box was empty. He could not suppress his irritation when he told his daughter, "Don't you know that when you give someone a present, there's supposed to be something inside it?"

The little girl looked up at him with tears in her eyes and said, "Oh Daddy, it's not empty. I blew kisses into the box. All for you, Daddy." The father was crushed. He put his arms around his little girl and asked her forgiveness.

This father kept the gold box by his bed for years. Whenever he was discouraged, he would take out an imaginary kiss and remember the love of the child who had put it there.

Whether we realize it or not, each of us has been given a gold container filled with unconditional love and kisses from our children. If you have ever asked a child for forgiveness, you have undoubtedly experienced that overwhelming rush of love. And if being reassured that we are loved is so powerful for us, can it be any less so for our children?

"Oh, my kids know I love them," most parents will say. "I tell them so all the time." Just saying the words, however, may not be enough. Some interesting studies have shown that what communicates love most powerfully isn't what we say but what we *do:* making eye contact, touching in affectionate ways, spending time together, building a child's sense of belonging and significance. Ruffling a daughter's hair as we pass by the chair where she's studying, or giving an unexpected hug to a son as he dutifully does the dishes says "I love you and I appreciate you" in a wonderful way. Saying "yes" instead of "no" occasionally,

SENDING THE MESSAGE OF LOVE

Expressing love to children is so important, and there are so many creative (and inexpensive) ways to do it! Here are a few suggestions, which may prompt you to discover some of your own:

- Send notes. Try tucking a note in your child's lunch box to tell her she's in your thoughts, or put a "sticky note" in her backpack when she goes to her other parent's home. A funny poem, an "I love you," or just a "smiley face" tells her she's special.

- Make use of technology. In these computerized times, many parents have discovered that technology provides many ways to stay connected. Try sending your child an "electronic greeting card" if she uses the Internet; if your teen has a pager, type in a short message instead of a number.

- Use objects as symbols. One night, a mother told her little boy, who was upset, that he could tell his troubles to his little stuffed bunny and the bunny would always understand. For years, whenever the boy left home, he would find the bunny hidden somewhere in his belongings and would remember the mom who loved him.

- Spend "special time" together. Nothing says "I love you" as well as regular time spent one-on-one with a child, sharing thoughts, playing, or just being together.

especially when it's least expected, can delight children and make everyone feel more cheerful. Even the most inexpensive treat (a pack of gum, some baseball cards) takes on magic when it is given just to say, "You're special."

> The hassles of daily life with our children can seem less bitter and overwhelming when we manage to communicate love in the midst of them.

A song from the movie *Mary Poppins* tells us that a "spoonful of sugar helps the medicine go down." The hassles of daily life with our children can seem less bitter and overwhelming when we manage to communicate love in the midst of them. You may find it necessary to use some Positive Discipline methods when your children make unfortunate choices, but you can still smile or give an affectionate touch that says "You're still my child and I love you."

Some families find that a nonverbal signal, such as pointing to the heart, can express love and reassurance even during the most heated discussion. Whatever may work best for you and your family, be sure you take the time to let the message of love get through—it can make all the difference in the world.

Laughter *Is* the Best Medicine

ONE OF THE BEST (and healthiest) ways of expressing love and togetherness is through laughter. It's sometimes easier said than done, but nurturing your sense of humor, learning to recognize and enjoy the silly side of life, and finding ways to laugh with your children can make an astonishing change in how life *feels* for all of you.

Pete was giving his wilted petunias a shot of water one summer evening when Tyler and Travis, his twin sons, wandered out into the front yard. "We're bored, Dad," they moaned. "There's nothing to do and it's too hot in the house. And we don't want to go to bed—it's still light." Both boys flopped onto the front porch with perfectly matched frowns.

Pete felt a flash of annoyance. They'd had this same conversation at least twice already this week. They'd brainstormed about things to do, and they'd agreed to purchase a fan when there was enough money in the budget; yet here the boys were, at it again. He was looking over at his sons with irritated words on the tip of his tongue when the sight of the two identical grumpy faces struck him as funny.

"Here," he said with a grin, "this might cool you down." And he gave the boys' bare legs a squirt with the garden hose.

Both boys leaped up with indignant squawks. "Da-ad!" they shrieked, running into the house and slamming the door behind them. *Oh, great,* Pete thought, *now I've gotten them mad.* He was just getting ready to turn off the hose and go inside to talk to the boys, when Travis and Tyler appeared around the corner of the house—armed to the teeth with their high-powered squirt guns.

For the next fifteen minutes, the neighbors were treated to the sight of pitched battle in Pete's front yard. And by the time the combatants finally collapsed in a heap on the grass, all three of them were soaked to the skin.

"Well," Tyler said soberly, looking down at his dripping T-shirt, "I guess I'm not hot anymore." Something in his voice tickled his brother and father and all three began to laugh, trooping into the house together for showers and bed.

Josie and her three children decided to have an ongoing contest in their family to see who could be the first to find the humor in a situation. The ground rule was that it had to be the kind of humor that would get them laughing "with" each other instead of "at" each other. One day, as the family was returning from a family picnic, Josie was stopped by a policeman for speeding and was given a ticket. She felt very upset about the fine she would have to pay.

> Nurturing your sense of humor, learning to recognize and enjoy the silly side of life, and finding ways to laugh with your children can make an astonishing change in how life *feels* for all of you.

One of her children quipped, "Well, Mom, you are always telling us mistakes are wonderful opportunities to learn. You just received a wonderful opportunity." Another child added, "Hey, that's right. And that policeman may have saved our lives by teaching you to slow down. That ticket may be a small price to pay for our lives." Josie chimed in, "Well, I'm always going to workshops for personal growth. It looks like I just provided us with a private seminar. Now I won't have to lecture you guys about slowing down because I just demonstrated the consequences." They all laughed—and learned.

Josie and her children also decided to make a cartoon scrapbook. They all scanned newspapers and magazines and cut out their favorite cartoons and pasted them in the scrapbook. They closed each family meeting by sharing the latest additions to the scrapbook. Every member of this family developed an excellent sense of humor.

> Will laughter solve all of your problems? Of course not—but it certainly does make them seem less overwhelming.

Will laughter solve all of your problems? Of course not—but it certainly does make them seem less overwhelming. It's important to realize that there is a difference between shared laughter and ridicule. You'll know if you listen to your inner wisdom, when laughter is positive and when it's hurtful.

Using your sense of humor and a little creativity can take the hassle out of much of daily life. A spontaneous pillow fight or tickling match, or making a funny face at an unexpected moment can remind parents and children alike that life can still be pretty wonderful—even when there are chores to do. Sometimes a child who balks at picking up toys will hurry to do so when it becomes a game. Sometimes a smile and a "Bet you can't pick up those toys (or put on your pajamas or brush your teeth) by the time I count to ten" makes the task an occasion for fun rather than a power struggle. Sometimes just trading jokes and silly stories gives everyone an opportunity to smile together, something that doesn't happen nearly enough in most of our homes.

The Value of Spirituality

EXPERTS WHO STUDY healthy families tell us that one quality many of these families share is a sense of spirituality. For some families, this means identification with an organized church. For others, it may mean something entirely different.

A famous theologian once defined *spirituality* as "an active sense of identification with something greater than oneself that gives life meaning and purpose." Religion and spirituality may not be the same, but such things as patriotism, a belief in God or a higher power, or concern for equality or the environment may be deeply spiritual in nature.

For most people, a spiritual life is a source of strength, a foundation on which to build, and an effective way of creating a sense of belonging to something greater than oneself. You and your children may find that prayer, or the practice of what you believe, unites you with each other and with a larger community.

The form of spirituality you choose is less important than simply having something that you believe in. However you define it, creating a spiritual practice for yourself and your children is an important part of strengthening your identity as a healthy family.

Building Memories to Treasure

SOMETIME WHEN YOU have a quiet moment, think back on your own childhood and see what it is that you most enjoy remembering—or what you wish you had to remember. Will your children have laughter, celebrations, and other good times to look back on? Creating those special times is easier (and less expensive) than you might think. It can actually become a way of life and it can transform the atmosphere in your home. Making space for ritual, tradition, laughter, and shared memories will make your family *feel* like a family, and will help you create a home where people want to come and stay awhile.

> Making space for ritual, tradition, laughter, and shared memories will make your family *feel* like a family, and will help you create a home where people want to come and stay awhile.

None of us gets to choose all of the circumstances of our lives. There is an old adage that tells us: "Into each life a little rain must fall"— for some of us it seems to have been a veritable flood! Still, as yet another saying tells us: "The heart would have no rainbow had the eye no tear." Whether or not being a single parent was your choice, your family is your family. It will be whatever you have the courage to make it. Believe in your heart that it can be something wonderful, take whatever steps you can, and celebrate!

CONCLUSION

WE HAVE COME to the end of a book, but it's only the beginning of a journey. Single parenthood may have been your carefully considered plan—or it may be a trip you never wanted to take. You may find it frightening, confusing, or overwhelming. Or you may be realizing that like most trips, this one will have some rough spots but will hold some wonderful moments as well.

Parenting is almost always more of a learning experience for the parent than for the child, and single parenthood offers special opportunities for growth and change. Both adults and children may approach it reluctantly; they may be shattered and hurting, or simply unsure they can make it work. But at its best, single parenthood is the chance to build something beautiful, to create a new vision of family life, and to see it to its fruition.

> Parenting is almost always more of a learning experience for the parent than for the child, and single parenthood offers special opportunities for growth and change.

Yes, it *is* possible to raise responsible, respectful, resourceful children as a single parent and to watch them mature into capable, happy adults. It is our hope as authors—and as parents—that you now possess skills and understanding that will help you reach that goal. You *can* build a home that is secure and loving, a place where you and your children can thrive and learn. It will not always be easy, but the rewards for you and your children can be so great.

You have the opportunity to give your children the ability to face life and all its challenges with love, wisdom, and confidence. You can teach them to be human by living an honest life in their presence and by doing your best to be sure your actions support your words. Your children can learn that despite its occasional hardships and challenges, life is an adventure to be savored.

Being a single parent may be the hardest thing you ever have to do, but it is also undoubtedly the most important. Single or not, you are first and foremost your children's *parent.* Nothing you ever do is likely to make as much of an impact on this world as the legacy you leave through your children.

It is tempting in the rush of everyday life with youngsters to wish mightily for the next stage, whatever it may be. When they're babies, we look forward to toddlerhood (no more diapers!). When they're preschoolers, we wish for the school years. As we face the challenges of adolescence, we may long for the day when our children are on their own.

Most parents find, hard as it may be to believe now, that the day comes when they want only to slow down the process, when they cannot believe the little child with the eternally untied shoes has become a capable, independent young adult who no longer needs his parent in the old ways. Learning to slow down, to appreciate and live each moment with children, is something all too many parents discover too late. Yes, being a single parent is a tough job sometimes—but there is also no greater joy than sharing your life with a child.

> Each single parent must eventually find his or her own way, learning to trust his or her own wisdom, to change what seems necessary when it seems right.

Remember our cypress tree? If that tree could speak, it might tell us that there are times it wishes it were anywhere else, when hanging on to the rock takes more strength and perseverance than the tree seems to possess. It may be tempting to give in to the wind and the storm, to simply let go.

But both the cypress tree and the single parent possess a strength that comes from the storm itself. They endure and they grow, and they provide shelter, beauty, and inspiration for those who gather beneath their branches. And when the sun breaks through, the sight is a wonder to behold.

Each single parent must eventually find his or her own way, learning to trust his or her own wisdom, to change what seems necessary when it seems right. Mistakes and discouragement are inevitable—but what truly matters is not where you are, but where you are going. None of us will ever be perfect parents; our children are highly unlikely to be perfect children. If you're doing the best you can, making occasional mistakes but learning from them, and loving your children all along the way, you'll know you're headed in the right direction. That is all any parent can ever do—and yes, it is enough.

INDEX

FOR MORE INFORMATION

Workshops, seminars, and facilitator trainings are scheduled throughout the United States each year. Workshops include:

Teaching Parenting the Positive Discipline Way
(a two-day workshop for parent educators)

Positive Discipline for Parents
(a one-day workshop)

Positive Discipline in the Classroom
(a one-day or two-day workshop for teachers and school personnel)

Dates and locations are available by contacting:

Empowering People
P.O. Box 1926
Orem, UT 84059-1926
1-800-456-7770
E-mail: JaneNelsen@aol.com
Web Site: www.positivediscipline.com

The authors also provide dynamic lectures, seminars, and conference keynote presentations. For more information or to schedule a presentation, call 1-800-456-7770.

ORDER FORM

To: Empowering People, P.O. Box 1926, Orem, UT 84059-1926
Phone: 1-800-456-7770 (credit card orders only)
Fax: 801-762-0022
Web Site: www.positivediscipline.com for discount prices

BOOKS

	Price	Quantity	Amount
Positive Discipline for Your Stepfamily, by Nelsen, Erwin, & Glenn	$16.95	_____	_____
Positive Discipline for Single Parents, by Nelsen, Erwin, & Delzer	$16.95	_____	_____
Positive Discipline in the Classroom, by Nelsen, Lott, & Glenn	$16.95	_____	_____
Positive Discipline: A Teacher's A–Z Guide, by Nelsen, Duffy, Escobar, Ortolano, & Owen-Sohocki	$16.95	_____	_____
Positive Discipline for Preschoolers, by Nelsen, Erwin, & Duffy	$16.95	_____	_____
Positive Discipline: The First Three Years, by Nelsen, Erwin, & Duffy	$16.95	_____	_____
Positive Discipline, by Nelsen	$12.00	_____	_____
Positive Discipline A–Z, by Nelsen, Lott, & Glenn	$16.95	_____	_____
Positive Discipline for Teenagers, by Nelsen & Lott	$16.95	_____	_____
Positive Discipline for Parenting in Recovery, by Nelsen, Intner, & Lott	$12.95	_____	_____
Raising Self Reliant Children in a Self-Indulgent World, by Glenn & Nelsen	$15.95	_____	_____
Positive Time-Out: And 50 Other Ways to Avoid Power Struggles, Nelsen	$12.95	_____	_____
From Here to Serenity, by Nelsen	$14.00	_____	_____
Positive Discipline in the Christian Home, by Nelsen, Erwin, Brock, & Hughes	$16.95	_____	_____

MANUALS

	Price	Quantity	Amount
Teaching Parenting the Positive Discipline Way, by Lott & Nelsen	$49.95	_____	_____
Positive Discipline in the Classroom, by Nelsen & Lott	$49.95	_____	_____

TAPES AND VIDEOS

	Price	Quantity	Amount
Positive Discipline audiotape	$10.00	_____	_____
Positive Discipline videotape	$49.95	_____	_____
Building Healthy Self-Esteem Through Positive Discipline audiotape	$10.00	_____	_____

SUBTOTAL	_____
Sales tax: UT add 6.25%; CA add 7.25%	_____
Shipping & handling: $3.00 plus $0.50 each item	_____

(Prices subject to change without notice.) **TOTAL** _____

METHOD OF PAYMENT (check one):
_____ Check made payable to Empowering People Books, Tapes, & Videos
_____ MasterCard, Visa, Discover Card, American Express

Card # _____ Expiration _____ / _____

Ship to _____

Address _____

City/State/Zip _____

Daytime phone (_____) _____

ABOUT THE AUTHORS

Jane Nelsen is a popular lecturer and co-author of the entire POSITIVE DISCIPLINE series. She has appeared on *Oprah* and *Sally Jesse Raphael* and was the featured parent expert on the "National Parent Quiz" hosted by Ben Vereen. Jane is the mother of seven children and the grandmother of fifteen.

Cheryl Erwin is a marriage and family therapist in private practice. For the past nine years she has also been a consultant, writer, and speaker on parenting issues. Cheryl lives with her husband and fourteen-year-old son in Reno, Nevada.

Carol Delzer is a family law attorney-mediator, Certified Law Specialist, and Marriage, Family, Child Counselor. Her case load includes divorce and child-custody cases. She is a single mother and lives with her daughter Jessica, who inspired her to help write this book.